Alpine Plants of Europe

The Matterhorn

Alpine Plants of Europe

A Gardener's Guide

Jim Jermyn

With photographs by Wilhelm and Dieter Schacht

Timber Press

To both Wilhelm and Dieter Schacht, for sharing with me so much of their botanical knowledge about these plants and providing such a unique pictorial record.

Photographs by Wilhelm and Dieter Schacht unless otherwise noted.
Map adapted from Mountain High Maps. Copyright ©1993 Digital Wisdom, Inc.

Mention of trademark, proprietary product, or vendor does not constitute a guarantee or warranty of the product by the publisher or author and does not imply its approval to the exclusion of other products or vendors.

Published in 2005 by
Timber Press, Inc.
The Haseltine Building
133 S.W. Second Avenue, Suite 450
Portland, Oregon 97204-3527, U.S.A.
www.timberpress.com
For contact information for editorial, marketing, sales, and distribution
in the United Kingdom, see www.timberpress.com/uk.

ISBN-13: 978-0-88192-734-4
ISBN-10: 0-88192-734-1

Designed by Dick Malt
Printed in China

Library of Congress Cataloging-in-Publication Data
Jermyn, Jim.
  Alpine plants of Europe : a gardener's guide / Jim Jermyn ; with
photographs by Wilhelm and Dieter Schacht.
      p. cm.
  Includes bibliographical references and index.
  ISBN 0-88192-734-1 (hardcover)
  1. Alpine garden plants–Europe. 2. Alpine gardens–Europe. I.
Title.
  SB421.J47 2005
  635.9'528'094–dc22
                        2005008019

A catalogue record for this book is also available from the British Library.

Contents

Foreword

Over the years, we have derived great enjoyment from photographing plants in several of our favourite European mountain ranges. Fortunately, Europe boasts a variety of rock types—limestone, granite, and mica schist—giving rise to a wonderful range of mountain flowers. Surprisingly, several new primulas have recently been described from isolated mountains in northern Italy, with *Primula albenensis* being a particularly attractive species with silvery farina on the leaves and flowers in shades of lilac with a white eye. Like most of the European primulas, this one seems quite easy in the garden and makes a lovely show plant.

Here in Scotland, a few years ago we had three nights of hard frost in late April and noted that our European alpines were totally unharmed, whereas Himalayan rhododendrons, cassiopes, and other plants were severely damaged. Actually, on 5 July a few years previously we had camped on a mountain in northern Italy and awoke the following morning to find 15 cm of fresh snow. When this snow was scraped aside, we found primulas with undamaged flowers; our Europeans are accustomed to changeable weather! Whereas primulas, gentians, and most European plants thrive in the garden, others, like *Eritrichium nanum* and *Viola cazorlensis*, are a challenge for the most expert gardener. This is where Jim Jermyn steps in.

Jim started at Ingwersen's Nursery in Sussex, followed by a traineeship at the Munich Botanic Garden with Dieter Schacht. He then worked at Jack Drake's Nursery in Aviemore until he was asked to help Rudolf Wurdig set up his nursery on the side of Lake Garda. Our friendship started with trips to Edrom Nurseries to help the enthusiastic new proprietor. Small groups used to visit at weekends, armed with picnics to be shared in the old Nissen hut where Jim then lived. His friendly personality attracted help with weeding, pricking out, or whatever needed doing, and of course there was a chance to buy some choice plants. During his time at Edrom, Jim was famous for his award-winning naturalistic displays of alpines at flower shows. Enjoy growing these plants with Jim's advice from his years of experience. Walk around any nursery or rock garden in spring to admire the wide range of European primula species and their natural or man-made hybrids. Vibrant-blue *Gentiana verna* and *G. acaulis* transport you back to your first alpine holiday. As the season progresses, dwarf daphnes scent the air, followed by many species of dianthus. Recently we found a mountain in the French Alps where *Dianthus pavonius* grows in a range of colours from white to soft pink and deep cerise. These 5 to 19 CM cushions are easy to raise from seed or cuttings and make wonderful plants for a sunny position. There are many more good Europeans, including the gorgeous pink *Ranunculus parnassifolius*, which can be seen at Nuria near the eastern end of the Pyrénées and also in the Puerto de San Glorio in the Picos de Europa.

Gardeners tend to follow fashions. A few years ago, Andean alpines were in; at present, China holds that position. Folk tend to forget the immense variation of the alpine flora just across the Channel. Grow our Europeans and try to visit our mountains to see plants in their native habitats—an unforgettable experience made easy nowadays by the use of the Euro in every sensible bit of Europe.

Margaret and Henry Taylor
Invergowrie, Scotland

Introduction

I am sure it would be a fascinating exercise to ask an avid plantsperson which plant or flower triggered their interest in gardening. In my case, I well recall travelling to London on a family outing and being introduced to Foyles, the bookshop on Tottenham Court Road. My sister and I were invited to choose a book—where on earth would we start? Would I be drawn to a sporting volume or a book on trains? I suspect I was encouraged to choose something different for a change, so I selected an attractive looking encyclopaedia of garden plants.

The train journey home was spent eagerly devouring the pictures in the first section of the book, the subject matter being "alpine and rock garden plants". I remember fixing my eyes on an illustration of a curious little plant called a soldanella, in fact *Soldanella pusilla*. So that was it. I was so beguiled by the flowers and the nature of the plant that I was curious to find out more about this highly specialised group of plants. I guess this experience took place some 35 years ago, before I left school, and now having been fully immersed in a horticultural career I am greatly indebted to my parents for initiating that trip to Foyles.

Over the last 20 years, my profession has given me the opportunity to visit the mountains of Europe, which allowed me to rekindle my passion for its alpine flora. There is, though, a great feeling observing one's favourite plants in nature but another quite different perception as we take up the challenge of growing these plants in our own garden.

I cannot possibly relate in full how privileged I have been encountering so many of the choicest European alpine plants grown to perfection in private and public gardens across Europe as well as in Canada and the United States. It is my belief that most attempts at growing these plants in our gardens are really, by definition, contrived. In recent years a number of highly innovative formations of rock work have been constructed in gardens, illustrating not only how these specialised plants can be grown but more importantly that they can be grown successfully.

Most of my encounters with European alpines in gardens have involved visiting some of the world's finest growers, and this can, quite naturally, present a somewhat elitist view of these plants. It is for this reason that I will endeavour to present, throughout the pages of this book, a more down-to-earth approach for growing both the rarities and familiar species embodied in this title.

The aim of this book, as with my previous work, entitled *The Himalayan Garden* (Timber Press, 2001), is to help readers to see ways of growing a wide range of the most popular and exciting plants without becoming overwhelmed by their status in nature. Too often I perceive the notion that if a plant has a label of exclusivity about it, this will indicate a greater challenge in cultivation. Not so. Once we can fully grasp the different habitats our favourite plants prefer in nature, including the altitude, soil type, and pH (measure of acidity or alkalinity), we will be better able to grow a wider range of plants successfully.

Most of us garden at lower levels, where extremes of temperature can greatly affect the cultivation of alpine plants. Some readers will have a naturally sympathetic climate gardening in cooler conditions, due to their geographic location. I know I am not alone with experiencing a change in climate and this in turn presents new challenges. If global warming is to blame, then it is important that alpine gardeners prepare to adapt to the prevailing conditions. This may entail incorporating more rocks in a landscape than we have been used to, thus creating a cooler microclimate for our plants. Many alpine houses constructed at the beginning of the 20th century were designed with the foundations about 1 M beneath the ground. This innovation created an environment with less extremes in temperature, ideally suited for successful alpine plant growing. In today's extremes of temperature, most notably in the summer months, we may well benefit from digging deep and creating a more amenable microclimate.

I hope that the subsequent pages will offer some helpful advice enabling any reader, whether from the U.K., Europe, or the Americas, to succeed with a wide range of European alpine plants. More than that, I want to show how we can flower a soldanella, enjoy success with both the familiar and the choicest gentians such as *Gentiana froelichii* and *G. pyrenaica*, as well as find a position of natural charm for such treasures as *Daphne petraea* and *Jankaea heldreichii*.

For beginners, my advice is never give up, keep trying, adapt, and eventually a new position will bring success. To the seasoned grower and expert, I say share your experiences; most secrets have been borrowed from nature. I have travelled to some wonderful locations in Europe and always learned anew. I am particularly grateful to my wife, Alison, for her patience, supporting me in my quest to search for these plants in nature and putting up with the years of trying to grow them. Without her support and enthusiasm, this second volume could not have happened. I am also very thankful to Johanna McLeod for her tireless work with the typing and editing.

1: A History of European Alpine Plants and Their Geographical Distribution

Each time I return to the mountains and the location of my favourite European alpine plants, I marvel at the apparent way that these plants seem to be at peace with the madness of the world round about. Then, in that moment of peace, I reflect on how many generations may have shared this same feeling of excitement and tranquillity, whether it is encountering a meadow sheeted with *Primula glutinosa* at its pristine best or perhaps an isolated mat of *Androsace alpina* clinging to life in the cruel environ of a scree amidst a local oasis of gritty humus sufficient to support its fragile existence. Maybe we chance upon the elusive albino form of *Jankaea heldreichii* in a cool grotto of limestone; how rare is that? All of these are recent experiences, but surely others have shared them for centuries as humans advanced across Europe, colonising the rich valleys with their agricultural expertise and making forays into the mountains. Surely someone else has seen this same albino jankaea. It is my experience in alpine localities that the native population rarely seek an intimate knowledge of their own flora. Yes, they appreciate their own heritage and, as a result of a mushrooming explosion in tourism, will take even more pride in their traditions. When did people start to take note of these alpine jewels accessible to most able-bodied humans? How far back can we find an awareness of the choice plants about which I am going to write?

An early reference was made a few hundred years before Christ, when Greek philosopher Theophrastus wrote about cyclamen plants in his classic literature. Later, Dioscorides, a writer on medical botany in the first century AD, draws the reader's attention to a saxifrage, probably *Saxifraga granulata*. Other individuals who have not figured in history will have exploited the medicinal properties of alpine plants in Europe, showing that these values featured more strongly than the aesthetic value of the plants in past history.

This belief of mine is further backed up by a personal experience, when I first tasted the "heart-warming" Enzian schnapps. I had arrived for my apprenticeship in Munich, Bavaria, in the autumn of 1974. The kindness and hospitality shown to me by fellow colleagues in the Munich Botanic Garden, where I was

Gentiana lutea with Enzian schnapps

training, was one of the highlights of my life. We would meet up for exhilarating walks, followed by the customary visit to a well-placed hostelry to enjoy the local fare. Part of this hospitality was the local tradition that on our arrival at our host's dwelling, we would be welcomed with a small tray with little glasses containing a clear, slightly viscous beverage. On the first occasion, I must have looked a trifle bewildered, but the pretty lady beckoned to me, so I, too, accepted my little glass. I glanced at my friends and noticed that before I could say "*Auf Wiedersehen*" they had knocked the contents of the little glass down in a "oner". My stony British resolve came to me at once and I followed suit, and all seemed well for a split second until the schnapps passed from my throat to the lower regions. There was a brief, warm sensation, and on reflection, it was mildly uplifting. Was this a drug—would I become addicted? These were questions I was asking myself. Then I got the bitter after-taste—not really pleasant. So, no, I would not become addicted. I turned to my friends, who were all looking my way—pursed my lips and smiled. I was now totally accepted, all would be well, and so would my stomach! As an afterthought—this product of the yellow gentian, *Gentiana lutea*, is indeed good for settling the stomach, but while this book will not contain any thoughts about cultivating dessert pear trees, let me strongly recommend the very special Williams Pear schnapps, much nicer than the product distilled from the roots of a gentian. This experience bears out the fact that from early times, many of these plants were used for their medicinal properties rather than their place in the garden.

Moving rapidly on—back to alpine plants and their history—it is interesting to note that the medicinal properties of the yellow gentian are purported to have been noted as early in history as the second century BC. Both Dioscorides and Pliny tell us that King Gentius of Illyria, an ancient region on the eastern shore of the Adriatic Sea that included the former Yugoslavia and present-day Albania, caused a remedy against plague to be prepared from the roots and leaves of *Gentiana lutea*. It is thus so that the plant was named in honour of Gentius. I would say this is a great honour, considering the horticultural import of this wonderful genus.

One of my favourite European primulas of the *Auricula* (*Auriculastrum*) section is *Primula clusiana*, endemic to southeast Germany and the northern

Primula clusiana

calcareous Alps of Austria, commemorating the Flemish botanist Carolus Clusius. Sometimes known by his French name, Charles de L'Ecluse, he was born in 1526 and is often referred to as a renaissance man. He fittingly takes us on in history during a time of Reformation and counter-Reformation, and clearly his books influenced subsequent botanical researchers, including Carl Linnaeus.

The year 1573 saw Clusius commence a period of 14 years based in Vienna. He worked for Habsburg Emperor Maximilian II of Austria as director of the imperial court gardens in that famous city. Little wonder that with such an optimal base he began exploring and botanising the following year in and around the celebrated Schneeberg and then ventured farther afield into Hungary.

He was to find an impressive number of alpine plants, including *Gentiana clusii*, *Primula clusiana*, and *Dianthus alpinus*, all discovered in what we now recognise as the Eastern Alps of Austria. He had a particular love of primulas and was largely responsible for introducing the sumptuous and often fragrant *Primula auricula* into cultivation.

My love of Austria today is bound up not only with the mountains but with the pristine cleanness of the cities and the tradition of beautiful music and fine pastries. In Clusius's day, I doubt these joys had been so refined, but imagine visiting the markets, patronised by court ladies, keen gardeners seeking plants of the humble auricula. Clusius gave the name of *auricula ursi* to the primula because the leaves resembled bears' ears. (Well he may have come across the native bears, too!) He sent roots of this primula, along with the hybrid *Primula ×pubescens*, to his friend Van de Delft in Belgium, and the plants soon spread to England and throughout Europe, becoming very popular as they still are today in their highly developed forms.

While reading about this famous early botanist, I appreciated his difficulty in cultivating *Rhodothamnus chamaecistus* in Vienna. I also have much to learn when it comes to growing it. Clusius founded his botany on personal observations rather than classical authority. How I wish more botanists today would do likewise, rather than basing so much of their studies on herbarium material, of chromosome numbers, DNA, and the like. Each of these scientific discoveries and records will add weight to a botanist's work, but surely there is no substitute for personal observation in the field. There is a need for both groups to work more closely together through the botanic gardens. Clusius used the reproductive system of plants to clarify them; for example, he studied the colour and number of stamens. His nomenclature approached the binomial system in its simplicity, providing the groundwork for Linnaeus's significant elaboration in the 18th century.

Clusius died in 1609 at the age of 83 and was buried in Leiden, Holland, home to a very fine botanical garden with which he had been very much involved. My gaining knowledge of this man, who latterly became a professor of botany, has given me a greater appreciation for the early pioneer work carried out on the classification of our favourite garden plants. Yet despite being moved by scientific curiosity, Clusius was a humble man who enjoyed peace of mind, a keen gardener who believed in God and the Resurrection. He went beyond science—he looked at the plants and saw their beauty when others thought only of their medicinal properties. By drawing attention to them all those centuries ago, he has spurred others on to explore these plants farther afield.

Pulsatilla alpina subsp. *apiifolia*

Moving on in time we reach an important landmark in history with the life of Swedish botanist Linnaeus (Carl von Linné, 1707–1778). It was Linnaeus who established the binomial system of biological nomenclature that forms the basis of modern classification as we understand it today. During his lifetime, the European Alps were being explored by contemporaries Haller and Allioni, and significant introductions of familiar alpine plants were trickling into gardens across Europe. By the advent of his written work, *Species Plantarum* (1753), Linnaeus had described 10 species of daphne and 37 species of saxifrage, just to mention two genera.

The first alpine plant collector of note was a Scot, Thomas Blaikie. Son of a market gardener, he was born in Corstorphine, Edinburgh, in 1750. He was commissioned to collect plants for two wealthy London physicians, Drs. John Fotthergill and William Pitcairn, both very keen gardeners. His collections in 1775 were concentrated in the Swiss Alps and included the following plants sent back to London: *Aquilegia alpina*, *Gentiana verna*, *Geum montanum*, *Pulsatilla alpina* subsp. *apiifolia*, and *Viola cenisia*—not a bad start! Plants introduced by Blaikie for the first time include *Campanula cenisia*, *Leontopodium alpinum*, and *Ranunculus glacialis*.

While Blaikie's exploits are well documented, it is important not to overlook the undocumented exploits of fellow Europeans, perhaps due to there being no record in the English language. For example, when writing on the *Histoire des*

Plantes de Dauphine (a former province of southeastern France) in 1787, Dominique Villars gives accurate information about some of the cultivated species of gentian in the section *Thylacites* (acaulis group) including *Gentiana angustifolia*. A century later in 1899, botanist A. Jakowatz covered the same section of gentian in his monograph, *Die Arten der Gattung Gentian* (The Species of Gentiana).

Spurred on by their close proximity to the Alps, the formation of alpine plant nurseries would follow the introduction of endemic species. This was the case with that great name, Sundermann, a nursery specialising in saxifrages in Lindau, southwestern Germany. Franz Sundermann produced his first alpine plant catalogue in 1886, in which he listed 94 different species of saxifrage.

As these plants and many others became established in private gardens, they would have undoubtedly been the catalyst behind William Robinson's *Alpine Flowers for the English Garden*, published in 1870. This volume makes fascinating reading, and from it we can discern that the most fashionable alpine plants at that time were from the European Alps, including androsace, primula, saxifraga, sempervivum, and sedum.

It can be stated with safety that the following 100 years would mark the golden age for plant collectors. Robinson's publication preceded Farrer's *My Rock Garden* by 37 years, and it is Robinson who should be credited for the revolutionary approach to alpine gardening that would now see its dawn. At that time, it was the general opinion that alpines simply could not be cultivated in the garden. Robinson had been on a trip to the Alps in 1868 and described how the long roots of "the choice jewellery of plant life, radiated in all directions through crevices filled with grit and soil". He maintained that the failure of these plants to thrive in gardens could be "attributed to a false conception of what a rockwork ought to be and of what the true alpine requires". There can be no doubt that despite Robinson's assertion, there would have been individuals in Europe who had already come to a similar conclusion, and it is no surprise that the much revered Botanic Garden in Munich began major work on its rock garden at the beginning of the 20th century, along with its famous Schachen garden situated in the Wetterstein Mountains above Garmisch-Partenkirchen, southern Germany.

The most outspoken of all alpinists must surely have been Reginald Farrer (1880–1920), whose two volumes of *The English Rock Garden* (1919) will be regarded by many alpine plant lovers as their garden bible. I must say that I generally agree and love to return to several of his works, most notably, *The Dolomites*, first published in 1913. His prose is quite inimitable, and from time to time I will quote his words. His writings have had more impact on alpine gardeners than those of any other writer.

In 1870 William Robinson had listed almost 500 species predominantly from the European Alps, whereas by 1919, when Farrer's *The English Rock Garden* was published, he covered some 600 genera from the mountains of most continents. As a permanent student of alpine gardening, I find myself making constant reference to the bulletins of the Alpine Garden Society, founded in 1929. In 1933 the Scottish Rock Garden Club was formed and likewise its journals have given me endless insight into the European alpine flora. Both societies have in many ways motivated me both to travel and attain greater success and pleasure in growing the plants. More recently I have joined the North American Rock Garden Society and, having become acquainted with many of its members, now have a clearer picture of the challenges involved with cultivating European alpine plants in the diverse climatic extremes of the United States.

It never ceases to amuse me how various fashions take root. In my short span of alpine gardening, I have, for example, seen great strides to succeed with the cultivation of *Primula allionii*. Memories come to me of private collections displayed at RHS (Royal Horticultural Society) shows in Westminster, London, during the 1960s and 1970s consisting of immensely proportioned plants displayed in clay pans the size of breakfast bowls. These almost perfect domes of flowers seemed a little surreal; could mere mortals succeed, too? An alpine house was essential for such treasures. Then on 13 March 1978, I would first experience a unique glimpse of this alpine jewel flowering in all its beauty in its native Maritime Alps on the Franco-Italian border. To see the plant in its native habitat growing on vertical cliffs gave me a new perspective. I found, on my return to the U.K., that I was frowning at plants grown in clay pans and clearly other growers have also been motivated to dispense with pans and plant the primula in tufa cliffs with winter protection. So another fashion has taken hold, with the tufa cliff, quite popular amongst gardeners now. As this feature becomes further refined, many other European endemics will succeed in this artificial garden environment.

Just as plants come into fashion, they can also fall from it. As I write today, bulbous species clearly top the popularity charts. Daphnes have made a welcome resurgence; Kabschia saxifrages have, too. These latter plants, sometimes known as the Porophyllums, were all the rage for nearly 50 years, but by the 1970s they fell from popularity in the U.K. Yet individuals such as Lincoln Foster in the United States, and the outstanding growers in the Czech Republic together with some British hybridists, were creating stunning new hybrids which have relaunched this popular group of plants again.

So what of the future? I hope that plants native to the European Alps will make a continued resurgence. Keen growers in the U.K. and Europe, North

America, Canada, and Japan, together with Australasia and New Zealand, will form their own specialised societies promoting individual genera as we already see with saxifrages, daphne, and various bulbous genera. This is all to be welcomed and encouraged. With such a wide distribution of alpine plants in Europe, which areas and types of plant will this book cover?

As we sit down and ponder the map of Europe, it is tempting to conclude that there is little left still to discover or learn about its mountain flora. How wrong could we be! Not long before the death of one of Europe's greatest alpinists, Wilhelm Schacht (1903–2001), I had the privilege of sitting down beside him in his home and listening to him reminiscing about some of his favourite trips into the mountains. Listening intently, I realised how scant our current knowledge is of the intimate floras of, for example, the Romanian Carpathian mountains or the Balkan regions of Greece, Bulgaria, and Albania. So often the greatest gardeners, including Herr Schacht, can go unnoticed in the mass media. From 1928 to 1944 he served as director of the Royal Bulgarian Parks and Gardens under the direction of King Boris III, who put him in charge of a staff of 100. It was he who was responsible for introducing so many European plants into the Munich Botanic Garden, where he was curator from 1948 until his retirement in 1968.

When he spoke to me about the habitats of such classics, including *Daphne blagayana*, *Dianthus callizonus*, *Corydalis solida* in its stunning Transylvanian forms, or *Dianthus simulans* from Ali Butusch in Macedonia, I reflected on the botanical potential still untapped in these mountainous regions. Add this to the array of plants recently discovered from the Apennine Mountains, as well as two newly discovered primula species of the section *Auricula* (*Auriculastrum*) in recent years, and it becomes clear that research in many areas will reveal interesting information and new species are still to be discovered.

As respects the boundary of *my* Europe, the reader will note from the map in chapter 2 that I will follow the guidelines of *Flora Europaea* (Tutin 1964). It is my objective to discuss the cultivation of species confined to the most familiar areas in Europe with the exclusion of the Caucasus Mountains. It is therefore planned to look closely at plants of the Alps, the Pyrénées, as well as the Cantabrian Mountains, taking in the Maritime Alps to the south, moving east to the Dolomites, and covering the Balkan region and the Carpathians.

I am well aware that specialised books abound on orchids and bulbous plants, and for this reason I will generally keep fairly clear of them, without excluding their mention, but my personal experience allows me to focus on fibrous-rooted species which will form the backbone of this volume.

Plant hunting in Europe often conveys to the reader an idea of individuals seeking out rare plants with hammer, chisel, and trowel in hand. Not so; walking in the mountains and searching for plants can be fully appreciated with a camera and notebook. To help the reader both fully appreciate and discern the best means of growing these plants, I will write at length about how these species perform in nature; as we gain understanding of these needs, our success in the garden should increase proportionately.

By way of concluding this chapter, I have to say that the scenic beauty of the mountains along with its friendly human population, and above all its exciting array of plant treasures, fascinate me to an equal degree. Let's now take up the challenge of growing them wherever possible according to their true character in nature. It will be helpful to have a look at the ecological zones from which we will make our choice of plants and in so doing, understand a little better how and where we will position these plants in our gardens.

Dianthus callizonus

Snowline 3000 to 4000 m

Alpine zone 2400 m

Subalpine zone 1800 m

Figure 1. The ecological zones in the Alps

2: Ecological Zones in the European Alps

As a grower of both mountain and true alpine plants, I endeavour to cultivate my chosen specimens so that they appear as true to their natural character as is feasible. I have made reference to mountain plants in order to encompass species that do not fall into the classic confines of a "true alpine plant". This latter term, by definition, is a plant which grows above the treeline (timberline in North America). Many alpine species also occur in meadows or open areas below the treeline, in some cases right down to sea level, but these are exceptions. In Europe, the altitudinal band in which we will locate most of the popular species to be covered in this book is between the permanent treeline (2400–3000 м) and the permanent snowline (3000–4000 м). See figure 1.

For those readers who are determined to succeed with European alpine plants, there is no substitute for understanding their habitat in nature. When visiting the mountains at the prime flowering time, it is possible to see a population of many hundreds of plants and compare forms. It is also feasible to study the exact habitat, including the microenvironment and type of rock on which they are growing. When travelling to the mountains to seek out our favourite alpine species, two important factors are immediately apparent in the true alpine zone: the cool temperatures experienced and the constant air movement around the plants, even at the height of summer in this unique environment. How many of us, having climbed up to the alpine zone, in blazing heat, have been tempted to shed some clothing? The usual experience is a sudden feeling of chill, and this will be accentuated when the clouds gather and the wind blows. Those with experience in the mountains will be prepared for the sudden changes in the weather, but even when the days are bright and sunny, there is the near certainty of frost at night. Once we are aware of these dominant features in the alpine zone, we can appreciate how challenging it will be to cultivate some of these true alpine plants in our lowland gardens.

After a number of visits to the Alps, we will observe a pronounced influence on plants within their own microenvironments. For example, snow beds frequently occur in hollows and depressions, retaining the snow much longer than on exposed ridges. Plants adapt to these extremes of condition, with *Loiseleuria procumbens* (the alpine azalea) coping with a drought-tolerant environment. The tight, cushion-forming *Diapensia lapponica* native to the Scandinavian tundra and a few sites in northwest Scotland falls into this category in nature yet adapts well to a cool position in a trough in cultivation.

In contrast to these exposed conditions, the alpenrose (*Rhododendron ferrugineum*) and the calcicole *R. hirsutum* are both intolerant of drought. They prefer to grow on steep snow beds and depressions, and when the snow melts earlier than usual, plants are highly susceptible to drying out; it is not unusual to find plants suffering from severe burning, dieback, or even death.

Rhododendron hirsutum

Another key factor we need to understand in our quest to grow these plants successfully is the difference between the quality of light which alpine plants receive at high altitudes in the wild and that which they must cope with at low elevation in our gardens. It is often stated that light intensities are higher in the mountains, notably in the spectrum of ultraviolet (UV). This may well account for more congested growth and an increased number of flowers on plants at high altitudes. I have, on occasion, managed to raise young plants of *Eritrichium nanum*, but the results are disappointing. A lax, open cushion, lacking the tomentose look of its habit in nature are just a few reasons why it is hopeless to try it in more typical lowland gardens. I have recently seen improved specimens growing in a low-altitude rock garden in southern Germany in close proximity to the mountains, and the improved light levels together with clean air and many weeks of snow cover must contribute to this success. Other examples of European species that seem to defy success at lower levels are *Androsace helvetica* and the two primulas, *Primula minima* and *P. tyrolensis*. The former primula will grow successfully, but flowering is somewhere between disappointing and nonexistent. A friend who gardens at higher altitude, near Aberdeen, northeast Scotland, has experienced success with the flowering of this species, which further argues the need for better light levels coupled with a cooler growing season.

Figure 1 on page 20 shows a cross section of a mountain scene in Europe with each of the ecological vegetation zones identified. I hope this will help readers discern the differing altitudinal bands. I must emphasise, though, that this is only a basic guide, as these altitudes vary significantly throughout the Alps.

I often recommend that alpine plant lovers make use of the numerous lifts when heading up into the alpine zone. This allows the individual more time at a higher level to study and enjoy the alpine flora. Persistent use of lifts, though, has its drawbacks. An early breakfast allows the genuine walker to set off early, and making an ascent from around 1200 M as the starting point can be a thrilling experience. Leaving the bustle of village life, we amble through lowland meadows, where cultivation is well advanced at the beginning of June. Spring-flowering species, including lily of the valley (*Convallaria majalis*) and the common oxslip (*Primula elatior*) now give way to composite species and cranesbills (*Geranium*). The first *Lilium bulbiferum* may be making their appearance with the daytime temperature rising fast. Our walk next takes us into the lowland woods, first of all the more refreshing feel from the deciduous species of tree, including beech and sweet chestnut. A gradual ascent brings a change of fragrance from deciduous woods to coniferous species including spruce, larch, and pine. A careful search in this more densely shaded woodland, where light is just able to penetrate, affords a glimpse of the single-flowered wintergreen (*Moneses uniflora*) and a few orchid species, including the helleborines (*Epipactis*).

Polygala chamaebuxus var. *purpurea*

As we approach the 2000 M point on our altimeter (typically in the Dolomites), there is a marked change in the vegetation. The forest opens up to lower growing species of pine (*Pinus mugo*), and grasses predominate. Higher light levels bring a greater range of subalpine plant species including *Clematis alpina* and *Polygala chamaebuxus*. Although we are progressing well, it is now approaching 10:30 a.m. and is getting much warmer; our exertions, together with the rise in temperatures, make for heavy work. We have now left the subalpine zone and have risen above the treeline. The terrain may well be rocky with cooler spots still covered with snow. By mid to late June, these locations will abound with newly emerging soldanellas, crocus, primulas, and the first sign of alpine buttercups.

In recent years it has been challenging to advise botanical tour operators when it is best to visit the top spots in the Alps. Traditionally I would plump for the last week in June and the first in July and experience few disappointments. The year 2003 saw a rise in spring temperatures with an early snowmelt. Alpine flowers burst into flower and the high summer temperatures caused all but those from the highest levels (more than 2500 m) to be well past their best by mid-June. Each new season must now be taken in isolation and, where possible, an assessment made at the end of spring as the snows begin the recede.

At the peak of the flowering season within the alpine zone (between 2400 and 3200 m) during late June through to August, a wide range of species can be found. In specialised habitats, the growing season at this altitude is short, perhaps compressed into a period of some 100 days. This allows a plant to emerge after the snows recede, to flower as well as to set seed with its subsequent dispersal before the autumn snows return. Within this final vegetation zone, true alpines may be found in high alpine turf, in scree, on boulders nestling in fissures of humus, or as ultraspecialised cushions growing on cliffs.

Some plants have adapted to withstand severe competition in nature, such as the lovely royal blue–flowered bellflower, *Campanula pulla*, growing in alpine turf. When species such as this are taken out of this environment and planted, for example on a raised bed, they will soon spread to dangerous proportions. They are thus best planted in a prison of rocks or on a wall or allowed to compete with comparable species in an artificial alpine lawn.

Another notable change in the character of plants takes place in the alpine zone. It involves the root system. It is well known that alpine plants enjoy a deep and cool root run, and the higher we go, invariably the deeper delving the root systems. Their root-to-shoot ratios are generally higher than those of other plants, varying from about 2:1 to 6:1, compared to values of 1:1 or less for most plants from lower altitudes. This immense root system acts mainly as a store for carbohydrates, providing a reservoir of energy to tide the plants through the long winter and prepare for the sudden surge of growth which takes place as soon as the snow melts. This understanding will again help the grower when considering the correct conditions for favourite species from this alpine zone. One of the best examples is the immense root system associated with alpine buttercups, *Ranunculus*. Creating an ideal location in the garden for species such as *R. parnassifolius*, *R. glacialis*, and *R. seguieri* is challenging to say the least.

It never ceases to astonish me when I encounter immense, flat shrublets of *Daphne petraea* hanging off limestone cliffs with no vestige of soil or humus. The same could be said of *Primula allionii* or *Campanula morettiana* amongst many species which grow in these stark conditions. It seems that they are extremely efficient at retaining nutrients once they have acquired them. I have observed a plant of *D. petraea* growing on an exposed limestone cliff where a layer of rock had eroded away, exposing about 90 sq. cm of root system lying vertically on the inner rock face. How much longer could it survive, I wondered? Over a period of many decades, this ancient plant had not only survived but thrived as a result of its vast, penetrating root system perfectly adapted to ensure a cool root run.

It is only by studying these specialised microenvironments that we can better understand how to adapt to our own conditions in lowland gardens in order to succeed with these wonderful species.

Having arrived at a truly alpine location in the mountains, perhaps at around 2500 m in the Dolomites, we may have the privilege of admiring fine specimens of *Eritrichium nanum* occupying a cleft in an alpine boulder or cliff beside the more modest *Saxifraga squarrosa*. Logic might suggest that if we are to obtain seed or nursery-grown plants of both these species, we could grow them both in the identical spot in our garden. Not so. The little saxifrage is quite amenable to cultivation and is best tucked in between rocks on a trough or raised bed—no problem. But the eritrichium defies cultivation, and there is no logical explanation as to why this disparity should take place. While this is an extreme example, many species grow cheek by jowl in nature, yet defy ease of cultivation when grown in close proximity in a garden setting.

Another significant observation from the vegetation zones relates to the terms *sun* or *shade*. As a former nurseryman who wrote many descriptions for species in my plant catalogues, references were made to the ideal position in full sun or dappled shade. But what does this really mean? Does a "sunny aspect in nature" mean that a plant must be given just such a position in the garden, or will an open, cooler position work as well? Add to this our definition of *shade*. Does it comprise just a little shade with a free sky over plants or a position on the leaside of a boulder?

Let me highlight a few examples. I well recall visiting the Maritime Alps on 13 March 1978 in search of the very local *Primula allionii*. It was at its pristine best, flowering in hairline fissures on south-facing cliffs. In sharp contrast, there were exceptionally ugly, truncated plants growing in full shade with a few flowers, yet still quite content and healthy. Successful cultivation requires a marriage of both of these conditions, but either of the extremes will generally prove unsuccessful in low-altitude gardens. There is also a marked difference in the mean daily temperatures experienced in central Scotland and the south of England, so an open, sunny spot in Scotland might suit well, but in the south of England plants could be severely scorched.

A visit to the Rhodope Mountains in Bulgaria will undoubtedly allow an encounter with that classic mountain plant, *Haberlea rhodopensis*. It is possible to find plants growing in water-moistened moss in dense shade under trees. Again,

Primula allionii
Photo by Paul Matthews.

by contrast, it is also possible to find plants in dry, sunny rock crevices. Although the plants in sunny crevices are tinder-dry in summer, they survive and flower profusely. The plants growing in dense shade produce a sparsity of flowers. Again, when we translate this example to our gardens, there is a case for balance. In my experience, this plant and its related genera, including *Ramonda* and *Jankaea*, prefer a cooler position but not too much shade to prevent free-flowering.

Careful observation of the natural conditions in which the plants described in this book are growing will enable us to make prudent choices. It may be that offering the physical property of plant association is another determining factor in order for wild plants to survive in artificial conditions in our gardens. The proviso of a little shade may be the difference between success and failure, although we may have to accept a little less than perfect flowering.

One of the major influences on alpine plants and their success in gardens relates to geology, rock type, and land form. For gardeners and plant hunters alike, a little geological knowledge is useful. Recognition of the substrate in which a plant is growing can seriously influence the plant's identification. Our first concern is the soil pH. Is the rock type or rooting substrate alkaline or acidic? We must be cautious at jumping to swift conclusions. A plant may be growing in a limestone boulder environment, but the shallow root system may be spread out in a thin layer of acidic to neutral humus, as, for example, with

Rhodothamnus chamaecistus. I will make regular reference to the term *dolomite*. We automatically think of it as limestone, but it is really made up of calcium magnesium carbonate. The influence of magnesium is so beneficial for many plants.

So as we bend down to study and photograph our favourite plant, a basic awareness of the rock type will help us as gardeners to make the correct choice of soil or aggregate. When, for example, observing an igneous rock of a porphyritic texture or schistose rock, it will often be lime-free, while white marble and dolomite are of calcareous nature. More experience in the field will add to our knowledge of the local geology, and this will further influence us in succeeding with alpine plants in our own gardens.

There can be no doubt that on each occasion in which we visit the mountains we will make another valid observation that will help us in our quest to grow these highly specialised plants. There will be plants which we either fail to grow successfully or which grow satisfactorily but refuse to flower. An example of this, in my experience, is a familiar plant of the European Alps, *Dryas octopetala*. Without a great deal of effort, I can produce a pad of luxuriant foliage and a paucity of flowers. An observation consistent over many years of this same species in nature alerted me to its preference for spreading its flat mat of foliage over a slab of limestone. The exact type of rock is not essential in the garden, but limestone is clearly what it prefers. It works a treat!

Dryas octopetala

Corydalis solida subsp. *solida*

3: Early Spring in the Garden

Most readers would agree that one of the greatest thrills we can experience in the garden emanates from plants we call the "harbingers of spring". I suppose this is partly because of the relief as we emerge from the dull winter months. Interestingly, most of my favourite spring flowers, both alpine and subalpine, seem to be native to the European mountains. Early spring will mean something quite different to gardeners in, for example, the United States and Canada by comparison to those from the milder regions of Europe, including the south of England. With the unpredictable nature of seasons now, I will assume for the purpose of writing this book that early to midspring commences in early February and runs through April in Europe and North America.

On a trip to southern Germany in mid-March 2004, the winter snows were just receding. This coincided with a rapid rise in temperatures to record levels (25°c), bringing an acceleration of emergent growth and flowering of many species.

Never before have I appreciated just how rewarding a relatively small area, 10 m by 10 m, of grass can be when planted with spring-flowering bulbs along with other fibrous-rooted species. Typical in private gardens in this part of Germany are naturalised plantings of *Leucojum vernum*, *Crocus tommasinianus*, *C. chrysanthus* and its cultivars, along with the winter aconite, *Eranthis hyemalis*.

Corydalis

Whilst staying with Dieter Schacht during the same period, I observed a similar choice of planting in his Bavarian garden, which, not surprisingly, included a range of more challenging subjects, amongst which were a wide array of colour forms from the much confused *Corydalis solida* subsp. *solida* (formerly *C. solida* var. *transylvanica*, which is now regarded as an invalid name). This subspecies includes a group of plants which, quite properly, have been elevated amongst the most sought-after of all spring-flowering bulbs, with botanists recommending group status for the deeper red forms (Sunset Group) and for paler pink ones (Sunrise Group). Let me dwell on them for a moment. Dieter was growing a variety of forms seeding naturally in short grass around the base of plum trees. He simply rooted out the less dramatic seedlings, paying particular attention to removing any with the purplish-mauve colour that rather muddies the beauty of this variable plant.

Congested clumps of tubers can be increased by lifting and dividing during the dormant season (mid to late autumn). A number of clones have been given cultivar names, and as a result of the proliferation of this practise a word of caution should be issued. Soon after the flowering of these plants, it will be noted that the green seed capsules begin to mature and by late spring they pop open, shedding numerous shiny-brown seeds amongst and around the parent plants. To give an example of a popular cultivar I will focus attention on the brick-red *Corydalis solida* subsp. *solida* 'George Baker'. The resulting seedlings from this one will vary greatly in colour from reds through to purplish pinks. Once the seedlings have matured and formed tubers, they will merge into the parent clumps, creating a major problem when lifted during dormancy, particularly if each tuber is potted up and offered either to friends or to the nursery trade. There will now be a mixture of tubers deviating from the original brick-red. I have taken time to emphasise this situation, because in recent years, there are many impostors being offered in the U.K. with cultivar names which bear no resemblance to the correct plant, in this case the cultivar 'George Baker'.

Some of the finest red and pink colour forms of this corydalis originate from a rather local area in Romania. They were first introduced by the well-known Dutch bulb firm, Van Tubergen, in 1925. Tubers were then distributed to the Munich Botanic Garden in the 1940s, from whence some of the best forms have been subsequently distributed.

The first cultivar name was given to 'George Baker', which was awarded a First Class Certificate (FCC) by the Royal Horticultural Society in 1988. The RHS also conducts trials of various groups of plants, and in 1997 a trial of tuberous-rooted corydalis took place at the RHS Garden Wisley in Surrey, England. The Award of Garden Merit (AGM) is the society's symbol of excellence given to plants of outstanding garden value. Amongst the cultivars recommended for this award were *Corydalis solida* subsp. *solida* 'George Baker' and *C. solida* subsp. *solida* 'Dieter Schacht', a rich, apple-blossom pink form that I named from a batch of seedlings given to me by Dieter whilst he was curator of the alpine department at the Munich Botanic Garden. This cultivar has proved to be the best and most widely distributed of the current pink forms. It is compact, vigorous, and free-flowering, commencing in early spring, with its flowers held well

Corydalis solida **subsp.** *solida* 'Dieter Schacht'
Photo by Jim Jermyn.

above the finely divided, glaucous green foliage. It enjoys both dappled shade or a sunny aspect amongst deciduous trees and can be a wonderful addition to the woodland garden. I would strongly recommend the deeper crimson selection 'Wilhelm Schacht' along with the startling red cultivar 'Latvian Zwanenburg', and 'Maggie Mathew' with warm red flowers and a hint of orange. My initial love of these corydalis was spurred on after viewing a frame of potted plants at the Munich Botanic Garden, including many of these coloured forms plunged in sand amongst a selection of golden-yellow flowered forms of *Narcissus bulbocodium*. Quite a sight!

Named after *korydalis*, Greek for lark, as the flowers are said to resemble that bird's crested head, corydalis belong to the family Papaveraceae. They are commonly known as fumitories. The European species and each of the abovementioned cultivars are fully hardy and easily grown with the following proviso: the cooler and damper the conditions during the summer rest period, the more exposure they will take. It is summer heat and drought that often leads to the loss of tubers. I would personally recommend working into the soil plenty of gritty sand along with leaf mould at the time of planting, and top-dressing annually during the summer dormancy with leaf mould. Most species and cultivars, as already mentioned, can be propagated by division of tubers when dormant and also from seed which should be sown as soon as it is ripe.

Early spring colour is traditionally associated with bulbous species, and it is not my intention to write at length about these subjects due to the abundance of specialist books already available on the subject. Plant association is, though, such a pleasure with these bulbous plants, and as the spring warmth draws these species out of their dormancy, there are a few more I want to highlight.

Eranthis and Galanthus

Here in Berwickshire, Scotland, flowering in my garden commences with the winter aconite (*Eranthis hyemalis*) and the earliest of snowdrops (*Galanthus nivalis* and *G. elwesii*). The two genera combine wonderfully when they are allowed to form drifts amongst deciduous trees or planted in short turf. Winter aconites have been grown in gardens for more than 400 years, providing colour before most plants have ventured above ground. It is my experience that wherever we garden, a typical neighbourly greeting in late winter or early spring can be initiated by a conferring of "isn't it a joy to see the first aconites and snowdrops, a sign of spring". A real talking point!

The characteristic, yellow buttercuplike flowers set against a frilly, bright green ruff of leaves are easily recognised. Although cultivars are rare, a few have appeared in plant catalogues of late. Despite their charming beauty, the winter aconite is one of the most poisonous plants we grow in our gardens. Related to the monkshood (*Aconitum*), the poisonous nature of these plants may be known to some readers, but I felt it was worthy of mention to those unaware of their toxic properties.

This little member of Ranunculaceae is native to France, Italy, and the Balkan region, where it can be found in deciduous woods and rocky places. It is also widely naturalised in many parts of Europe. *Eranthis hyemalis* is by far the most commonly grown species, with stems reaching up to 15 cm tall, including the golden-yellow flower, which has up to eight petals (sepals) and six nectaries. During the past century there have been some attempts to raise hybrids, and in 1923 *E. hyemalis* (Tubergenii Group) 'Guinea Gold' was raised in Haarlem, in the Netherlands. This cultivar has proved to be absolutely sterile in my garden and is altogether a larger and more robust plant bearing the qualities of both parents (*E. hyemalis* × *E. cilicica*). It is this sterility which commends us this plant when only a small area is available. It is from its Turkish cousin, *E. cilicica*, that this hybrid inherits the quality of emerging shoots tinged with bronze. Plants of *E. hyemalis* will increase very rapidly from seed in cool, moist conditions; it is best moved in full growth for maximum success, and divided plants must be well watered. The sterile hybrid, 'Guinea Gold', should be allowed to establish for several years before dividing clumps during the dormant season.

Much has been written about snowdrops (*Galanthus*) in recent years, with an ever-increasing enthusiasm for these charming plants. The human disorder relating to this passion is now known as "Galanthophilia", and most of us who love spring flowers will admit to suffering from it to a greater or lesser degree. It should come as no surprise that at present there are some 700 named cultivars of snowdrop in circulation.

Most good new snowdrops arise amongst swarms of seedlings produced where compatible parents are growing in quantity. In my locality of southeast Scotland, this situation exists in grounds of country houses and in undisturbed deciduous woodland. Where several species grow—most notably, *Galanthus elwesii*, *G. nivalis*, and *G. plicatus*—the greatest fun begins to unfold. I well recall my restrained joy when visiting the garden of the late Miss Diane Aitchison in Northumberland, England, where her deciduous woodland was amassed with

Galanthus nivalis with *Eranthis hyemalis*

good plants, including many snowdrops. Diane calmly drew my attention to a flowering clump of plicate-leaved hybrids, each bearing exquisite flowers where both the inner segments and ovaries were golden yellow instead of green. I gratefully accepted the offer to dig up a plant of the finest specimen, which I later named 'Spindlestone Surprise' (commemorating her nursery garden), a form showing a striking resemblance to *G. plicatus*. It was awarded the coveted FCC by the RHS when exhibited quite beautifully by Dr. Ronald Mackenzie in the spring of 2004.

My preference is to enjoy a naturalised swarm of the species along with a few of the finest cultivars amongst *Eranthis hyemalis* and the easy to please *Crocus tommasinianus*. If I were asked to choose a few of my favourite cultivars to complement the aforementioned species, they would include the following: *Galanthus* 'S. Arnott', a lovely, tall snowdrop was given an Award of Merit (AM) by the RHS in 1957. It is noted for its sweet scent and vigour. *Galanthus* 'Bertram Anderson' is an outstanding *G. plicatus* hybrid awarded an AM in 1996. *Galanthus* 'Mighty Atom' is a cultivar with an outrageously large flower. These are just a few choice cultivars, but here I must stop and be satisfied with the simple beauty of the naturalised species. Each one of these cultivars is best divided in the green, soon after flowering.

Crocus

I mentioned *Crocus* species as a virtuous companion, and the more I visit established gardens in early to midspring, the more I appreciate the simple beauty of this genus. Anyone who has had the pleasure of encountering a vast meadow of *Crocus vernus* subsp. *albiflorus* in the European Alps, forming a carpet of white or purple as soon as the snows recede, will appreciate the beauty of this simple flower. The European mountains are home to many more exciting species. I would recommend a selection from the following early spring-flowering species to complement a colourful planting amongst the aforementioned genera. Native to western Italy is the lilac-flowered *C. etruscus*, mixing well with golden-yellow *C. chrysanthus* from the Balkan peninsula. A selection of some of the best cultivars of *C. chrysanthus*, such as 'Cream Beauty', 'Snow Bunting', and 'Zwanenburg Bronze', are outstanding when planted in groups around deciduous trees with corydalis and snowdrops. *Crocus tommasinianus* naturalises well in short grass but has a tendency to flop due to its slender flower stems. Native to the Balkan region, this lilac to purple-flowering species may be found in woods and shady hillsides. From the same region is the popular *C. sieberi*, much smaller in habit, with flowers in various shades of lilac to purple with a yellow throat.

Crocus vernus subsp. *albiflorus*

Each of these species, along with the widely available cultivars, can be planted as dry corms in the autumn or planted in flower, when offered as potted plants in the spring. A patch of short grass amongst trees planted with a range of the above species and cultivars is a special joy as the spring sunshine encourages the flowers to open and attract the first activity of bees in search of nectar amongst the bright array of colour.

Erythronium

Whilst helping to develop a nursery on the side of Lake Garda, northern Italy, I had the privilege of finding fine stands of *Erythronium dens-canis*, the dog's tooth violet, flowering in early spring. They were growing in grassy meadows amongst mature specimens of sweet chestnut trees (*Castanea sativa*). Known to

Erythronium dens-canis

gardeners for centuries for its medicinal properties, *E. dens-canis* has been advocated as a cure for worms of the stomach! It is widespread in Europe, flowering in open meadows as the snow melts from April to June. In the garden, I grow it either in humus-rich beds in full sun amongst deciduous trees or in short grass. Care should be taken to avoid planting bulbs in too much shade, as clumps of lush foliage may predominate at the expense of flowers.

In its best forms, I feel that the maroon and brown mottling of the foliage promotes *Erythronium* as one of the finest bulbous species for the early spring garden. It is, however, on the basis of flower colour that most of the cultivars can be distinguished. The nodding flowers are usually held singly on a 10 CM stem and are made up of a perianth of six segments. The colour varies from a glowing pink to purple and white. My choice of cultivars would include the purple-flowering 'Frans Hals', 'Pink Perfection', and 'Snowflake'. These are all vigorous and reliable in the garden.

Narcissus

I wonder how we could possibly rationalise our choice from the outstanding genus *Narcissus*, a member of the family Amaryllidaceae. With an ever-increasing number of people spending their holidays looking for plants, there is clearly a need for specialist books to meet the demands of these individuals. It is not my intention to fill this need, and I am relieved at the number of excellent monographs covering individual genera—notably those of a bulbous nature. The one written by John Blanchard (1990) on the subject of narcissus and published by the Alpine Garden Society (AGS) is no exception. In his foreword, he writes about the problem of identification within this genus, and this is not an observation that is unique to narcissus. Amongst the alpine flora I plan to write about, bulbous species, including allium and the vast array of orchids, sempervivum, linum, viola, and grasses, are often very difficult to identify. When encountering these plants in the field, the difficulties can be compounded when several species come together, resulting in a hybrid swarm.

When the same process occurs in the garden, we are generally overjoyed, and I will highlight a few hybrids that typified the diversity of this wonderful genus. Each year I eagerly await the emergence and subsequent flowering of our display of daffodils. I am sure we would agree with the words of the English poet William Wordsworth, who wrote

> I wandered lonely as a cloud
> That floats on high o'er vales and hills,
> When all at once I saw a crowd,
> A host, of golden daffodils;
> Beside the lake, beneath the trees,
> Fluttering and dancing in the breeze.

While his experience took place near his home in the Lake District, northwest England, and involved the naturalised *Narcissus pseudonarcissus*, we, too, could share this experience in the mountains of Europe. The most often encountered species is *N. poeticus* var. *poeticus*. It comes from a wide altitudinal range from near sea level to about 2000 M in many parts of Europe. Although the variety *N. poeticus* var. *recurvus* with its swept-back petals is accurately referred to as the pheasant's eye daffodil, I refer to all forms of the species by this common name. To experience a vast meadow of this plant in the mountains of central Europe, and most notably the Pyrénées, is a sight to savour, but the fragrance is simply wonderful. Fields of them in nature can extend to hundreds of acres containing literally millions of bulbs. In nature they flower from March until July according to altitude and the season. It is the disc-shaped corona, with its red edge set amidst white petals on up to 36 CM stems, that makes this species so attractive and desirable.

In sharp contrast is the most easily identified dwarf *Narcissus cyclamineus*, with its bright green leaves and pendant flowers. The specific name describes the way the petals are reflexed, and this feature is persistent in many of the most desirable dwarf hybrid daffodils of the cyclamineus section. The species was first described in 1816, and partly due to overzealous collectors, it has become scarce in the wild. It is so easily raised from seed that one hopes that all collecting in its native Portugal and northern Spain will have ceased. Bright yellow flowers are held on 10 CM stems over spreading green foliage. It grows naturally in damp, heavy soil and in my experience thrives in a cool, dampish, acid soil. When happily growing in these conditions, it will naturalise and spread by seed. When planted amongst the pink-flowered corydalis around the base of trees and shrubs, this association is one of the real thrills of spring in the garden.

I strongly recommend adding a few hybrids from this section, as their result-ing vigour will produce clumps more rapidly. I am at present growing a cultivar by the name of *Narcissus* 'Mitzi' that always draws the eye with its yellow trum-pet and cream-coloured petals. A final species I would also strongly recommend is the widely available *N. asturiensis*. It is native to northern Spain and the west-ern Spanish Pyrénées. It may be found flowering from February to mid-May in the Picos de Europa as soon as the snow melts, at an altitude of about 1500 M. The solitary yellow flowers are held on 7 to 15 CM stems. It hybridises freely with *N. cyclamineus* and resultant plants are given the name *N.* 'Minicycla'. I have exercised considerable restraint with my choice here.

Leucojum

From one outstanding genus to another, I now wish to extol the virtues of the spring snowflake, *Leucojum vernum*. In his much-revered book, *The English Rock Garden* (1919), Farrer referred to it as follows:

> By far the best of all is *L. carpaticum*, [now recognised as *L. vernum* var. *carpathicum*] which sends up ample, cosy, wide cups of pure white, tipped with gold in earliest spring, hanging from stout stems of 8 to 10 CM and incomparably more cheerful than those chilly snowdrops, more warm and brilliant in its white, set off by that golden tip to each segment, more hearty in the shape of its flower and more luxuriant in the bright green gloss of its broad foliage.

I thought some of my sentences were somewhat lengthy, but I do not feel so bad if the great man can wax so lyrically! I agree wholeheartedly with his sentiments, but fortunately we do not need to seek out exclusively the Carpathian form of spring snowflake. I would not go as far as to malign humble snowdrops, though.

On a recent trip to southern Germany, I was enchanted by the great quantities of the species *Leucojum vernum* choosing dappled shade amongst deciduous woodland, while often found in luxuriant forms along the banks of streams growing side by side with *Galanthus nivalis*. It flowers there from March to May as soon as the snow melts. Typically, the flowering stems are 15 to 20 CM, each carrying a single nodding head with a green spot on each petal. Yellow-spotted forms will be found in large populations, yet the form *L. vernum* var. *car-pathicum* does tend to display consistent yellow spotting, while the more robust and taller variety *L. vernum* var. *vagneri* from Hungary generally has two flow-ers to a stem and green spotting.

Leucojum vernum

I feel that this variable species is still very much underrated as a garden plant and, apart from its strong aversion to drying out, can easily be propagated by division of the bulbs in the green. Indeed, it deserves to be much more widely planted, notably where moisture prevails.

Anemone

Flowering in the garden from early to midspring is the most attractive and easy to please wood anemone, *Anemone nemorosa*. Found growing in woods and shady hillsides in northern Europe, this species may be looked down upon by some as the lowly white-flowering wood anemone, but it should rightly join the proudest beauties of this great family Ranunculaceae. With so many fine cultivars available in catalogues, each form will associate admirably with hepatica, hacquetia, and narcissus. Closely related to *A. nemorosa* is another species from northern Europe, *A. ranunculoides* with golden-yellow flowers. The two species occasionally meet in the wild and produce a most desirable lemon-yellow flowered hybrid, *A.* ×*lipsiensis*. The cultivation of species, hybrids, and the named cultivars is straightforward in a moisture-retentive soil. Large mats of creeping, twiglike rhizomes soon form near the surface of the soil, from which emerge deeply cleft leaves in loose clusters. Flower stems vary in length from 8 to 30 cm and of the garden forms I will now recommend, most are widely available in the nursery trade.

Amongst the white-flowering forms, I have found that *Anemone nemorosa* 'Lady Doneraile' is the first to flower, often in midspring, producing 15 cm stems, each carrying an immense, pure white, nodding flower. It combines so well with *Hepatica nobilis* and the late, pink-flowering *Corydalis solida* forms. A whole host of blue-flowering cultivars are available in the trade, but it is difficult to verify the validity of their naming. They set much seed which will, in part, germinate amongst the mature clump of rhizomes, giving rise to future variation in colour and form. This said, the cultivar 'Allenii' has soft blue flowers with a lovely scent. A very fine double white by the name of 'Vestal' is a favourite, while the hybrid *A.* ×*lipsiensis* 'Seemannii' has bronze emerging foliage along with lemon-yellow flowers.

Hepatica

If asked about my absolute favourite early-spring flowering plant, it would be *Hepatica nobilis*, another member of the buttercup family, Ranunculaceae. As with many of the species described thus far, this one fits into the subalpine ecological zone, where it inhabits both lowland and mountain woods. A search through beech woods in southern Germany towards the end of March will often reveal the first flowers amongst the previous season's trilobed foliage. The colour of flowers varies greatly, and while blue is the dominant colour, many woods will support populations of red, pink, and whites interspersed with blue. In the French Pyrénées, forms are often found above the treeline with white flowers and marbled foliage.

In nature, it is my belief that despite the fact that they grow best of all in a well-drained, humus-rich soil, there is a strong preference for an alkaline soil. The upper 10 cm of soil is generally made up of rotting leaves. It is this part of the equation that I feel is of utmost importance to recreate in our own gardens. On my acid soil I find that without the leaf mould, European hepaticas perform poorly. A number of growers report success with applications of well-rotted mushroom compost, the basis of which is generally horse manure and added lime. It should preferably be of a well-rotted consistency.

The name *hepatica* is taken from the Greek *heppar* meaning the liver, alluding to the shape of the lobed foliage. In Germany they are popularly known as *leberblumchen* (liver flowers). The species *Hepatica nobilis* is widespread throughout most of Europe from Spain, Italy, through to the Balkans. Although, as already mentioned, they generally grow in lowland woods, hepaticas can be found growing quite happily at altitudes of up to 2200 M.

The varietal name *Hepatica nobilis* var. *pyrenaica* is often given to a compact form from the Pyrénées with beautifully marbled foliage. The dominant colour tends to be white, but pale blue forms may also be found along with a particular favourite of mine which has been named 'Apple Blossom'. The flowering stems in all forms are generally some 8 to 10 CM in height.

Propagation of *Hepatica* could not be easier, as an abundance of seed is usually set, enabling a sowing to be made as soon as it can be harvested in the green. With flowering taking place from late winter to midspring, seed begins to set through late spring and early summer and, once ripe, quickly falls to the

Hepatica nobilis

ground. The new season's growth of foliage may partially hide the ripened seed heads, so a careful search needs to be undertaken. When the seeds are ripe they will fall away; caught in an egg cup, they should be sown immediately. I would recommend sowing onto a mix made up of a John Innes seed compost (or a loam-based proprietary mix) with added leaf mould. I then sieve a thin layer of compost over the seed and then finally sprinkle a layer of flint chick grit on top, carefully label, and then water from the base. The seed pots should be plunged in sand and left in the open with dappled or artificial shade and kept moist.

Seeds will generally germinate the following spring. I do not prick out the seedlings for another year until they are well established. I will repot the whole pot of seedlings into a fresh mixture and feed with a liquid, low-nitrogen tomato fertiliser. The seedlings can then be separated as they break into growth the following spring, but I prefer to separate the roots, as with all members of Ranunculaceae, in a pail of water to wash away the soil. Where space is not an issue, I would also suggest an alternative method: sowing the seeds individually in cellular trays, so that the developed seedlings can be potted up or planted out without any root disturbance. Once we have mastered the craft of raising hepaticas from seed, the next stage is to select the best flowering strains from seed, developing, for example, deep blues, dark reds, or pure white ones.

Generations of hepatica lovers have paid serious money and traded swaps for the much sought after, double-flowering forms. These are available in small numbers from specialist nurseries and can be grown in exactly the same way as single forms. Division of established clumps should be carried out during mid to late summer.

From the mountain woods of central Romania comes the more robust and spreading *Hepatica transsilvanica*. Forming large clumps, this species differs in structure from *H. nobilis* with its crenate to dentate leaf lobes. It will thrive in somewhat drier conditions and spreads by creeping rhizomes. The flower stems are longer than those of *H. nobilis*, often as much as 15 CM. A number of fine forms of *H. transsilvanica* are available from specialist nurseries, with the following being those that I would recommend: 'Ada Scott' is a vigorous clone with a deep blue flower named by Valerie Finnis. 'Eisvogel' is an excellent white form with a pale blue flash on the reverse of each petal. 'Elison Spence' is a semi-double blue form thought to have originated in Ireland.

In 1916, the late Ernest Ballard raised a quite outstanding hybrid between the two European species, named *Hepatica* ×*media* 'Ballardii'. The hybrid has very large, ice-blue, velvetlike flowers up to 5 CM across on 10 CM stems and received an AM in 1938. I have specimens planted amongst *Narcissus cyclamineus* and the compact form of *Daphne blagayana* 'Brenda Anderson', and the floral association in late March to early April is quite special. With the sterile hybrid producing no seed, clumps can be divided during the summer months, provided the plants are not suffering the stress of drought. It is beneficial to soak a plant the night before division is planned in order to promote a successful transition after propagation. Although generally found in woodland conditions in nature, I have found both the species and forms perform admirably in open positions as long as the soil is not allowed to dry out too much. Dappled shade is perhaps a safer recommendation for this outstanding spring-flowering member of the buttercup family.

Hacquetia and *Daphne blagayana*

Hacquetia epipactis is an early-flowering member of the carrot family, Umbelliferae, that I prefer to plant amongst hepaticas in dappled shade. The genus commemorates an Austrian writer on alpine flowers, Balthasar Hacquet (1740–1815), and may be found in deciduous woods throughout the Eastern Alps. It is a glabrous perennial forming creeping rhizomes with attractive trifoliate leaves in neat tufts. The golden-yellow flowers are in the form of a boss sitting on a frill of lime-green bracts.

Hacquetia epipactis
Photo by Jim Jermyn.

Solid clumps can be divided during the late summer whilst moist, allowing propagules to develop a new root system before dormancy. An observant eye will also spot developing seed in the early summer, which should be rubbed off when ripe and sown at once.

Many gardeners experience a love-hate relationship with variegated forms of a popular plant. It takes quite a bit for me to become excited about a variegated plant, but I have a great fondness for *Hacquetia epipactis* 'Thor', which is a lovely companion to so many blue-flowered subjects. It is it little stronger growing in my acid soil than the type species, and both the foliage and bracts are variegated, giving the plant a justifiably expensive price tag. I have planted it close to the deepest gentian blue–flowering form of *Pulmonaria angustifolia* 'Blue Ensign', where they both complement each other nicely, flowering in late March through April.

The genus *Daphne* will receive fuller coverage later through the geographic chapter headings. It is, though, wholly appropriate to describe the early spring-flowering *D. blagayana* at this stage. It was originally discovered in 1837 by Count Blagay in part of his estate on Mount Lorenziberg in Slovenia. It is often found amongst *Erica carnea* on calcareous soils, and this combination works extremely well in the garden where space provides. The bright red-flowering *E. carnea* 'Myretoun Ruby' contrasts well with the creamy white flowers of the daphne. It seems to have been introduced into European gardens around the 1870s. When exhibited by Messrs. Veitch in 1880, it received the distinction of an FCC; how well deserved that award has proved to be.

This daphne is easily grown on either acid or alkaline soils, and it loves to ramble in a cool, well-drained, humus-rich soil. A regular top dressing of leaf mould will further enhance the quality of its flowering. Long, trailing stems ascend to a height of some 15 to 30 CM each, one with a terminal head containing up to 30 very fragrant, creamy white flowers. The stems are clothed with dark green alternate leaves. After flowering, which takes place from late winter to early spring, some two or three new growths will sprout from the terminal shoot, thus extending the spread.

The species enjoys a wide distribution from southeast Austria into the Balkan region, as well as the Carpathian mountains, where it is often known as the *königsblume* or king's flower, as a king of Saxony is reputed to have made a special journey to Transylvania in search of it. One very distinct form is in cultivation, notably more compact in nature than the type species. It was introduced by well-known plantswoman Brenda Anderson, who, along with her husband, gardened in the Carse of Gowrie near Dundee, Scotland. She found this compact form on the slopes of Mount Durmitor, Montenegro, and it is now available

Daphne blagayana

from a few specialist nurseries and appropriately named *Daphne blagayana* 'Brenda Anderson'. I have been growing it for several years, and it maintains a neat little shrublet, in sharp contrast with its cousin, which, if allowed, will cover several square metres. The eminent botanist and former director of Kew Gardens, Sir George Taylor, grew a colony in his Hertfordshire garden which reputedly reached more than 5 M across.

Despite its ease of cultivation, the species is seldom offered in nurseries. Propagation is best achieved by taking semiripe cuttings, the timing of which in my experience is fairly critical. I take them in the late summer or when stems have reached about 10 to 15 CM in length. They should be dipped in a liquid fungicide and then inserted into a mixture of equal parts peat and perlite. They should root easily over bottom heat in the shaded propagator. Care should be taken to ensure that cuttings are not in contact with each other, thus reducing the spread of fungal disease. This fine species will likely feature in many a gardener's top ten list of most popular European alpine plants.

Helleborus niger

Helleborus

If there is such a thing as a real vogue plant, then at the time of writing it must surely be the hellebore. The European mountains are host to some of the most sought-after species and much of eastern Europe seems to be the natural epicentre for many of them. I will highlight a few for their early spring display. My firm favourite is *Helleborus niger*, the Christmas rose. My parents always pick a posy of flowers for Christmas from their garden at around sea level on the east coast of Scotland. A few miles inland and my plants regularly flower in March. I still love to see their pristine white flowers whenever they open.

Hellebores have been known to man for more than 2000 years, for Theophrastus (372–287 BC) used the name freely as if it were well-known in Greek history. In more recent history, around 1565 in *De Materia Medica*, Matthiolus illustrated *Helleborus niger* as well as *H. viridis*. It is important to mention the poisonous properties of hellebores, most notably amongst the following species: *H. argutifolius*,

H. foetidus, and *H. orientalis*. It may be that when collecting seeds there will be some nasty side effects to the tips of the fingers, and wearing gloves would therefore be advisable.

For me, there can be no finer sight than a well-proportioned clump of *Helleborus niger* with its perfectly created, nodding flowers held above those glistening, dark green leaves. Classified as *H. niger* by Linnaeus in 1753, in the wild it is found in mountain woods on calcareous formations as well as grassy alpine meadows from 400 to 2000 m. It is most commonly located in Austria, southern Germany, northern Italy, and the Balkans. It flowers as soon as the snow melts in early spring onwards. The best forms should be propagated by freshly sown seed. As soon as the pods (follicles) split open, usually in late spring in cultivation, the seeds should be sown and the pots plunged in a cold frame. The seeds should be covered with a thin layer of grit. Germination usually takes place the following autumn or winter.

I well remember fine clumps of the form *Helleborus niger* subsp. *macranthus* growing and seeding about on the rock garden in the Munich Botanic Garden. This form is native to northern Italy, with the foliage a little more glaucous in colour.

Helleborus niger subsp. *macranthus*

Helleborus argutifolius

Where space provides, I could not be without stately plants of *Helleborus argutifolius*, the Corsican hellebore. It produces a woody stem bearing attractive foliage and a terminal inflorescence made up of cuplike, pale green flowers. When carefully positioned in the garden, it draws attention as an architectural plant and is one of the earliest to flower in midwinter.

My final choice from such a celebrated genus is the species *Helleborus multifidus*. The specific name makes reference to the foliage, the leaflets of which are divided to varying degrees. In the wild, *H. multifidus* is a plant of sparse, deciduous woods and open, grassy hillsides subject to extensive drying out in the summer months. The pendant, greenish yellow flowers tend to precede the foliage. The largest flowering form is the southern Italian variant, *H. multifidus* subsp. *bocconei*, which is most striking, and I would recommend that keen growers of this genus look out for it.

The type species is native to the Balkans in the central region of the Adriatic coastal mountains. Plants generally reach 20 to 30 cm in height at flowering time, from late winter to midspring in cultivation. All forms are easily raised from seed.

Pulsatilla and Adonis

Early spring is associated with another two exciting genera, *Pulsatilla* and *Adonis*, both members of Ranunculaceae. I will describe a few lowland species from both genera. Many keen plantsfolk in the south of England will make an annual pilgrimage over the Easter period to look for pasque flowers, *Pulsatilla vulgaris*, in its few remaining stations. Across the channel, the same species, along with the closely related *P. grandis*, is more common and enjoys a very wide distribution. Often frequenting chalk downland and open grassland, plants form tufts of carrotlike foliage with rich purple, erect or nodding flowers on 15 CM stems. The familiar flowers are followed by fluffy seed heads, which, when ripe, will fall away in the hand and can be sown at once, providing the best means of propagation. Cultivated plants should not be allowed to become waterlogged, and they strongly resent root disturbance. A showy red-flowering cultivar is named *P. vulgaris* 'Rubra'.

Pulsatilla vulgaris 'Rubra'

Associating well with purple-flowered pulsatillas are *Adonis* species. The first European species to flower in cultivation is the very rare *A. cyllenea* from a few isolated stations in southern Greece. As well as being desperately rare in nature, it is not yet widely available in cultivation—one to look out for! It was first discovered by the botanist Heldreich in 1848 and later described in 1856. After 1893, no more observations were recorded and it was thought to be extinct. Then in 1976, Greek botanist George Sfikas was presented with flowers by a friend who had found the plant on Mount Parnas. In more recent decades, continued threat of overgrazing endangers this species. It is found growing in full sun or dappled shade at the base of limestone rocks, where a cooler root run can be provided. I can best describe the plant as sensational, growing up to and in excess of 45 CM, with attractive pinnate foliage and huge, bright yellow flowers, consisting of 8 to 12 wide petals. In cultivation it flowers in early to midspring and should be planted in pride of place, providing an open, sunny, sheltered position in a freely drained soil.

Adonis, like the genus *Ranunculus*, produces fruit in the form of many achenes.

Adonis vernalis

After flowering, the keen grower of this genus will watch the ripening achenes very carefully. As the late spring moves into summer, they ripen and can be carefully prised from their seating into your hand or an awaiting egg cup or envelope. Adonis seeds are large, green, and valuable. They should, as with all members of the family, be sown at once on to a loam-based compost, given a generous covering of grit, and then be plunged in a sand frame. The seed may germinate sporadically, commencing the following spring, but the seed pot should be retained for several years, as certain conditions may suddenly provoke a break in dormancy. It is my experience that old seed rarely germinates.

More widely available is the lovely species *Adonis vernalis*, found in stony grassland and scrub throughout much of Europe. I know of a favourite site just north of Munich, southern Germany, where it grows in acres of dry, grassy meadow along with *Pulsatilla vulgaris*. This site is protected by the Nature Conservancy and is carefully managed in order to preserve this desirable species along with its associated biodiversity. Flowering stems generally range from 20 to 30 cm and are unbranched with sessile leaves concentrated toward their tips.

The golden flowers are up to 8 CM across, with established clumps producing a fine show. Once again, a sunny, well-drained position is essential, and patience is a virtue in order to establish plants. Care should be taken to protect all pulsatilla and adonis from the attention of slugs.

Vernales Primulas

Many experienced and keen growers of alpine plants agree that it is often the simplest and most common plants that provide the greatest pleasure. It should therefore be no surprise that I will now give due attention to a few early-flowering members of the *Vernales* section of *Primula* according to the classification of primulas by Wright Smith and Fletcher. The various species which give equal pleasure to both the plant hunter and gardener alike include *Primula vulgaris*, *P. veris*, *P. elatior*, and *P. amoena*. With the exception of the last named species, *P. amoena* (synonym *P. elatior* subsp. *meyeri*), all are widespread in Europe. Because of its great beauty and value as a garden plant, I will describe *P. vulgaris*, despite daring to stretch my geographic boundary into European Turkey.

Primula vulgaris is surely one of the best loved of all wildflowers. Known as the common primrose, it is widely distributed across Europe, preferring open woodland and shady meadows, especially by streams and ditches, often preferring to grow on alkaline soils. Neat rosettes of foliage form a lovely base for the posy of sulphur-yellow flowers, opening from early to midspring in the wild. Cultivation in the garden is not always straightforward, and I find that clumps may be short lived in my acid soil.

A firm favourite of mine is its geographic variant from central Greece and farther east into Turkey and Armenia—the very variable *Primula vulgaris* subsp. *sibthorpii*. It differs from the type species purely in its diversity of flower colour. I well recall sitting in the home of the late Dr. George Smith, looking at slides from a recent trip he had made to Turkey in search of primulas. To this day, I still look at these slides that he kindly gave to me, in utter bewilderment. The sheer abundance in which they are growing and the range of colours is breathtaking. Jim and Jenny Archibald collected seed from this population of plants, and for many years I grew a range of coloured forms including lemon-yellow, pure white, and soft pinks to a glowing purple. Some were sweetly fragrant to add to the pleasure of growing them. In some woods, all the colours could be found growing together, but often, as the contours changed, so, too, did the flower colours. This variation is well described in *Curtis's Botanical Magazine*, 1966–68, and is a fine example of polymorphism displayed within this well-known subspecies.

Primula veris

Primula elatior
Photo by Jim Jermyn.

Primula amoena
Photo by Jim Jermyn.

The cowslip, *Primula veris*, is one of the most widespread of all primulas in Europe. In the best forms it is a thrill to find its great colonies on grassy embankments, beckoning us to bend down to enjoy its unique fragrance.

Closely related to the foregoing, but easily distinguished, is the oxslip, *Primula elatior*. Once again widely distributed, it prefers, by contrast, damp meadows and open woodland but ventures to higher altitudes in the Alps and Pyrénées, up to 2200 m. I have seen fine stands of this species in southern Germany in damp meadows, and a finer sight it is hard to imagine, with its umbels of lemon-yellow flowers. It is the easiest of this section to grow in the garden, and fine populations may be raised from seed, with plants flowering from early to mid-spring. The finest of all the geographic forms that I grow is *P. elatior* subsp. *pallasii*, which is to be found right on the border between Europe and Asia, from the Ural Mountains. I am growing solid clumps of this subspecies raised from the Archibalds' seed, and subsequent generations from seed show no sign of variation. The lemon-yellow, sweetly fragrant flowers are quite immense, and it associates admirably in the garden with blue-flowered *Hepatica transsilvanica*.

My final choice is the closely related *Primula amoena*, sometimes sunk into *P. elatior* subsp. *meyeri*. It varies considerably in colour of flower and in its best forms has stunning reddish purple flowers. I have this colour form growing close to *P. elatior* subsp. *pallasii* and some of the resulting seedlings have wonderful lemon-yellow flowers with dark maroon calyces. It is widespread in the Pontic Mountains of northeast Turkey. As with all members of this section, propagation is achieved from seed.

Androsace villosa

4: The Pyrénées

Commencing my journey across the European mountain ranges, I will focus first of all on some familiar plants from the Pyrénées. I must point out that my own view of growing alpine plants is far from scientific. I prefer to grow a range of plants in the open garden, simply and naturally, with a minimum of fuss and an absence of paraphernalia. Where possible, I try to persevere with a favourite species despite experiencing disappointment, and I try to apply the proverb, "If at first you don't succeed try, try again."

I will travel across the Alps from west to east, concluding my journey with a closer look at some favourite species from the Carpathian mountains. Whether we are travelling in the Pyrénées or elsewhere, it is worth reiterating that the most useful knowledge from which we can benefit is an understanding of the nature of the soil, with the most obvious contrast being between calcareous and noncalcareous formations. It is for this reason that I will often make reference to whether a plant is found on a calcareous (limestone) substrate—that is, a calcicole plant—or the contrasting calcifuge species, which grows on a lime-free or acid soil.

When translating all this to our lowland gardens, it appears that plenty of plants are equally happy on limy or nonlimy soils, despite the fact that in nature the same plants exhibit a clear preference for one or the other rock formation. With experience, as growers, we will soon grasp which species have a genuine demand for limestone in the garden or a lime-free soil.

The Pyrénées form a mountain barrier some 350 KM between France and Spain, extending from the Bay of Biscay to the shores of the Mediterranean. The highest peak, the Pico de Aneto, rises to 3404 M on the Spanish side of the frontier.

Panoramic peaks are not the highlight of the Pyrénées by comparison to the more picturesque Dolomites and Swiss Alps, yet they do support a wide range of exciting plants, many of which are endemic, not occurring anywhere else in the Alps.

The Cantabrian Mountains and the Picos de Europa

Forming an east-west ridge along the north coast of Spain are the Cantabrian Mountains, creating an ill-defined point of separation from the western Pyrénées. Around the centre of the cordillera, the range rises to its greatest height in a dramatic block of mountains, the Picos de Europa. It is my observation that this part of Europe is still relatively little known or botanised by keen gardeners, but I hope that I will be able to highlight a few species that will perform well and truly place this area on the European map.

The treeline fades out between 1300 and 1500 m, with the woodland zone being made up mainly of hardwoods comprising ash, oak, and beech. In no part of these mountains does the altitude attain truly alpine levels, yet such is the range of plants found here that gardeners will be keen to try growing some of them.

In the east of the range the rocks are predominantly acidic slates and quartzites, while in the Picos de Europa, limestone is the principal rock type with the highest peak, Torre Cerredo, at 2648 m. A trip to these mountains at the end of June and early July will reward the plant hunter with many alpine treasures.

I will describe a few plants that have given me a great deal of pleasure. One of the finest spots in the Cantabrian Mountain range is on the south-facing slopes of the Pena Vieja, 2613 m. A plant encountered there is a species with a wide distribution across the Alps, *Androsace villosa*. With neat cushions of congested rosettes, it is a showy plant with clusters of sweetly scented white flowers, the centre of which often turns a reddish colour before fading. Grouped taxonomically into the section *Chamaejasme*, it is a species I find performs well on a trough or raised bed in full sun. The hirsute nature of the rosettes makes it susceptible to losses due to winter wet, and for this reason I would recommend a cloche cover during the winter months.

Apart from the highly desirable dense, cushion-forming drabas, few members of this genus excite the avid alpine grower who gardens solely in the open. Yet here in these rich and rocky limestone formations is the compact, cushion-forming *Draba dedeana*. I remember first receiving material of this geographic form from the late Eric Watson, and what a fine and easy plant it was. It forms a dense tuft of tiny leaves and crowded corymbs of clean, white flowers on 5 cm stems. This is a choice species to be positioned between small pieces of limestone on a trough, and it is easily raised from seed. It is an example of a plant that from this particular locality is superior to other forms, and for alpine gardeners just starting out with alpines, it highlights the need to be both observant in the field and selective when purchasing plants.

Whilst carrying out my initial apprenticeship at Ingwersen's Nursery in Sussex, England, I paid careful attention to the best-selling alpine plants of that

Draba dedeana
Photo by Kees Jan van Zwienen.

era (the early 1970s). Close to the number one spot came *Lithospermum* (as it was then), now *Lithodora diffusa* in its vigorous forms, 'Grace Ward' and 'Heavenly Blue'. More recently, Ron McBeath and Jim Gardiner introduced a fine compact form, *L. diffusa* 'Picos', from this locality. Here it grows on rocky outcrops and screes with its gentian-blue flowers contrasting against the white limestone rocks. I have found it prefers a lime-free, well-drained soil in full sun. Its wide, evergreen mats spread widely and are seen at their best when positioned at the perimeter of a raised bed, where the dark green, hairy foliage can tumble over the wall. The type species flowers earlier than the popular and more upright-growing cultivars, often as early as midspring, and continues well into the summer months. It makes a stunning display with its myriad of blue flowers. Both the species and its cultivars can be propagated by either softwood or semi-ripe cuttings inserted into a mix of equal parts gritty sand, peat, and perlite. Once the cuttings have rooted and are ready for potting up, the tips should be nipped out to encourage a neat and compact plant.

The westernmost form of the acaulis group of gentians that is often found in the limestone meadows and amongst rocks in these parts is the variable *Gentiana occidentalis*, closely related to *G. angustifolia*. I have raised both deep blue forms and purple forms, and the best plants should be retained for the garden. *Gentiana occidentalis* may be readily identified by its distinctly narrow leaves.

Geranium cinereum
Photo by Margaret and Henry Taylor.

Two highly desirable plants often found growing together on open, sunny limestone formations are *Geranium cinereum* and the wonderful, pale blue-flowering *Linum narbonense*. The geranium is a classic alpine species and will surely feature in many alpinists' top ten. But, a word of warning: please give it space. A small plant purchased in a 7 CM pot will, at flowering, extend to some 45 CM in breadth. I hardly know of a European alpine plant that flowers for a longer period through the summer months, but more of this later.

The closely associating *Linum narbonense* deserves wider recognition as with its close relatives. It is a tall, 30 CM, graceful, and handsome blue-flowered flax which forms neat clumps, with slender, arching stems clothed in small leaves and an abundance of funnel-shaped flowers. Together with the geranium, they look their best in a sunny rock garden and are best raised from seed.

Another choice but slightly more demanding species of flax is *Linum viscosum*. I would position this one amongst dwarf willows on a raised bed or rock garden, where it forms neat clumps with 30 CM stems and large, open, pink flowers with the salix offering valuable support. The linums can be propagated from softwood cuttings as well as seed.

There is a danger that as alpine gardeners we may tend to overlook members of that great family, Compositae. Many of its species can be a little invasive or deemed too large for the alpine garden. What, though, about some of the near stemless thistles? Could we find space in a well-drained rock garden or raised bed for them? I will mention two thistles which can be raised from seed and should become more widely recognised in gardens.

The first is the near stemless, lemon yellow–flowered *Centaurea lagascana* with attractive green pinnatisect foliage. The second, *Jurinea humilis*, has a similar habit with pink flowers held on short 4 CM stems. Both are often found in gravely turf in nature and warrant a position in a freely drained, sunny position. I rate these thistles highly and recommend that the reader look out for them in a seed list.

There can be no doubt that the high point for visitors to these parts is a trip to the large acidic mountain, Pena Prieta, approached from the Puerto de San Glorio. Giving a hint of a more temperate climate, at 1600 M the tree heaths, *Erica arborea* and *E. australis*, are in full flower by early July. Although the well-known *Fritillaria pyrenaica* is often found on limestone formations, here solitary plants are dotted about on the grassy slopes with striking purple, yellow-throated flowers.

At 1900 M, where the surrounding acidic screes are made up of stones of varying sizes—mostly around 5 CM in diameter—there is evidence of one of the supremely beautiful alpine plants native to Europe. It is immediately recognised by its huge, kidney-shaped leaves, slate green and hairy, almost disguised in the surrounding stones. Let me unveil *Ranunculus parnassifolius* in its most imperious form, seen here with flowers carried on 15 CM stems, but often shorter. The huge white and pink-flushed flowers are heavily veined with red on the outside, to such an extent that they appear from a distance to be red. Quite stunning! Now here lies the challenge—that is, how to grow it in our gardens. The scree here is mobile and deep and supports little in the way of a flora. If I were lucky enough to obtain a plant, I would plant it in my good soil with a generous addition of quartz gravel and say a prayer. What about you? Apart from wishing to show it and receive a Forrest or Farrer medal, nothing would possess me to want to containerise such a plant and grow it in an alpine house, but perhaps—just perhaps—there may be a case for growing it in a deep clay pot, plunged in sand.

As far as propagation is concerned, once this Pena Prieta form becomes available, having established it, look out for seed. As soon as it is ripe and the follicles are changing colour, they can be rubbed off and sown immediately. Only well-established clumps should be divided after flowering. As alpine gardeners, we are indebted to those individuals who not only discovered this sensational plant but also described it in the pages of the alpine journals. I am very grateful to my friend Kees Jan van Zwienen for telling me all about this plant in nature, although it was Ron McBeath who first brought our attention to this outstanding form.

Ranunculus parnassifolius 'Pena Prieta'
Photo by Kees Jan van Zwienen.

Before concluding with plants from this region, I will highlight another variable buttercup which should be given pride of place in the rock garden, *Ranunculus amplexicaulis*. This species is again to be found from the Puerto de San Glorio Pass in superior forms to its Pyrenean cousins. Perhaps the rich minerals associated with this acidic rock formation contributes to the quality of plants found here. At flowering time, stems will rise to 30 cm in height with the leaves less pointed and noticeably less glaucous than the more eastern representations. The tall, branching stems carry several large, soft pink, heavily veined flowers up to 4 cm across. It is apparent that the forms associated with the Picos mountain range are distinct and provide gardeners with a highly desirable race of plants. We are greatly indebted to Henry and Margaret Taylor for introducing and distributing this superior form of such a fine species.

I will now move into the main body of the Pyrénées and discuss some favourite alpine species that we cannot overlook.

The Central Pyrénées

Travelling eastward into the main body of the Pyrénées, certain plants leap into the minds of alpine gardeners. If I were to focus on just a few endemics, my choice would have to include *Saxifraga longifolia*, *Ramonda myconi*, *Aquilegia pyrenaica*, *Daphne cneorum* var. *pygmaea*, *Adonis pyrenaica*, *Fritillaria pyrenaica*, and two androsaces: *Androsace ciliata* and the rare *A. cylindrica*. It is interesting to note that each of these endemics has its own specific cultural requirements. This is a fact that cannot be overlooked if we are to enjoy success when growing most of our favourite European alpine plants.

Saxifraga longifolia

Let me commence our tour in the Pyrénées in the west and then move eastwards, incorporating the little state of Andorra as I go. For those readers who wish to visit any of the locations mentioned, I hope that the simple map provided here will serve as a useful guide.

I have already drawn the reader's attention to the endemism (indigenousness) associated with the Pyrénées, yet it is interesting to note that some of these

An alpine house

As already stated, I am very much an outdoor gardener and do not possess an alpine house. I am not sure that I can envisage the need for one, although that view may change with both my age and the changing climate. I well recall a telling comment from the late Jack Drake; whilst working at his nursery, he stated, "An Alpine House is really a place for humans to enjoy their plants, not a place for growing alpine plants." Perhaps he had a point, as he spent a lot of time in his alpine houses. The management and good husbandry involved with such a project is a serious undertaking. Consider first of all the temperature and moisture control for the plants, as well as the added concerns of pest and disease control under glass. Do you have good neighbours or friends who will pay heed to these important matters while you jet off to the mountains for a couple of weeks during the summer months? Such affairs are worth considering prior to investing in an alpine house.

Alpine map of Europe

species are to be found only in the west of the range while others are confined to the east. This can be explained by the climatic variance. The western part of the range has a higher rainfall and a milder climate, influenced by the close proximity of the Atlantic Ocean. The east, however, enjoys some influence from the Mediterranean with a climate of extremes: more heat in the summer and most of the rain falling in the winter months.

So let us look a little closer at some of these Pyrenean gems. A rewarding drive through the West Pyrénées, or the Pirineos Occidentales, might commence with a search for flowers on both sides of the Col du Somport. Four attractive garden plants can be found hereabouts: *Hypericum nummularium*, *Asperula hirta*, *Petrocoptis pyrenaica*, and *Saxifraga longifolia*, of which the latter is to be seen in spectacular form here.

Alpine hypericums tend not to receive many popular reviews in my opinion, but a number of alpine and subalpine species are deserving of a sunny, well-drained position in our gardens. *Hypericum nummularium* may be frequently encountered on limestone in the Pyrénées growing on rocky outcrops. It forms a neat clump, eventually spreading to some 30 to 45 CM, with masses of golden-yellow flowers held on 15 to 25 CM stems. Its great forte is the extended period of flowering, from late spring until late summer. It may be readily propagated from seed.

I would find a home for a number of pretty little asperulas in a raised bed or trough. *Asperula hirta*, a Pyrenean endemic, is sometimes recommended for a scree, where I am sure it will soon establish a fine mat. My personal view is that a scree is generally viewed from a distance, despite a few stepping stones enabling closer inspection. The soft pink flowers provided by this species are best enjoyed in the closer proximity of a raised bed, tucked in between stones. Forming a prostrate mat of short stems with attractive foliage, it is seen at its best in mid to late spring, when the whole mat is covered with pink buds, opening to soft pink and then white. Asperulas may be propagated from soft cuttings taken after flowering.

A member of the family Caryophyllaceae that should not be overlooked is *Petrocoptis pyrenaica*. It is often encountered in the western Pyrénées occupying cliffs and rocky outcrops, sometimes preferring dappled shade. A position in the garden should be chosen avoiding open exposure to excessive winter wet, and a vertical position between rocks should prove ideal where the glaucous foliage sets off the short stems, each bearing a terminal cluster of pale pink flowers in spring. As with other members of the pink family, this species can easily be raised from seed.

It has already been noted that the great epic of Pyrenean endemics, *Saxifraga longifolia*, is super-abundant on the French side of the Col du Somport in the western Pyrénées. This outstanding species is restricted to the central Pyrénées on the French side, but in Spain it has a wider distribution, reaching the area just south of Andorra. In nature, it does have one simple insistence, that of growing on limestone cliffs ranging from 800 to 2400 M. It has a number of popular names, including queen of the saxifrages, glory of the Pyrénées, and crown royal, in Spain. Who would argue? It was first recognised in 1689 by Sherard and later described by French botanist Lapeyrouse in 1801. By the late 19th century, it was offered by a few British nurseries. The fact that *S. longifolia* is monocarpic, or dies after flowering, must have frustrated early alpine gardeners, who paid around one shilling and sixpence for a plant from James Backhouse and Son of York, England. By 1905, Reginald Farrer charged two shillings and sixpence for "exhibition plants" from his Craven Nursery.

A member of the silver, or encrusted, section of *Saxifraga* (or, for the more scientifically minded, *Ligulatae*), mature plants have been observed with rosettes some 14 CM in diameter containing around 200 leaves, and, in some cases, flower spikes with 700 to 800 flowers on one spike! I wonder who would have had the patience to carry out such an analysis. At the end of June, in its native habitat, it may be seen flowering at its best, and of the many favourite locations for this outstanding alpine saxifrage, one of the most sensational is the famous Vallée d'Ossoue, a little to the west of Gavarnie. Soon after the approach to the valley, one is confronted with a huge limestone cliff, some 800 M high. It is covered with many thousands of saxifrages. Each plant eventually erupts with immense multibloomed, conelike panicles of glistening white flowers, arching out of the cliff to a distance of 60 CM. It is surely one of the floristic wonders of the Pyrénées, and, as Wilhelm Schacht so aptly put it, "the finest and most wonderful flower in the Pyrénées is undoubtedly *Saxifraga longifolia*, with its long white inflorescences like bursting rockets".

To experience this spectacular display is one thing, but to master the successful cultivation of this species in the garden is quite another. The first hurdle is to decide where to plant it in order to show off its extravagant beauty. Here are a few suggestions. I first experienced this plant, growing in all its glory, whilst training in the Munich Botanic Garden. It was seeding about naturally on steep, tufa cliffs in the famous rock garden there. The magnificent, symmetrical rosettes of narrow, lime-encrusted leaves lay perfectly in crevices and on the flat faces of porous rock.

Although relatively expensive, tufa is widely available, and having visited gardens utilising it in many parts of Europe, the United States, and Canada, I would make this material my first choice in the garden for growing this plant.

Saxifraga longifolia

Two-year seedlings can be planted directly into the boulders of tufa by excavating small holes, some 3 to 5 cm in diameter at 45 degrees to the rock face. Wedge the seedlings into the holes singly, packing a mixture of soil, sand, and tufa dust with a few small pieces of tufa to hold the soil and seedlings in place. Water in well. Each year, the rosettes will slowly grow, until after about five years the flower spike appears. What a thrill! Few of us possess a naturally high wall of limestone, so tufa is an ideal substitute.

Another idea would be to position young plants at the perimeter of a raised bed, wedging the plants between pieces of limestone. I have not found that this particular saxifrage has a notable preference for a cooler position.

In nature, multirosetted plants can often be spotted with each rosette emanating from the central rootstock. While this is not the norm, it most certainly is a characteristic of the outstanding man-made hybrid *Saxifraga* 'Tumbling Waters'. While the true species can be propagated only from seed, the sterile hybrid must be vegetatively propagated from cuttings. The hybrid was raised in 1913 by Captain B. H. B. Symons-Jeune. He crossed a very fine form of *S. callosa* subsp. *lantoscana* (now *S. callosa* subsp. *callosa* var. *australis*) with *S. longifolia*. The rosette takes after the male parent (*S. longifolia*), growing to an even greater size, and the flowering spray is even larger than that parent. It received a well-deserved AM in 1920. I would recommend removing and propagating side rosettes before the main rosette commences flowering. The cuttings can be rooted effectively with a short basal stem when taken in late spring and placed in a mixture of sand and perlite and kept shaded and cool. A three to four year wait is required before the rooted rosettes will flower. I believe anyone who has grown this plant will agree that every effort is repaid in perpetuating this wonderful display.

I am not fussy whether I grow the monocarpic species *Saxifraga longifolia* or the superior hybrid *S.* 'Tumbling Waters', but either will rank in my top 20 most desirable of European alpine plants.

A plant often associated with *Saxifraga longifolia* (from a geographic point of view) is another endemic, *Ramonda myconi*. It is a classic European alpine but in my view rather overshadowed by its sumptuous Balkan relative, *R. nathaliae*. That apart, the Pyrenean species is far more widely available in the nursery trade, easy of cultivation, and in its best forms an undeniably attractive alpine plant for the garden.

Ramonda myconi
Photo by Jim Jermyn.

If there is just one simple, golden rule to ensure success, it is to provide a cool, vertical position for all ramondas. I have grown some wonderful plants which have matured into sizeable, multirosetted clumps, tucked in between rocks making up a wall of a raised bed. Perhaps more aesthetically pleasing is a rocky outcrop created by a collection of tufa boulders beside a water feature. The added humidity and the porous properties of the rock combine to provide optimal conditions for this variable species. I say *variable*, for flower colour may provide a range of hues from violet-blue, mauve, pink, to pure white. For me, there is just one colour for a perfect ramonda, and that is the pristine, clean violet-blue. There is something about the dark green, hirsute, and leathery leaf rosettes that create a sense of class, reminiscent of a very choice primula. The short 10 cm flower stems generally bear one to six wide-petalled flowers with a yellow centre, strongly resembling an African violet (*Saintpaulia*). It is because of their variable flower colour that I would advise readers to choose their plants in flower.

Named for Louis Francis Ramond (1753–1827), a botanist and traveller in the Pyrénées, this member of the botanical family Gesneriaceae is most commonly encountered in the central and eastern Pyrénées. Here, it inhabits shady rocks of limestone in great colonies, nestling in deep crevices.

Flowering in early and midsummer, *Ramonda myconi* can be propagated easily by a variety of means. Simple division of large, multirosetted clumps is by far the easiest method and can be carried out during a damp spell after flowering. On no account should mature plants be handled when undergoing stress, as, for example, during a period of drought. I have at times drenched clumps of ramonda or the closely related haberlea with a can of water in the evening prior to division. At the time of division, a deep seed tray or some pots should be ready and waiting. When carefully teasing apart the rosettes from the mature clump, a reasonable amount of decaying foliage can be discarded; at the same time, a number of healthy leaves with a complete petiole or stem will become detached. (By the way, when carrying out this task, bury your nose into the clump of foliage—I love the pungent smell, somewhat reminiscent of moorland bracken—*Pteridium aquilinum*.) The detached foliage may be inserted in a tray or pot filled with a mix of moistened peat and perlite. I like to work with a pencil and make a hole into the compost at 45 degrees and carefully insert the leaf cuttings. Some propagators will cut the main blade of the leaf in half to reduce transpiration, but I have not found this to be in any way essential. Leaf cuttings can also be inserted around the rim of a pot filled with the same cuttings mix. Either receptacle should be well watered, covered with a thin film of polythene, and placed, if possible, over a heated bench or propagator. Members of the gesneriad family generally prefer shade, and this is certainly the case for propagation as well as cultivation. The main divisions can be replanted or potted up.

Now, to seed. Many nursery customers used to ask me how to raise ramondas from seed, as copious quantities of seed are produced on mature plants. Here is a simple method; but I must openly admit to the fact that I am not good with handling tiny seedlings—my wife would probably say it has something to do with a lack of patience! Whilst training at Jack Drake's Nursery in Aviemore, Scotland, I experienced this method of seed propagation at its very best, for Jack Drake and John Lawson were masters of this art of raising alpines from seed. Watch out that the ripening seed capsules do not shed their fine seed prior to collection. As soon as they mature and just begin to open, cut the decaying flower's stems and place them in a paper bag with absolutely no holes in the corners (such is the fine nature of the seed). Prepare your seed pots at the normal time of seed sowing with a peaty mixture containing a small percentage of sand and perlite— or, better still, a mixture containing sphagnum moss that has been sterilised in a microwave and rubbed through a sieve. The seed should be sown thinly on to the surface of the compost and placed in a propagator and covered with a thin layer of polythene. I must say that the milky or slightly opaque colour of polythene is preferable for propagation, as it offers a little shade as well as maintaining humidity. Gentle bottom heat will speed up germination thereafter, and the seedlings will mature, provided they are given constant care, including some winter warmth and shade. The growth of moss must be controlled.

So where would I rank this classic Pyrenean species, *Ramonda myconi*? Right up with the best—easy of culture, beautiful in form, and rewarding in flower. What more could a gardener wish for? And there is a bonus: how many alpine plants prefer a cooler site?

The wonderful Cirque de Gavarnie is one of the main attractions in the central French Pyrénées just north of the Ordessa National Park over the border in Spain. A very popular centre for plant lovers, this spot is home to a number of Pyrenean endemics already described, such as the saxifraga and ramonda. But there are more. One means of gaining altitude from the village of Gavarnie up to the base of the magnificent cliffs is by donkey. At the base of the cliffs, we can raise our eyes to contemplate the awesome view of the cirque and its 425 M waterfall (the highest in Europe). Not too far above these great cliffs one can find an androsace endemic to the central Pyrénées—in fact, one of the choicest and most attractive of all the Aretian species. Too high for the donkey, I'm afraid! It is *Androsace ciliata*, with its glowing pink flowers over a neat, compact rosette. It has often been written of this species (as with *Eritrichium nanum*) that it never occurs on limestone. In this location above Gavarnie, it may be found in

Androsace ciliata
Photo by Margaret and Henry Taylor.

its natural habitat on limestone, and I believe that seed-raised plants from this origin may well prove to be more resilient in cultivation. It favours high, open, rocky ridges and is more often found on acidic formations from about 2500 to more than 3200 м, and it forms a continuous mat consisting of clusters of cushions. I have not experienced such a performance in cultivation.

It is my experience that plants are not long-lived and are particularly prone to attacks from greenfly (aphis or aphid). I would recommend purchasing young plants and positioning them between rocks in a cool position on a trough or raised bed and providing winter protection in the form of a cloche cover. It is a prolific flowerer, and I suspect that pot-grown specimens often flower themselves to death. In other words, due to the lack of time, the plants have little in reserve due to having no established root system protected by a cool root run between rocks, as they would experience in nature. The flowers are sweetly fragrant and produce a generous amount of seed, which provide the best means of reproduction. It is variable in flower colour and the best forms can be selected from seed.

Although this species is a personal favourite, it is not alone among endemic species of androsace. Having introduced the reader to two species thus far, I feel it would be helpful to highlight a very simple breakdown of the taxonomic differences within the genus. The species are grouped into a number of sections with close affinities. I will list below those which are to be covered in this book, according to their sections as outlined in Smith and Lowe's *Androsaces*, published by the Alpine Garden Society in 1977. Hopefully, this simple guide to the taxonomy of this outstanding genus with its many gardenworthy species will help readers appreciate their close affinities. This may well offer a few clues to the individual needs of the related species, as we transfer them into our gardens.

Section *Aretia*
    Subsection *Dicranothrix*
      Androsace hedraeantha
      Androsace carnea
      Androsace laggeri
      Androsace pyrenaica
      Androsace obtusifolia
    Subsection *Aretia*
      Androsace wulfeniana
      Androsace alpina
      Androsace hausmannii
      Androsace ciliata
      Androsace vandellii
      Androsace helvetica
      Androsace pubescens
      Androsace hirtella
      Androsace cylindrica
    Section *Chamaejasme*
      Androsace villosa
      Androsace chamaejasme

I shall now describe the cultivation requirements for a few species that may be encountered in the Pyrénées, some of which have sadly become very rare in nature. From time to time I will draw the reader's attention to the rarity of certain favourite plants in their wild habitats. Their conservation must be understood by plantsfolk, because ultimately it is only we, as gardeners and avid growers of these rare species, that create a demand for the unscrupulous collector to carry out his overzealous methods of collection. Sometimes it maybe assumed that the old practice of collecting with a hammer and chisel is the only act causing the immediate denudation of a specialised habitat, but that is not the case. Although sadly this practise still occurs, the overzealous collection of seed from a very localised habitat can also seriously affect the conservation of a species. Fortunately, this is not the practice of most specialised seed collectors, including those recommended at the conclusion of this book.

I have recently visited several locations in Austria; on this trip I was keen to study the habitat of the rare *Androsace wulfeniana* in the Nockberge national park. My colleagues and I agreed that should there be a desire to collect seed of this species (outwith the national park), then a few seeds from three or four cushions or mats would suffice, given the very limited demand for such a challenging and rare species. It is therefore a matter of concern when seed merchants offer sizeable portions of seed of rarities that have been collected in the wild.

I must also bear some responsibility, for when writing about these desirable rarities, I may create a further demand on a potentially endangered species. I hope, though, that I will recommend a few ways that most of us can give these specialised species a fair chance of success in our lowland gardens.

The two most successful ways of growing them out in the open garden are by employing a raised bed or troughs. Before the recent death of Duncan Lowe, perhaps the most successful grower of a wide range of true alpine plants, I spent some time seeking his advice on the cultivation of androsaces. He gardened in a relatively cool and moist region in the northwest of England. He created the most wonderful raised beds, and I believe that, along with troughs, they represent the most satisfactory method of succeeding with nearly all the plants covered in this book. There is a case for growing the choicest and most precious of the true alpine plants, most notably cushion-forming species, in an alpine house. Specialised books on this subject are available, and as I have little experience of such a culture, I will apply my experience of growing alpines in the open garden.

When I first started growing alpine plants about 35 years ago, I recall visiting a market stall in the city of St. Albans, England, where I studied horticulture. A softly spoken, elderly gentleman was often to be found selling a wide range of alpine plants from his stall, and it was from his range of species that I made my very first purchases. He offered prudent counsel to the unwary customer like myself, and off I went with a shoe box filled with a mixture of treasures. Included in my first collection was an alpine pink, a few rhodohypoxis, and a perfectly budded androsace (*Androsace cylindrica ×hirtella*). The kind gentleman implored me to provide good drainage for the plants. The best I could do in my relative ignorance, too lazy to build a rock garden, was to hollow out pockets between my parents crazy paving! Can you imagine my androsace carefully planted in an especially sandy mix between slabs of paving, along with its label? Well, the plant grew, despite the interests of our little Jack Russell terrier's raised leg. (I absolutely adore Jack Russells, but their first trip to the garden in the morning can be fatal for a cushion-forming alpine plant. I prefer the female version, as they tend to trot out gamely on to the lawn, lower themselves in a ladylike manner, nose in the air; look around; scratch the lawn; and seek out alternative mischief that causes no harm to the defenceless alpine plant. I apologise to dog lovers for my prejudice against the male version of the Jack Russell terrier.)

Returning to the androsace: not only did it flower, but it also grew rather satisfactorily until its first encounter with a dampish winter period of dormancy. A cloche cover (quite impractical in the circumstances) may have increased the plant's longevity. As it was, I learnt from my mistakes and persevered with growing alpine plants, but next time I chose a raised bed (see chapter 9).

Let me now return to the cultivation of a few Pyrenean species of androsace. My first choice is the rare *Androsace cylindrica*, native to the western Pyrénées. Ingwersen's Nursery specialised (during my time of tuition) in a wide range of alpine plants, from the easily grown to the choicest of species. I well recall the terraced layout making up the sales area: A narrow path passed between a bed well-planted with many choice subjects and a row of small greenhouses, the first of which housed a wide range of cushion plants. Among the collection in the greenhouse were rows of carefully plunged clay pots containing such treasures as *A. cylindrica*, *A. cylindrica* ×*hirtella*, *A. pyrenaica*, and the variable *A. carnea* ×*pyrenaica*. As these subjects began to produce their flower buds, I remember my fascination passing on to disbelief at the abundance of flowers. When seen at their best, they are simply stunning. Let me add, then, a little meat to the bones regarding the cultivation of these Aretian androsaces, many of which have fragrant flowers as an added bonus.

Androsace cylindrica is a species confined to calcareous locations, choosing habitats along the subalpine zone in the western half of the Pyrénées. It was Monsieur De Candolle who named this species, identifying the dry, old leaves which form cylinders. It is one of the most sought-after of all androsaces, with each individual rosette producing as many as ten pure white flowers. I have never found the true species to be successful outdoors in our Scottish climate without effective winter cover. When planted beside *A. hirtella*, the resulting hybrids produced from seed are far easier to please. The true species must be afforded effective winter cloche cover. Propagation is best carried out from seed, with great care required throughout the process to ensure excellent drainage and avoiding overhead watering during the dormant period.

If *Androsace cylindrica* presents a challenge to the gardener operating purely in the open, then *A. hirtella* will prove easier of cultivation. Finding a plant true to name may be more of a challenge. Once again, it is comparatively rare in the wild, located in the northern side of the Pyrénées. Preferring a northwest aspect in nature, it also chooses complete shelter from overhanging rocks. It is a calcareous species and one of its added qualities is the almond scent of its white flowers. It forms tight cushions which can be grown best of all on a raised bed. A few well-placed rocks (in this case, limestone) can provide just the shelter this cushion-forming species requires.

In marked contrast to the foregoing species and its hybrid is another Pyrenean endemic, *Androsace pyrenaica*, a more challenging species in the garden. A calcifuge species preferring granitic formations, it is found in fissures at altitudes in excess of 2500 м. Given the provision of winter cover, I have found this rarity to perform well in a trough when positioned vertically, wedged in between stones, producing a fine show with its white flowers. It is not long lived in my experience, and those able to offer more tender loving care in an alpine house will undoubtedly enjoy success with added longevity.

I well recall fine plants of the hybrid *Androsace carnea* ×*pyrenaica* whilst working at Jack Drake's Nursery. Many of them produced soft pink-coloured flowers on tight cushions but were highly variable. The influence of both parents may be evident, with single blooms to multiflowered umbels. When raising this hybrid artificially, great care is required to select the best forms, both in flower and those with a tight cushion. Not surprisingly, the hybrids are much easier to please on either a trough or raised beds. I will describe the other parent, *A. carnea*, in the form of its subspecies *laggeri* (now given specific rank as *A. laggeri*) when describing the species found in the eastern Pyrénées.

Each one of these cushion-forming androsaces is susceptible to attacks from greenfly (aphis), but this is less serious outdoors than in the confines of an alpine house. I find it very satisfying collecting seed of androsaces, but great care must be taken to watch out for the ripening capsules as the time for collection approaches. It is best to carry out the task with a pair of sharply pointed scissors, thus avoiding damage to the cushion. The seed can be carefully separated from the capsules and then sown immediately on to a John Innes type seed compost. The seed should be covered with sharp grit and the pots plunged in sand and kept in a cool, open position. With the seeds rarely germinating in a uniform pattern, it may be prudent to wait until there is a significant germination or carefully ease out seedlings as they germinate. The pricked out seedlings must be kept moist and shaded for a week or so until they have established, after which they can be given full exposure.

Of the Pyrenean androsaces, my favourite is the hybrid *Androsace cylindrica* ×*hirtella*, combining the qualities of its illustrious parents but proving much easier of cultivation. In truth, they are all challenging but worth every bit of the effort in cultivation.

Let me highlight a few more choice garden plants from the central Pyrénées. Few of us are not captivated by a spreading shrublet of daphne, filling the late spring air with its special fragrance. *Daphne cneorum* must surely top the bill for popularity, ease of culture, and "payback" to the cultivator. This freely branching, evergreen shrublet popularly known as the garland flower is widespread in both subalpine and alpine Europe. In nature and in cultivation it seems quite indifferent to the pH of the soil and seems either to thrive or die suddenly. My feeling, having experienced both success and failure, is that effecting a good start is essential. Daphnes, with few exceptions, require good air movement and no immediate obstruction in the form of overhanging foliage from neighbouring plants. The soil must be well-drained and yet moisture-retentive. *Daphne cneorum*,

Daphne cneorum

as a straight species, received an AGM in 1927 and, given its ability to spread, would rank as a perfect choice for the rock garden, positioned in full sun. I also favour planting it at the edge of a raised bed where it will sprawl over the border. Mature plants can be clipped back to form an appropriate shape for the chosen position. Given its ability to spread, I hope that the following advice does not seem too contradictory. In mid to late summer as the wood begins to ripen and present a fine framework for next year's flowering, I apply a well-diluted, liquid seaweed fertiliser. This will not be necessary with a particularly vigorous clone such as *D. cneorum* 'Eximia'. Any action taken to prune this species should be taken only once the plant is well established.

I have described this outstanding species at this stage in order to introduce a choice variant often encountered in the Pyrénées and in the French and Swiss Alps. It is *Daphne cneorum* var. *pygmaea*. In a number of locations close to Gavarnie, this special form of the noble species can be found. It represents a true alpine variant and can thus be given a special position between small rocks on a trough or a raised bed. It can now be admired in pride of position for its wonderful fragrance and the surprisingly tight mat it forms, in sharp contrast to the type species.

Specialised forms such as this one and cultivars of dwarf daphne species are best propagated by grafting on to a rootstock of another daphne—for example, *Daphne acutiloba*. On this subject I am no expert and would direct readers to the expert grower Robin White of Blackthorn Nursery, Hampshire, England, and his fine book on the genus *Daphne* (*Daphnes: A Practical Guide for Gardeners*, Timber Press, 2006). Both the type species and its dwarf variant are outstanding European alpine plants and will rank highly in our wish list.

A plant sadly rather overlooked in favour of its more illustrious hybrid children is *Saxifraga aretioides*. This Kabschia saxifrage is endemic to the central and eastern Pyrénées, where it is not uncommon. It is a remarkably consistent species, choosing to inhabit limestone fissures in rock faces at altitudes from 900 to 2000 M. This compact, cushion-forming plant takes many years to assume a sizeable, firm, green hummock, some 10 CM across. In late spring in cultivation, 2 to 6 CM tall stems are produced in loose corymbs of up to seven greenish yellow flowers. It is a valuable member of this popular section of saxifrage with many famous hybrids having been created with it as one of the parents. *Saxifraga aretioides* performs well when planted in tufa.

Some of the best known hybrids involving *Saxifraga aretioides* include *S.* ×*anglica* 'Myra Cambria', a lovely pink; *S.* ×*boydii* 'Faldonside', deep yellow; and for me one of the finest man-made creations, *S.* ×*megaseaeflora*, raised by Holenka, which includes the gorgeous 'Karel Capek' with huge apple blossom–pink flowers. Each one of these superb Kabschia saxifrages can be grown with ease in a trough or on boulders of tufa rock. I will give a more detailed description of this valuable dimension to alpine gardening in chapter 9.

A free-flowering plant for the alpine garden is the somewhat variable Pyrenean endemic, *Geranium cinereum*, mentioned earlier. I note that *Flora Europaea* (Tutin 1964) records two subspecies of the type. This surprises me from a horticultural point of view, since the two subspecies are *G. cinereum* subsp. *cinereum* and *G. cinereum* subsp. *subcaulescens*. I would have thought that the lovely *G. argenteum* was much closer to the type species than the Balkan *G. subcaulescens*. For my part, I will take the horticultural route and separate the three species, closely related as they certainly are. The European alpine geraniums are both promiscuous and prodigious seeders. For this reason, I would wish to issue the reader with a word a warning: When possible, one should avoid planting any of the three species together if the goal is to obtain progeny that are in any way true to their parents. The more vigorous forms of *G. cinereum* will form clumps that spread to an excess of 45 CM. The leaner the treatment in the garden, the tighter the resulting clump, and all forms should be given a position in full sun. Where space provides and pureness of a species is not important, mixed planting will provide a vibrant show of colour over a long period throughout the summer months.

A vigorous perennial, *Geranium cinereum* produces neat mounds of deeply cut, grey-green foliage and beneath the soil a stout, branching rhizome. The flowers are quite stunning, and generally the petals are a pale lilac colour etched with pink veins. In nature it is often found in turf intermingled with *Dryas octopetala*, a lovely sight! White-flowering forms are also found and make a valuable addition in the garden.

Whilst running my nursery, I had many friends who used to arrive, sometimes quite unexpectedly, with a bounty of exciting plants for me. On many occasions they would be offered on a commercial basis. One such friend used to arrive with his delightful wife and children (who were more eager to get down to the nearby beach) and a few tomato boxes filled with his prize seedlings of *Geranium cinereum*. We agreed a price and off he went, assuming that I would immediately offer them for sale. There was a problem, however: Each one was a winner. I would play with each pot like an excited child, moving the best to one side for planting out and the rest back in the box for sale. The problem was that I kept moving more and more to the stock side, until hardly a single pot was for sale. This was a dilemma: I couldn't plant them all out, for that was just sheer greed. On the other hand, I didn't want the first customer to come in and go off with a prize form. If only I had a flare for marketing and was not such an avid plantsman, we may have made some real money in the nursery! The simple fact is that once you have an eye for these geraniums, be warned—it is difficult to pass another one by. I think its pastel shades of pink and lilac with the stunning venation cause all the trouble.

If the reader were to catch this geranium disease, I guarantee that trying to collect the seed will be fun. There is no rule of thumb as to when to collect it; it is simply a case of watching for the exact time and applying experience. The seed pod, or ovary, is, in the case of a geranium, made up of five united carpels, and at the time of fruiting this separates into mericarps—all rather technical, I know! But it is at the time of separation that the seed is exposed and very quickly falls or is propelled to the ground. With experience, one soon learns when to sever these carpels and place them in a secured paper bag, where the seed is released and can be cleaned ready for sowing. The very best forms can be propagated from stem cuttings taken after flowering or from root cuttings taken during the dormant season.

A member of the family Ranunculaceae that does not feature strongly in the European Alps, by comparison to its epicentre in North America, is aquilegia, the columbine. There is, however, one species of particular note, which is a Pyrenean endemic: it is *Aquilegia pyrenaica*. It abounds on calcareous soils on the northeast side of the Valle de Arán and is rather special. If it can be kept separate from its close relatives in the garden, it may be retained as a good species. Not far from the little village of Gourette in the western Pyrénées, it may be found growing with edelweiss (*Leontopodium alpinum*) and *Geranium cinereum*, still flowering in late summer with its clear blue, flat-faced flowers over neat foliage, some 25 CM in height. It is a choice species for the rock garden or raised bed and a plant deserving of greater respect amongst the alpine fraternity. As with all columbines, it is easily raised from seed as existing plants become exhausted and require replenishment.

The western Pyrénées is home to a rare endemic which is sadly all too rarely seen in our gardens: *Buglossoides gastonii* (synonym *Lithospermum gastonii*). This is a most attractive member of the borage family, Boraginaceae. Farrer extolled its virtues more than 90 years ago but recognised its reluctance to get established in some gardens. The finest specimen I have seen was spreading gallantly amongst limestone boulders in a bed of good soil in the Schachen Garden, southern Germany.

In nature, it grows just above the treeline around the 2000 M mark in amongst limestone boulders, where it thrives in ledges. The plant is typically rhizomatous, spreading with its underground root system through humus-filled crannies in the limestone. Here and there, 15 CM stems pop up with clusters of

Aquilegia pyrenaica

flowers 14 MM across. The clusters of two to five purplish buds open to the most lovely blue cup-shaped flowers with a white centre. After flowering, it is followed by a neat dome of dark foliage somewhat reminiscent of a pulmonaria—and then the whole lot disappears in late autumn.

I well remember that the first time I saw the huge flowers on this plant, I was immediately reminded of the king of the Alps, *Eritrichium nanum*. It is not yet widely available in horticulture, and this is partly due to its reluctance to set seed or, perhaps more accurately, a lack of awareness about its seed dispersal. The seed ripens whilst tucked down in the leaf axils and then falls away to the soil. Care must therefore be taken to seek it out. Apart from this challenge, the plant may be propagated by lifting during the dormant season and divided. Every effort should be made to please this choice species, giving it a humus-rich soil and then awaiting the special flowers.

From a taxonomic point of view, it may be necessary due to the number of variable species within a single genus to simplify their identification by classifying them into sections. It is therefore appropriate that the 118 or so species of saxifrage distributed through Europe should be divided into the following sections featured in this book as set out by Engler in 1891:

Section *Porphyrion*
   Subsection *Kabschia*
   Subsection *Engleria*
   Subsection *Oppositifolia*
Section *Ligulatae* (Silvers)
Section *Saxifraga* (Mossy)

I would like to draw the reader's attention to a very fine member of this celebrated plant family belonging to the section *Saxifraga* which deserves to be sought out for a trough or raised bed. *Saxifraga pubescens* subsp. *iratiana* can be found high up in the central Pyrénées at around 2600 M on granite cliffs. It is endemic to these parts, found near the Port de Venasque. It forms tight, grey-green pubescent and somewhat sticky cushions up to 30 CM in diameter. In mid to late summer, these cushions disappear under a mass of clean, white flowers with the petals veined red. I have found this subspecies a challenge to keep through our rather damp Scottish winters; but when accorded the respect due to similar choice cushion plants, a cloche cover, then longevity may be encouraged. I would recommend tucking it in between granite or silicaceous rocks in a cool position. It generally flowers in May here in Scotland.

For some 15 years now a very popular selection of the type species *Saxifraga pubescens* has been circulating on the British show benches. It is *S. pubescens* 'Snowcap', which received an AM in 1988. The pure white flowers of this cultivar are 1 CM across, unmarked but for the greenish yellow eye. Each stem carries four to seven flowers, and a well-grown plant will form an immaculate dome some 30 CM across. So here is a plant of distinction, but I would advise giving the plant winter protection to discourage damage to the cushion. This cultivar must be propagated vegetatively from cuttings and has proved to be a valuable introduction for both the garden and alpine house.

A genus that does not feature strongly in the garden, yet contains many European species, is *Arenaria*. The sandworts are not easily identified. When leading botanical tours in the Dolomites, I invited those partaking to bring along a few bits and pieces for identification after the evening meal. It was with fear and trepidation when I was presented with an unknown member of *Caryophyllaceae* and I would be left floundering trying to discern a native sandwort from its close relatives.

There is no such difficulty with *Arenaria purpurascens*, found primarily in damp, rocky habitats and scree conditions and widely distributed in the

Pyrénées. In the garden, I have given it a cool position amongst rocks on a raised bed, where it forms a loose mat of pointed foliage. In midsummer, a mass of rose-lilac–coloured flowers are produced on short stems. Cuttings root readily when taken after flowering.

Whilst proprietor of Edrom Nurseries, I was always a little nervous about offering taller growing species, those that are frequently encountered in an alpine meadow in nature. They can be challenging to position in the garden, both tastefully and successfully from a horticultural point of view. A few subjects that come to mind are *Gentiana lutea*, *Anemone narcissiflora*, *Asphodelus albus*, and *Paradisia liliastrum*.

The latter two species may be found in great quantity in the Pyrénées. Too tall for a raised bed, though, these plants are lovely in a ground-level bed of alpine plants or in a rock garden. Some writers have objected to finding a place for these taller subjects, but I feel that plants with some stature add greatly to a bed made up primarily of dwarf species. Why plant dwarf conifers solely for this purpose when a whole host of flowering subjects fit the bill? To witness a damp meadow amassed with tall spikes of *Paradisia liliastrum*, the lovely St. Bruno's lily, is surely memorable. This member of the lily family may be raised from seed, and what a fine sight it is when planted amongst *Pulsatilla alpina* subsp. *apiifolia* and *Gentiana acaulis*. It forms tufts of narrow leaves and tall stems carrying heads of lilylike, white, fragrant flowers. It can be raised from seed.

Similar in habit is *Asphodelus albus* with its grasslike foliage and stately spikes of white flowers. I would strongly recommend that the reader seek out this plant to add height amongst choice plants in the rock garden.

I grow a few plants in our garden which regrettably emit a very undesirable smell, amongst which are the black fritillary from Japan (*Fritillaria camschatcensis*), *Crassula sarcocaulis*, and possibly one of the showiest of all Pyrenean endemics, *Lilium pyrenaicum*. This latter species is vile smelling but well worth growing for its singular beauty of flower. Found more abundantly towards the eastern part of the range, it may be seen lining streamsides or flowering by the hundreds all over the hillsides, producing its showy yellow flowers with dark purple spots and purplish black papillae inside.

An endemic plant of which I am very fond is *Antirrhinum sempervirens*. It is a dwarf growing, pale-yellow snapdragon with lovely pink markings and tiny grey-green, hirsute foliage. It is really an aristocrat amongst this humble race of summer-flowering plants and can be found growing on rocks in full sunshine. I love to see it planted in a vertical crevice, where its flowers may be shown off to their best. It is easily propagated from seed.

I once became rather fascinated with the best forms of sea holly, *Eryngium*, but

Paradisia liliastrum

I soon realised that unless carefully dead-headed, they would seed around my scree. The result was a rather disagreeable number of bold, prickly, herbaceous plants with a deeply penetrating taproot appearing in the middle of choice mats of alpine species. I naturally became cautious of them thereafter. Having passed on this little note of warning to the alert reader, I will now extol the virtues of an especially attractive Pyrenean sea holly, *E. bourgatii*. It has deeply cut, silvery leaves and attractive blue, fluffy flowers during the summer months. Assuming heights from 40 to 60 cm, it is worth positioning with some care but is nevertheless a very attractive and permanent alpine species.

Many gardeners new to the challenge of growing alpine plants lament that, in their view, too many of them flower during a short period in the late spring months. That is a fair observation, given that in nature their period of flowering is reduced in order to maximise their chances of flower pollination, fertilisation, and eventual seed dispersal before the return of the snows. So it was always with some relief when I encountered new alpine species to lengthen my range of sales during the nursery season and to appease the aggrieved customer. Enter the many species of campanula, dianthus, and viola.

Viola cornuta var. *alba*

An endemic species of viola is the horned pansy, *Viola cornuta*. This simple plant is such a joy, both in nature and in the garden. It replaces *V. calcarata* in these parts, which is so abundant in the French Alps and often found studding the alpine turf in vast numbers. It flowers over a long period and is easily grown, which is more than can be said for some of its relatives, which I will describe later on. The fragrant flowers held on 10 CM stems are generally a lilac-blue or rich purple with a lovely pure white form, too (*V. cornuta* var. *alba*). The best forms should be propagated by soft cuttings taken from nonflowering shoots, and what an attractive plant it is, whether lining a path or positioned amongst similar bold species in a rock garden or an alpine bed.

As has already been mentioned, campanulas are a backbone genus for the summer months in the garden. The Pyrénées hardly abound with species from this noteworthy genus, but easily its most distinguished endemic is the recently introduced *Campanula jaubertiana*. A number of renowned growers' and plant hunters' names will feature strongly in this book. Most notably, when it comes to the Pyrénées, the plant hunters who come to mind are Harold and Winifred Bevington from the south of England, who introduced this gorgeous campanula from the Central Pyrénées. It shares cracks in limestone rocks with the ubiquitous *C. cochlearifolia*, but until now there are no known reported hybrids.

The Bevingtons first discovered it in late June 1989 growing in vertical limestone crevices in shade. It is extremely local, confined to a few dry Spanish peaks just south of the main Pyrenean chain. Henry and Margaret Taylor have, more recently, found a closely related subspecies in Andorra, *Campanula jaubertiana* subsp. *andorrana*. Winifred Bevington and her late husband, Harold, made regular pilgrimages to see the new campanula in its native habitat. I find it thrilling to learn of new species being recently introduced from Europe, both new to science and to horticulture. This is another campanula of outstanding merit that stands out prominently beside the greats, such as *C. zoysii*, *C. raineri*, *C. morettiana*, and *C. cenisia*. I have not yet grown this species but have seen a most wonderfully flowered pan filled with its glorious, blue bell-shaped flowers cultivated by Robert Rolfe. Flowering in the open garden during early and midsummer, *C. jaubertiana* should be given pride of place on a trough or raised bed, wedged in between pieces of dolomite limestone. Once satisfied, it will form neat clumps or mats with its typical creeping rhizomes. It is from the rhizomes that propagules may be carefully severed after flowering with a scalpel and either potted up or transferred to an eager friend.

Lest I should ever forget when describing choice members of Campanulaceae—beware of slugs. Even the tiniest form of these dreaded molluscs, or gastropods, will devour one's choicest bellflower in an hour or two.

I am always fascinated to see butterworts in nature, whether it is in our native Scotland or in the European mountains. Always frequenting damp places, pinguiculas are often found in wet turf or lining humus-rich, rock crevices. It is in the latter habitat that *Pinguicula longifolia* can frequently be seen in the Pyrénées. Along with long, sticky, yellowish green leaves, it produces very large, deep-blue flowers on short stems. Although it is not recommended to help oneself to armfuls of living sphagnum moss, I do admit to loving the smell and texture of this unique material used so widely in the lining of hanging baskets. It is its moisture-holding property that recommends this moss to those of us desperate to succeed with subjects such as pinguicula, *Primula deorum* and *P. glutinosa*, along with other desirable plants. A cool spot in the garden should be found where a mossy pocket can be created between rocks, or at the edge of a pool to accommodate this pretty Pyrenean endemic. Some winter protection for the overwintering resting buds is recommended. The closely related *Pinguicula grandiflora* is a plant I can also recommend, which is similar in all respects to the foregoing; it is a very pretty species found in the Pyrénées.

Andorra and the Eastern Pyrénées

A number of subjects are deserving of special mention from the eastern end of the Pyrénées, including the little principality of Andorra. I will now describe some plants that can be found in this independent state which lies between France and Spain. In the spring, the valley meadows are white with that loveliest of narcissus, the familiar pheasant's eye, *Narcissus poeticus*, filling the air with its delicious fragrance. Higher up in the alpine zone amongst the snow patches, flowering in June and early July, is one of my favourite alpine androsaces.

Belonging to the section *Aretia*, *Androsace laggeri* is found throughout the eastern Pyrénées. The closely related *A. carnea*, as found in the Central Alps, can be a tiny plant around 1 cm across, with rather disappointing pale pink flowers. What a contrast with *Androsace laggeri*, which forms large mats of dark green, needlelike leaves, covered with clusters of fine pink flowers from mid to late spring in cultivation.

Introduced into cultivation in 1975 by Henry and Margaret Taylor is a superior form which has been given the name *Androsace laggeri* 'Andorra', which will rank as one of the finest androsaces for the alpine garden. Why? Well, it is

Androsace laggeri 'Andorra'
Photo by Margaret and Henry Taylor.

extremely attractive, totally hardy, compact, easy to grow, and simple to propagate. What more could we ask of an alpine plant? Perhaps fragrance. No surprise, then, for the flowers also emit a sweet scent. It has deep pink buds which open to large, rose-pink flowers with a darker pink ring around the yellow eye. The short 1 cm stalks increase with age and generally carry up to six flowers. The cultivar name 'Andorra' commemorates its origin as it was found in the Val d'Incles at 2450 m. Nonflowering shoots root easily in a traditional cuttings mix of either sand and perlite or sand and vermiculite. I grow this choice cultivar on a trough, where its fragrant flowers can easily be admired. If there is one word of warning, it is the name of the only pest I expect to visit this plant: greenfly. Severely stunted and discoloured plants will have an infestation within the cushion. A systemic insecticide will solve the problem, and care should be taken to avoid allowing such an attack to kill the plant.

Some years ago I was invited to judge at a Scottish Rock Garden Club Show held in Milngavie, Glasgow. Once the main part of the judging routine was completed, it was time to select the most meritorious plant in the show, which would then be awarded the Forrest Medal (Farrer Medal in England). It is often the case that three or four plants will be brought forward to a table for final analysis. On this occasion, I recall a very fine pot full of a cypripedium and a pan of gentian labelled *Gentiana brachyphylla*. At that time, I would not have known the botanical differences that separated each of the verna group (section *Cyclostigma*) gentians. Sufficient to say, this specimen was outstanding, as we often experienced with plants submitted by Lynn and Ronald Bezzant. Yes, it won the Forrest Medal, added to which it was sweetly scented. It was this feature of the plant that provoked some ongoing discussion with the plant's owners. I discovered that this form had been collected as a wee cutting from a prominent limestone mountain in Andorra. In fact, the gentian was not *G. brachyphylla* (which prefers a lime-free substrate) but the rarely seen *G. pumila* subsp. *delphinensis*. Having passed on the whole story to the Taylors, they later visited the mountain and noted that a high percentage of the plants found there were in fact sweetly fragrant. This is surely an unusual but welcome feature for an alpine gentian.

This neat little plant is easily grown in a trough, where it forms a tiny, congested rosette of pointed leaves with the most intense deep blue flowers in mid to late spring. The rosettes increase slowly and are best positioned between small pieces of dolomite limestone in full sun. Look out for seed setting; collect it carefully and sow immediately. I find that with all the verna group of gentians, germination is improved from freshly sown seed, with the seed pots plunged in a sand frame.

Gentiana brachyphylla

Two more choice species of gentian are found in Andorra, but they are not exclusive to this principality. They are *Gentiana alpina* and *G. pyrenaica*. The first is an absolute brute to satisfy in a lowland garden. I say *lowland* because the Schachen Garden, situated at some 1800 M in the Bavarian Alps, is a garden where, despite its calcareous soil, this gentian does grow quite well. I have tried on several occasions to grow *G. alpina*, but without success. I must create an even more favourable spot, for it is quite one of the most beautiful of all European gentians. This species is unmistakable and found only in the Spanish Sierra Nevada, the eastern Pyrénées, and the Alps of Savoie and western Switzerland. It belongs to the acaulis group (section *Thylacites*) of gentians and is a true alpine plant, rarely found in nature under 2000 M, often ascending to 3000 M and more. It is generally intolerant of calcareous soils, and I would recommend finding a sunny position for it on a raised bed, giving it a well-drained but humus-rich mixture, and positioning a few flat, schistose rocks around the plant to afford the roots a little extra protection.

Gentiana alpina is readily distinguished by its small, undulate, and yellow-green foliage, somewhat reminiscent of *G. brachyphylla*. The flowers are really acaule (stemless) and are generally deep blue with green spots in the throat. There is no doubt that this species will present a challenge to most growers, but the reward for success will be great, indeed. Cuttings will root readily in a peat

Gentiana alpina

and sand mix, with added perlite to improve the root system. Seed is a useful alternative when available, but it must be sown as soon as it is obtained.

The second gentian, found both in Andorra and in the eastern Pyrénées, is *Gentiana pyrenaica*. It also occurs far away in the Rila mountains of Bulgaria, but more of this form later in the book. This plant presents a challenge to the grower, but I am more confident with its cultivation. I am convinced that part of this success is down to its symbiotic association with certain grasses and/or mosses. Of course, it is difficult to provide exactly what it associates with in its native habitat, but I have found it can be coaxed into some feeling of happiness when planted amongst sphagnum moss. it belongs to the section *Chondrophylla* as classified by Kusnezow in 1894.

With greater research into the subject of symbiotic relationships between alpine plants and grasses and mosses, we may be able to succeed with certain genera when previously we have failed. Much work has been carried out on the mycorrhizal association of fungi and higher plants, which most notably affects woodland plants and species of orchids. Yet what a thrill it would be to have a crack at growing alpine pedicularis, for example, giving them a better chance of survival in the garden.

Gentiana pyrenaica
Photo by Ronald Bezzant.

Gentiana pyrenaica grows fairly plentifully but seems quite particular to its preferred habitat. It is found in dampish hollows and on grassy banks but always amongst grass and generally avoiding a southerly aspect. It grows in a band between roughly 2250 and 2500 m; above this limit it is replaced with *G. acaulis* types and below by *G. verna* and its allies. *Gentiana pyrenaica* is readily distinguished by its violet-blue flowers, which appear to have ten, rather than the usual five, petals. This is of course an illusion, as on closer inspection, it can be observed that it is the plicae (folds between the petal lobes) which are more developed than most species of gentian.

Every effort should be made to succeed with this outstanding species, whether we choose the Pyrenean form or one from eastern Europe. I would create a specific spot for this gentian in a trough filled with a mixture of sphagnum moss, soil, and gritty sand in the ratio (by bulk) of 60:20:20, and plant it alongside *Gentiana alpina* and *Primula glutinosa*. Propagation of *G. pyrenaica* can be carried out by careful division of the plant in early spring, or from seed. Yes, it represents another challenge, but that is part of the fun of growing true alpine plants.

Whilst describing the cultivation of plants from the Cantabrian Mountains, I described two species of ranunculus, *Ranunculus parnassifolius* and *R. amplexicaulis*. Another spectacular form of *R. parnassifolius* is to be found in the eastern

Pyrénées close to the village of Nuria. For those planning a botanical trip to these parts, a great thrill can be experienced by taking the little rack railway from Caralps to the sanctuary of Nuria in the Spanish Pyrénées, where one may find excellent forms of *R. pyrenaeus* and the showy hybrid *R.×flahaultii*. Then there are *Senecio leucophyllus* and that ultimate treasure, *Adonis pyrenaica*. A truly rewarding area when visited in June to early July.

The local form of *Ranunculus parnassifolius* has been given the cultivar name 'Nuria' and received an AM in 1978 when exhibited by its collectors Henry and Margaret Taylor. It is locally abundant above 2300 M, growing in slaty, acidic scree. This scree in its structure varies from brick-sized slate to boulders the size of a garage, and beneath the rocks are large quantities of fine silt, providing a moisture-retentive material into which the plants can root. So the first require-ment becomes self-evident: a cool, deep root run. This wonderful plant pro-duces slightly hirsute, ovate basal leaves tucked in between glistening, micaceous rocks, giving it a look of distinction, even without flowers. The best is yet to come, though; short stems carry full-petalled flowers with pink veining both inside and outside the flower petals. Each plant is better than the last, but clearly the finest are to be found where there is a superabundance of cool moisture

Ranunculus parnassifolius 'Nuria'
Photo by Jim Jermyn.

Ranunculus pyrenaeus

at the roots. (How often do we hear or read about this challenging requirement? As I have found out to my own cost, one avoids this provision at one's peril; better to attend to the moisture requirements of a plant than admire a beautifully arranged pocket of rocks on a raised bed and an unattended label!)

Although Dr. Roger-Smith may have first brought the reader's attention to this fine form as early as 1953, and Henry Hammer introduced an analogous stock, it was the Taylors who introduced this fine plant to gardens. It is now well established and is easy in a trough, raised bed, or a scree. It multiplies well by division after flowering, or from freshly sown seed.

Closely related and widely distributed across the European Alpine ranges is *Ranunculus pyrenaeus*. My own experience of this species is not of fine forms, but outstanding variations do exist, most notably in the Pyrénées and the French Alps around Fontanalbe. The plant is always found in alpine turf, flowering just as the snows recede and usually in vast quantities. In its best forms it will make a fine

Alpine meadow with *Ranunculus pyrenaeus*

addition for the rock garden or scree where it produces an herbaceous clump of glaucous, linear foliage. The flower stems are some 12 CM tall with one or more, pure white, cup-shaped flowers up to 2 CM across. Propagation can be achieved by watching out carefully as the seed achenes ripen, and when ready they will fall away into a well-placed egg cup. They should be sown immediately as with most other members of Ranunculaceae.

These two species described above produce a variable hybrid *Ranunculus ×fla-haultii* with white to pink flowers. The foliage is intermediate in shape between those of the parent species, and the upper surface is dark blue-green and covered with white hairs. The flowering stems are 5 CM tall, each bearing groups of three flowers. In 1985, a cultivar name was given to an outstanding example of this hybrid, *R. ×flahaultii* 'Noufonts', found growing on acid turf at 2400 M in the eastern Pyrénées. The sterile hybrids can be multiplied satisfactorily by carefully dividing mature clumps either during the dormant season or after flowering. Divisions must be well watered in to encourage establishment.

One of the most striking endemics found in the eastern Pyrénées is *Senecio leucophyllus*. Some regard it as too challenging when encountered in nature as a shy scree dweller in the Val d'Eyne. But if we travel farther east to the Pic du Canigou, the more accommodating form of this illustrious species can be found at the lowest extremity of the alpine zone. It grows here in the grass amongst dwarf shrubs. It is widespread here at altitudes between 2300 and 2500 M, and rooted divisions collected should establish well in an open, sunny scree in the garden. This stunning plant with its intensely silver, divided foliage is susceptible to rotting off at the neck during the winter, and I would take the precautionary measure of providing winter cover. It is grown as a foliage plant, although it produces tight heads of yellow flowers. Short stem cuttings can be rooted easily in a sand bed with bottom heat, but I would not cover the cuttings with polythene in case of rotting.

My final choice from this outstanding mountain range is one of the most celebrated of all alpine plants, *Adonis pyrenaica*. This species, which is confined to the eastern Pyrénées and a few isolated stations in the Maritime Alps, provides one of the greatest thrills for plantsfolk visiting these parts. It is often sought out in the Val d'Eyne, which is a supremely beautiful valley with an abundance of flowers. The hillsides are shaded blue from *Linum alpinum* which is sharing space with *Aster alpinus*, *Rhododendron ferrugineum*, and *Delphinium elatum*—a truly spectacular sight. The speciality of this valley is unquestionably *Adonis pyrenaica*, which prefers to colonise inhospitable, barren hillsides or coarse, settled granite scree.

Adonis pyrenaica

In cultivation, *Adonis pyrenaica* is not difficult to establish, but patience is required, particularly since the best way to obtain it is from seed. If the seed is received from a friend, then it must be sown as soon as it is ripe. *Adonis* species all produce, at fruiting, a head of numerous achenes. Once mature, these achenes can be carefully prised away from their seating and collected in a small receptacle; I prefer (as the reader must now be aware) an egg cup. If the seed is going to be sown at home, this should be carried out at once; whereas, if some of it is going to be sent to a friend, then the following practice is advised: The large seeds (about the size of rice grains) should be placed within some slightly damp tissue and secured between bubble polythene prior to dispatch. Old seed is hardly worth sowing, as it will require specialised treatment and tends to germinate rather sporadically over several years. Fresh seed can be sown singly in cellular trays on a John Innes type compost with a covering of chick grit. If one prefers to sow the seeds thinly in a pot, then great care must be taken at pricking out; soaking the whole pot of seedlings in a pail of water to separate the seedlings prior to potting is a wise precaution.

I would choose a position for such a plant with great care, where the soil does not dry out. Incorporating a few rocks into the bed, whether raised or not, will provide a cool root run for the deeply searching root system. The mature herbaceous plants produce attractive, feathery foliage and 25 to 40 cm stems each bearing a huge, golden-yellow flower. In the Schachen Garden in southern Germany, a fine stand of this aristocratic species can be seen flowering from mid to late July. It is a sight to behold growing in deep beds amongst the endemic limestone.

I have still to visit many exciting locations in the European Alps, as well as classic locations in the mountain ranges (such as the Pyrénées) outwith the Alps, which I have read about in the pages of alpine journals. Several writers come to mind relative to the Pyrénées, including the well-travelled Taylors, but I frequently turn to the writings of Harold and Winifred Bevington. In 1993, Harold wrote about a trip he made with his wife based in the small town of Benasque in the middle of the Spanish Pyrénées. He said, "It is a very good centre in an area very rich in alpine flora."

I will conclude my Pyrenean sojourn, sharing some thoughts about growing these lovely endemics in our gardens, by highlighting where all of this experience in the garden starts. All the plants under discussion that we enjoy growing owe their origin to the Alps or the adjacent mountain ranges of Europe. Each one of them has been found by an intrepid plant hunter, and in most cases seed has been collected and introduced into cultivation. As we now move further into the 21st century, collecting etiquette has changed; almost gone are the hammer and chisels, and gone are the sack and hand trowel. Responsible seed collections are made; with the appropriate permits, cuttings and divisions are carefully collected and brought home for later dissemination. The results are clearly seen in botanic gardens the world over, on show benches in private gardens, and most importantly in nursery catalogues.

Let me offer the further words of Harold Bevington; writing about the area near to Benasque (1993), he enthuses,

> There is much more to see but we are in sight of the highest screes on Pic Castanesa for which we head with a quickened pace. As we approach, the seemingly barren slopes come alive with *Adonis pyrenaica* and an assortment of good plants such as *Vitaliana primuliflora* [synonym *Douglasia vitaliana*], compact cushions of *Alyssum cuneifolium*, *Crepis pygmaea*, *Androsace villosa* and *Oxtropis pyrenaica*.

What a thrill for the Bevingtons, the Taylors, and many others. There can be no doubt that the Pyrénées have given up many wonderful plants to our gardens. Some of these are still testing our skill as growers, but many are well established and provide the backbone to a colourful and rewarding alpine garden.

Cytisus ardoinii

5: The Western and Central Alps

Loosely, the Alps is a mountain range in south central Europe, extending more than 1000 km from the Mediterranean coast of France and northeast Italy through Switzerland, north Italy, and Austria, to what is now Serbia. The highest peak is Mont Blanc, at 4807 m. This great range will be broken down here into smaller components comprising the Maritime Alps, the Spanish Sierras, the French Alps, the Swiss Alps, and the Italian Alps, including the Apennine Mountains.

The Maritime Alps

This alpine range makes up part of the Western Alps in southeast France and northwest Italy. The highest peak is Argentera (3316 m). It is a botanically rich region owing to the diversity of rock formation. Only 40 km north from the Mediterranean, granitic peaks approaching 3000 m soar up through the crust of Jurassic limestone. It is on the sides of these limestone gorges and cliff faces that we find many exciting endemic plants. This is also a geologist's paradise, with shells and limestone chiselled from the sea floor being found up to 2400 m above sea level and scattered amongst the granite.

If the Pyrénées is famed for its *Saxifraga longifolia*, ramonda, or adonis, then the Maritime Alps' claim to fame will surely be the ultimate European primula, *Primula allionii*; another local primula, *P. marginata*; and an array of silver saxifrages, some proving more of a challenge in the garden than others.

As we take a closer look at the geography of the Maritime Alps and their close proximity to the Mediterranean, I am sure that a range of real sun-loving alpine plants come to mind. I will look at some of these species first.

In any of the limestone regions at lower subalpine levels, some fine plants can be found that we should consider growing in our gardens. Plants associated with sun-baked, grassy banks or rocky crevices in the lower reaches often prove versatile garden subjects. One of the real treasures in these parts is *Lilium pomponium*, which adorns the Col de la Sine. Easily raised from seed, this species makes an invaluable addition to the rock garden, standing out with its bright flower colour and providing some useful height to give a proportion to our alpine planting. In nature, it prefers to grow in open scrub or on established limestone hillsides, generally flowering in late spring. It cannot be mistaken with its waxy, scarlet-red flowers on 30 to 80 cm stems.

Another bulbous species which is often found in large numbers in the Maritime Alps but not confined to the range is *Fritillaria tubiformis* (synonym *F. delphinensis*). I have also encountered this attractive plant growing amongst *Anemone narcissiflora* in grassy alpine meadows in northwestern Italy. It may be found at an altitudinal range of 1500 to 2000 m, flowering in nature during late spring and early summer. The flowers are typically large and bell-like, a luminous rosy chestnut with a plum-coloured bloom towards the top of the flower, on 8 to 20 cm stems.

A rare form of this species may be found in this area, *Fritillaria tubiformis* subsp. *moggridgei*. It is very similar to the type species in stature, but it displays the most wonderful yellow flowers. Both are easily grown in the garden in a

Globularia cordifolia

humus-rich alpine bed and can be propagated either by seed (with a measure of patience required) or from division of established bulbs.

A genus of plants for which I think we all have a liking, but never quite get hooked on, are the rhizomatous irises. Perhaps it is the fleeting period of flowering relative to the space they occupy or the slight confusion over their nomenclature—I am not sure which. One point that is clear to me, though, is that they are easy of culture and in their best forms are fine garden plants. Often growing amongst the dashing *Lilium pomponium* on a limestone substrate is the attractive *Iris chamaeiris*, which in its best forms produce deep, velvety purple flowers held on 15 cm stems. It is closely related to the Balkan *I. reichenbachii*, but material of known geographic origin would give a clear identification. Division of the rhizomes after flowering is an effective means of reproduction.

My experience of the Maritime Alps is of hot, sun-baked meadows amidst rugged limestone scenery, and the flora often reflects this ambience. I would always find place in a rock garden or raised bed for plants of *Cytisus ardoinii*. I ought to bow to the botanical expertise of *Flora Europaea* (Tutin 1964), which chooses to remove an *i* from the specific name (*ardoini*). I believe that most readers are more familiar with the double-*i* spelling, however. Fortunately, neither spelling will affect the beauty provided by this dwarf broom. Forming a neat, gnarled shrublet up to 20 cm in height, with bright yellow flowers produced in axillary clusters, it can be given pride of place on a corner of a trough or raised bed, allowing it to tumble over the edge. Soft to semi-ripe cuttings root well in a sand and perlite rooting mixture.

Throughout the Alps a number of globularias will be encountered, often in a stony scree habitat or as flat mats tumbling over rock faces and wedged into crevices. I have found globularias accompanying *Daphne cneorum* along with the edelweiss, *Leontopodium alpinum*—a most attractive combination to reenact in the garden. The Maritime Alps are home to two species both deserving of a position in the rock garden or the more contemporary tufa wall: *Globularia cordifolia* and *G. repens*. The former is often offered in nurseries and is easy of cultivation. It is my experience that both species have a tendency to rot away in a damp, mild winter, despite forming strong mats of foliage. The best plants I have seen were planted directly into boulders of tufa. This situation provides the desired drainage and a leaner diet, which in turn helps to ripen the plants prior to our changeable British winters.

Globularia cordifolia is a flat-growing shrublet with dark green, evergreen, spathulate foliage. The spreading stems creep over both vertical and horizontal limestone rock faces in nature, and the same conditions will produce good results in our gardens. In early summer, when positioned in full sun, the mats

Challenges of photography

Plant photography can be a challenging hobby. Considerable skill is required when photographing pale blue to lilac-coloured flowers with a conventional 35 mm single-lens reflex (SLR) camera. It is my experience that trying to recreate the true colour of such flowers, including *Pulsatilla* 'Budapest Blue', ramonda, haberlea, and globularias, is more successful when the shot is taken out of full sunlight. Others have obtained good results when attaching a Wratten 82A pale blue filter to the lens.

are covered with a mass of pale blue globular heads of flowers, reminiscent of powder puffs, on short 2 to 4 cm stems. The plant is easily propagated from cuttings which can often be detached with roots, ready for transplanting or potting up. The shape of the flowers is almost unique, and I cannot resist planting it among appropriate forms of *Daphne cneorum*, with which it associates so well in its native habitat.

Globularia repens is closely related and similar in habit to *G. cordifolia*. It differs in forming a much tighter and denser mat of foliage with deeper blue or mauve flowers. It thrives when planted on a boulder of tufa rock, but it is a little more challenging to strike from cuttings due to the more gnarled habit of the mats.

Botanists and taxonomists have their work cut out at the best of times, but there are a number of genera needing some revision. An example of this could include a revision of the genus *Pulsatilla* or further refinements to the taxonomy of linums. And so to the very subject of naming linums. Who could venture to sort out this particular genus? One species which is to be found in the limestones of, for example, the Vésubie Valley, is the sun-loving *Linum suffruticosum*. In its dwarf manifestations, this is a choice plant for the garden with its showy white flowers. Several nurseries offer a plant with an awful lot of Latin nomenclature, *L. suffruticosum* subsp. *salsoloides* 'Nanum' (synonym *L. salsoloides* 'Nanum'). This is a fine form, producing flat carpets of neat linear foliage and masses of large, white, lilac-veined flowers on 5 cm stems. It is easily raised from cuttings.

Another linum of outstanding garden merit is *Linum campanulatum*. In *Flora Europaea* (Tutin 1964), it is assigned to the *Linum flavum* group. This is a species with a wide distribution, including parts of the Maritime Alps. Flat mats of branched, woody stems are made up of broad-leaved, glaucous rosettes. In its best forms, most notably one collected by the late Rudolf Wurdig, the flowers are held in an inflorescence of three to five bright, golden-yellow blooms. It flowers in the early summer and can be increased from cuttings taken after flowering from nonflowering (if possible) shoots. The plant requires an open, sunny spot and seems indifferent to soil pH.

A plant native to the same sun-baked limestone habitats is the pretty St. John's wort, *Hypericum coris*. It forms a dwarf evergreen shrublet up to 15 cm in height. The tiny leaves so typical of this genus are arranged in whorls along with an abundance of golden-yellow flowers during early to midsummer. This is a fine choice for the rock garden, providing valuable colour later in the season.

One of the real highlights of any trip made to the Maritime Alps in mid to late June are the fine array of silver or encrusted saxifrages (section *Ligulatae*). More than 90 years ago when writing his book *Among the Hills* (1911), Farrer extolled the virtues of these varied saxifrages, which he clearly collected at will and grew admirably in his North Yorkshire nursery and garden. He travelled from St. Martin de Vésubie through Lantosque and then down to Nice, along the Côte d'Azur and later northwards to Brigue and Tende. This was, and still is, an excellent route to travel in order to locate these wonderful plants. I will describe a few of my favourite species that are both distinct and valuable as garden plants in a variety of situations.

Linum campanulatum

It is my opinion that the encrusted saxifrages went through a barren patch in terms of popularity towards the end of the last century. Having visited the well-maintained trial beds, located under glass at the RHS Garden Wisley, I am not surprised at the downturn in popularity. There are far too many indistinct forms with a confusion of names that makes a visit to the specialist nursery so perplexing. This is not a problem confined only to this group of saxifrages. Whilst running Edrom Nurseries, I am sure I was guilty of offering far too many indistinct varieties from a particular genus—whether it was wood anemones, autumn-flowering gentians, or forms of *Primula marginata*.

This is where I particularly want to praise the work of the RHS Joint Rock Garden Committee. Perish the thought that this valuable committee would ever be amalgamated with another related committee, or even disbanded. The resulting awards should be embraced by nurseries and garden centres alike, providing the backbone of the many choice plants available in the nursery trade. All too often a vast array of cultivars are offered when most of them are very similar to one another. What the down-to-earth gardener wants is the "best doer". I do hope I am endeavouring to practise what I preach in the pages of this book. It is also my intention to alert gardeners whether a particular plant is better suited either to the beginner or to the avid collector.

The vast majority of saxifrages flower during early summer, with the exception of the ancient king, *Saxifraga florulenta*. Despite the fact that it is relatively easy to remove an offset of any saxifrage without damaging the mother plant, we are not at liberty to collect at will, with a number of specially protected areas existing in the Maritime Alps, including the Parco Naturale d'Argentera. Most of the subjects described here are readily available from specialist nursery catalogues, reducing the need for any collection in the wild.

I will describe five outstanding species, three from the section *Ligulatae*, one from the section *Porphyrion*, subsection *Kabschia*; another from the "mossy" section; and then finally the most difficult to classify, *Saxifraga florulenta*. Commencing with the silvers or encrusted species (section *Ligulatae*), I am back to the attention of the taxonomist. When Farrer wrote at length about these saxifrages, he was familiar with two notable forms of the species *S. callosa*, both of great merit: the first was *S. callosa* var. *lantoscana* and the second *S. callosa* var. *bellardii*.

The small town of Lantosque is the site of the first, which we must now get used to calling *Saxifraga callosa* subsp. *callosa* var. *australis* (the Latin word *australis* referring to the south, and having nothing to do with Australia). The original names were both simple and meaningful. The confusion was also prevalent in Farrer's day, for he, too, was lamenting the work of the taxonomist, saying,

"And now begins a controversy, which I cannot spare you. In the name of holy truth I beseech your patience" (Farrer 1911). Some things never change. But to come to the botanist's defence, the saxifrages are a difficult genus to sort out.

Fortunately, the two forms are sufficiently distinct, both geographically and morphologically, so let me discuss the fine form *Saxifraga callosa* var. *australis* (to reduce the name). Around the town of Lantosque, one can easily find a typically steep rock face amidst scrub, smothered in a vast population of this saxifrage. Although the plants are variable in leaf length and size of leaf-rosette, the common feature is the spathulate leaf, broadening at the tip and curving outwards. The foliage is greener than the form *S. callosa* subsp. *callosa* var. *callosa* (synonym *S. callosa* var. *bellardii*). The variety *australis* is more at home in cool, shady exposures. The flowers are carried more or less one-sided on their stems, with the spike rising to about 30 cm and bending under the weight of countless, brilliant, pure white flowers.

A very fine selection collected by Farrer, named *Saxifraga callosa* 'Limelight', is well worth seeking out, with its smaller rosettes and pale yellow-green leaves. Both 'Limelight' and its parent plant can be given a cool site in the garden,

Saxifraga callosa subsp. *callosa* var. *callosa*

tucked in between pieces of limestone. Allow room for the rosette to enlarge and sufficient height for the weight of flowering plumes to cascade down.

The second variety, *Saxifraga callosa* subsp. *callosa* var. *callosa*, is rather special. It is to be found around the Col de Tende (1930 M) on the French/Italian frontier. It grows on the cliffs above Tende and seems indifferent as to whether it has a sunny or shady exposure. So here is an advantage to the gardener with its amenability in cultivation. The rosettes of this variety are much larger than those of the variety *australis*. They form wider, denser tangles of silvery rosettes and have longer leaves of up to 20 CM in length. The spectacular sprays of white flowers commend this form to the alpine gardener, and its ease of cultivation, hardiness, and perennial habit gives *S. longifolia* a run for its money.

Another species I can strongly recommend is fairly local, being largely confined to the area around La Brigue and Saorge. It is the variable species *Saxifraga cochlearis* and may be found from the 'Major' to the 'Minor' forms of horticulture. In the hottest of habitats, it can become so condensed and minute as to be compared with the rare species *S. valdensis*. I find this species quite enchanting, simple in its appearance, with attractive, silver, lime-encrusted rosettes of spoon-shaped foliage. In the garden it is seen at its best tucked into vertical crevices of limestone or a boulder of tufa rock. Let it spread about at will and enjoy the 12 to 20 CM open panicles of white flowers on red pedicels.

This famous species was first described by Reichenbach in 1832 and was given specific status by Burnat in 1901. It is so restricted in its distribution that it should not be collected at all. It is represented by a number of cultivars in nursery catalogues, perhaps the best being *Saxifraga cochlearis* 'Minor', and as with the others is easily increased from cuttings.

From the silvers now to a choice Kabschia, *Saxifraga diapensioides*. Here is a species that was first recognised as distinct in about 1790 by Bellardi, who found it in the Maritime Alps. I am not quite sure where the connection is with *Diapensia lapponica* for its specific name, but that is of little significance. It is most closely related to the species *S. tombeanensis* from Lombardia, northern Italy, but the former species has a more pronounced glaucous incrustation to its foliage.

A careful search will need to be made to locate this species from a specialist nursery, and, if the search is successful, care should be taken to plant it in a cool position protected from the hottest afternoon sunshine. As with many Kabschia species, this one prefers to be wedged vertically between pieces of limestone, but it also likes best to get its roots into a humus-rich soil mixture. Tight, knobbly cushions are made up of compressed rosettes which vanish during flowering beneath 6 to 8 CM stems, carrying a short, loose corymb with three to five large white flowers. A well-flowered cushion in late spring is a sight of which to be proud. The plants can be propagated from seed or cuttings carefully prised away after flowering.

Although not located exclusively in the Maritime Alps, *Saxifraga diapensioides* is concentrated in the southwestern and west-central Alps, where it prefers shady limestone rocks at between 1700 and 2300 m, but descending in one location to 850 m. I would rate this species as a challenge to all but the most seasoned of growers, but let us rise to such challenges.

I have not left challenges behind yet. Here are two more exacting saxifrages that do not sit too easily among alpine gardeners. Let me tackle the very beautiful yet far from straightforward *Saxifraga pedemontana* first. It is a mossy saxifrage and a very lovely one, too. When I first enjoyed my apprenticeships, mossy saxifrages were justifiably popular. It was not unusual to visit a specialist alpine plant nursery and find a dedicated frame with an alphabetical selection of the finest species and cultivars from this popular section of saxifrage. Some of my favourites were *S.* ×*wallacei*, *S.* 'Winston Churchill', *S.* 'Ruth McConnel', *S.* 'Stansfieldii', *S.* 'Cloth of Gold', and of course *S.* 'Triumph'. A closer look at some of the species would then reveal the very choice *S. pedemontana*. So what has happened to them all now?

I recall that whilst still running Edrom Nurseries, a notable upsurge in the population of that awful little pest, the vine weevil, occurred in the mid-1980s, with the sudden withdrawal of the much-used pesticide Aldrin. Few of us would advocate the use of chemical pesticides if there were a safer biological alternative, but at that time no such option was available, hence the little horror went on the rampage. I suddenly found vine weevil shifting their nasty little noses from Primulaceae to Saxifragaceae, and, boy, did they like mossy saxifrages! I believe that the sudden onslaught of this rampageous pest added to the decline of this wonderful group of plants. I certainly hope that this can be reversed in due course. Thank goodness for a variety of both chemical and biological controls against vine weevil.

The first time I found *Saxifraga pedemontana* in nature was close to the Col de la Lombarde in the Maritime Alps. It was growing in deep shade in a damp gully, where the handsome, succulent-looking foliage contrasted well with the flowers. It was first described by the botanist Allioni in 1785 from the Maritime Alps, although it is not endemic there. Plants can be found across the southwestern Alps, both in France and Gran Paradiso in Italy, at altitudes of between 1500 and 2700 m. It prefers a lime-free soil and is often found wedged between granite rocks in full shade or exposed positions. To be quite correct, this form is named *S. pedemontana* subsp. *pedemontana*, as another three less attractive subspecies are found in other parts of Europe.

I would recommend positioning plants in dappled shade between rocks in a humus-rich mixture. Moisture retention is important. When plants are given full exposure, as with many mossies, the older foliage will assume a reddish colour, contrasting well with the fresh green rosettes. Whether this species is grown for its rather exotic green rosettes or the panicles of clean white flowers on 5 to 10 CM stems, it will prove to be a valuable addition in the rock garden. Nonflowering rosettes can be detached and rooted with ease to perpetuate the best forms, or seed can be saved as another means of propagation. A word of warning: If the foraging activities of blackbirds and sparrows are a problem, beware, for they love to tear apart the cushions of these mossies. Some wire netting protection may be necessary during their period of activity.

And now to something very special, particularly since I am about to describe one of the most outstanding of all European alpine plants, yet not for its floral performance. The ancient king, *Saxifraga florulenta*, is confined to the high granite or gneiss cliffs of the Maritime Alps, usually facing north or northwest, from 1900 to 3250 M. It is centred on the large massif known as the Mercantour with its two main summits, Argentera and Mont Clapier.

It is a monocarpic species (that is, it dies after flowering) that has not been known to science for a long time. In fact, it was probably discovered around 1810 by Bellardi. When Farrer first encountered the species in the early 1900s, he was quite awestruck. "I rent the welkin with a cry of triumph", he said (Farrer 1911), and went on: "For a moment I could not believe my eyes; for another moment I felt convinced, insanely, that some botanist must have put the rosette there as a practical joke, so monstrously apposite was its appearance at just that point." Yes, he was bowled over, just as I was when I saw a well-grown plant on an Alpine Garden Society show bench nestling between flat pieces of granite in a pan. I once raised the species from the Archibalds' seed, but as soon as they were saleable, I passed them on to safer hands and in doing so relinquished a weighty responsibility.

Saxifraga florulenta forms a dense rosette some 5 to 15 CM in diameter, with up to 150 leaves tightly packed and beautifully arranged. Seldom can we marvel at such a symmetrically stunning rosette in the alpine world. Nature seems to know no bounds. The foliage is dark green and smooth, and after many years an inflorescence will emerge from its awesome base in the form of a stout, glandular spike. The flowering stem is about 10 to 25 CM in length, with a dense, cylindrical inflorescence of flesh-pink flowers. In nature it flowers during mid to late summer, sets and disperses seed, and then the whole plant expires.

So how can we tame such a plant in cultivation? Not easily, I would hasten to reply. I might just recommend growing it in a freely drained acidic mix in a deep pan or pot, and plunge it in the alpine house. This said, if seed is made available, young plants can be planted out in vertical crevices of lime-free rock formations. I would also suggest providing autumn and winter protection from excessive rains and inclement weather. To boast, or even just to experience, a fat rosette of the ancient king is a feat in itself.

Saxifraga florulenta is a real alpine treasure; it is, however, a rare plant in nature and should be accorded all the rigours of conservation to preserve its natural beauty. It is protected by law in all its Italian stations, and for those of us able to seek it out in nature, as with many alpines, let us take some pictures and savour them forever, leaving the plant itself well alone.

If the reader feels a little exhausted after these sumptuous jewels, beware—the best is yet to come!

Before I conclude with the ultimate jewel of the Maritime Alps in the form of a primula, I will write about two challenging violas and an alpine pink found locally in the alpine zones of this region. I regard the truly alpine species from this genus of violas as precious as any comparable campanula, and for this reason I like to position them beside appropriate compatriots in a dedicated trough with a substrate to suit.

Viola nummularifolia is a local species found in the Maritime Alps close to the Franco-Italian border at altitudes between 2400 and 2800 м. It is not a pansy, but a violet, as Farrer was at pains to point out, and in his opinion it is "Queen of the violets" (Farrer 1911). This particular species is never seen below the highest alpine zone and is found only on granite formations. It is a plant of the moraine or scree, and once this fact is clearly understood, along with the rock type, we can reenact a special microclimate in a trough. A number of carefully positioned stones and a freely drained material, and we are all set. It spreads out its stems from a central taproot with a network of shoots clad in tiny round leaves. The flowers are freely produced on short stems of 3 to 5 см and are a subtle shade of cool-lavender verging toward lilac-blue, with fine lines of purple. It is an exquisite violet, and how well it would associate with a plant of *Primula minima* var. *alba* and perhaps a cushion or two of *Douglasia vitaliana* in its best forms. Careful observation of the maturing seed capsules will alert the best time for collection and subsequent sowing as a means of propagation.

Flowering from late June to August on gneiss formations in the Argentera massif is another treasure, *Viola valderia*. This one *is* a pansy. It is somewhat akin to a near relative, *V. cenisia*, in flower, but it is quite different in habit. While the Mont Cenis pansy races around in both calcareous and schistose shingles, the rare *V. valderia* makes a compact tuft of foliage from a single taproot and never sends out runners. The lilac-blue pansies are held on 5 to 10 см stems over attractive foliage. Once again, a trough is a fine place to position this treasure in full sun and with careful attention paid to the ravages of either slugs or an aphis (greenfly) attack.

One of my favourite alpine pinks is *Dianthus pavonius*, the peacock pink, once known as *D. neglectus*. It has a fairly wide distribution, commencing just north of the Mediterranean in the Alpes de Provence above Nice, through the Maritime Alps and the Savoie Alps to the Gran Paradiso. Wherever one finds it, there seems to be an abundance of its grasslike foliage and an awesome display of flowers in mid to late summer. It can be found at altitudes between 1200 and 2800 m and is particularly prolific from Mont Cenis south to the Maritime Alps. Depending on altitude, habitat, and aspect, it may be possible to find a variety of forms, neat and compact to rather straggly affairs, but they are usually intergrading in close proximity with one another. This was certainly my experience in the area around Mont Cenis.

I was disappointed to read that the RHS Award of Garden Merit Committee was considering removing this species from its listings. To obtain such an award, the plant should be of good constitution. I certainly feel this is not the place to open up a debate on such a judgement, but both my own experience and that of

Dianthus pavonius

many others is that with the same care we might accord to any outstanding alpine plant, *Dianthus pavonius* is a good doer. I would rate this as one of the finest of all alpine plants—but, on the other hand, my list is ever-increasing!

Farrer, when writing about his first sightings in the Maritime Alps (1911), recounted seeing the dianthus among golden arnicas. So massed was the pink, that he said,

> We stand on it, walk on it, lie on it; impossible to do otherwise, for half the turf is nothing but cushions of finest lawnlike foliage, from which, on stems two or three inches high, spring lovely huge rose-red flowers, round, delicately jagged at the edges of the petals, and lacquered on their underside with a clean coat of nankeen yellow.

Will Ingwersen clearly had a similar experience when he wrote (in 1949),

> A rocky slope covered over an area of many acres with *D. neglectus* [synonym *D. pavonius*] which was difficult to distinguish from the fine fescue grasses until it flowered, whereupon the whole slope was stained crimson. There was every conceivable variation of shape and colour to be found among the myriad of plants. Some were a shade of soft salmon-pink, and from this they ran through the whole gamut of pinks and reds to brilliant crimson.

These are the views of two of the most eminent alpine gardeners. I, like many others, have also experienced this memorable sight, but what is fascinating is how adaptable the species is, as it also sits very happily in tight cushions on stable scree formations and in rock crevices. Most recently, Henry and Margaret Taylor have further reported extreme intergrades in this region.

I have seen fine, scattered plantings of *Dianthus pavonius* both in the rock garden in Munich Botanic Garden and the affiliated Schachen Garden above Garmisch-Partenkirchen. It is a delight to enjoy neat clumps amongst rocks and an associated planting of campanula and edraianthus, for example. I have also grown it very successfully in a trough. It seems unfussy, for a calcifuge species, as to the soil pH in the garden.

I would advise the reader to pay heed to attacks from the local slug population, but apart from this pest, *Dianthus pavonius* will prove to be one of the most redoubtable members of this great genus. Seed is freely produced, and an alternative means for increasing outstanding forms is by softwood cuttings taken after flowering during mid to late summer.

Primula allionii
Photo by Jim Jermyn.

Primula allionii

One of the finest seedlings raised, possibly of hybrid origin with *Dianthus pavonius* as one of the parents, was spotted by the eagle eye of Jack Drake more than 40 years ago. He named the seedling *D.* 'Inshriach Dazzler'. It is a sterile hybrid of great merit, producing masses of deep, carmine-pink flowers over neat clumps during early summer. This hybrid of unknown parentage can easily be propagated by cuttings.

Few would contend that the rarest and most precious of all the European primulas is *Primula allionii*. I can recall first setting eyes on it as if it were yesterday. This was an extraordinary experience whilst working on the side of Lake Garda, northern Italy. My erstwhile employer, Herr Rudolph Würdig, approached me on the evening of 12 March 1978 and suggested we drive down to the Maritime Alps the next day to see whether *P. allionii* was in flower. Given the time of year and the amount of snow cover in the mountains, I thought he was going mad. He had visited these mountains in the French Tende Valley on many occasions but never at the optimum time of flowering for this endemic species.

So it was that we soon arrived in blazing heat, driving down the Roya Valley past acacia trees in full blossom, displaying their subtle but exotic beauty. We paused beyond a bustling little village, and I was still not convinced. Herr Würdig took out a telescope and raised it to his eyes. I cannot repeat his exclamation, but it may have borne many similarities to that of Reginald Farrer's the first time he saw the primula in flower, except in a different language. Over the road we walked at pace, with our camera equipment at the ready, across the river and through a certain amount of scrub and open deciduous woodland, mainly of chestnut, pausing briefly to inspect the foliage of *Hepatica nobilis*. We soon arrived a little breathless beside steep, sun-soaked cliffs with quite the most extraordinary sight I have ever beheld. Dotted about on these vertical cliffs were the most wonderful posies and clumps of stemless primrose flowers in a variety of shades, from midpurple to rose pink, some with a white eye, some without. Several plants were bereft of flowers, displaying their tight cushions made up of rosettes with sticky, greyish green, rounded foliage. We seemed to have timed our visit to perfection in order to enjoy these particular plants growing at an altitude of no more than 700 м.

The cliffs on which this primula grow are of a calcareous sedimentary type, and the rock type reminds me of a porous tufalike material. It is subject to erosion, and most of the cliffs are pitted with crevices, cracks, and caves. I found plants growing within these shady caves with somewhat truncated rootstocks; they were ugly in nature, and I concentrated my attention on the plants in open, sunny aspects.

There must be a degree of permeability in this limestone to permit water to percolate through the rock, allowing the plants to survive the vicious heat of the summer months. The extremely sticky nature of the foliage has adapted to withstand drought and reduce transpiration, but even more remarkable is the root system that penetrates the rock. Despite the little amount of moisture that can be retained amongst the rotting foliage of a mature clump, it is the deeply penetrating root system that provides a strategy for survival over many, many years. The finest plants, which may assume the size of a football, are highest up on the cliffs, which may well benefit from surface water trickling down the cliff face and around the base of the rosette.

Having created a picture of the primula's natural habitat, I hope it will be easier to translate its cultural requirements in the garden. The best way of growing it successfully is on a tufa wall. I hasten to add that this need not be constructed under glass, although a number of growers have reported great success with just such a venture. I have seen the most wonderful tufa cliffs constructed in an alpine house, and I will make reference to these methods in my bibliography. (As to utilising tufa in the garden, I will refer readers to the heading "Tufa in the Garden" in chapter 9.)

Owing to the variable character of the flowers, most notably their colour, a number of cultivars have been raised, and I will highlight just a few which I can strongly recommend. They are *Primula allionii* 'Apple Blossom', a rose-pink variety that won the AM in 1945; 'Anna Griffith', a pale pink, FCC in 1988; 'Avalanche', a pure white, AM in 1974; 'Crowsley Variety', a deep crimson; 'Edinburgh', purple with a white eye; and 'William Earle', lilac pink, AM in 1978.

A natural hybrid exists between *Primula allionii* and its close geographic neighbour, *P. marginata*; it is called *P.* ×*meridiana* 'Miniera' (formerly *P.* ×*miniera*). I say *close*, but this is only relative, because in one case the hybrid was found amongst *P. allionii* and the nearest *P. marginata* was some 188 km away. This is not always the case as the two parents do meet, but they very rarely flower together, with *P. allionii* peaking in midspring and its suitor well into late spring. It should also be pointed out that so early in the season there is little in the way of pollinating insect activity at these altitudes (700 to 1500 m). The hybrid was first found in 1927 by C. C. Mountfort and given an AM in 1979 and an FCC in 1988. This form has a strong affinity with *P. marginata* in the farinose margins to its foliage and several violet-blue coloured flowers.

As to artificial crosses between these two parents, I can recommend two that were raised by Jack Drake, who made use of the *Primula marginata* hybrid 'Linda Pope': the rose-pink *P.* ×*meridiana* 'Sunrise' and the dark purple *P.* ×*meridiana* 'Joan Hughes'. All of the hybrids should be treated in a similar manner to *P. allionii* and given winter protection.

Recently it has been brought to my attention that there has been a change of names to these hybrids. Rules for the naming of all cultivated plants are set out according to the International Code of Nomenclature for Cultivated Plants. This code does receive refinement over the years. As a result of this revision, a degree of orthodoxy now exists regarding the naming of hybrids. To help alpine gardeners, for example, with the naming of European primula hybrids, the binomial treatment is used. All hybrid plants of wild origin or known occurrence between the parents *Primula allionii* and *P. marginata* are named *P.* ×*meridiana*. The plant formerly named *P.* ×*miniera* is now a clone (identified as such for horticultural purposes) as *P.* ×*meridiana* 'Miniera'. Although this is a plant of wild origin, any artificially raised hybrids of this parentage would take the same binomial suffix.

If readers are able to create either a miniature tufa garden or the larger tufa mountain, there can surely be no finer sight than a rock dotted with flowering specimens of *Primula allionii* in its range of cultivars and related hybrids. This type of gardening presents a challenge and will involve a great deal of practice, but it will provide the grower with an exhilarating experience.

Propagating the species and hybrids is perhaps surprisingly straightforward.

The plants produce plenty of seed that will of course provide significant variation in its progeny. Plants may also be vegetatively increased either by stem cuttings taken at the end of June (early summer) or by division of plants that may tend to produce rather leggy plants.

Having now introduced perhaps the jewel of all European alpine primulas to the reader, I feel it would be appropriate to give some order to their classification to help with an understanding of their links as species. See the accompanying box (page 112) for explanation.

A second species of primula has a foothold in the Maritime Alps, but not exclusively to these parts; it is *Primula marginata*. Surely this is one of the most adaptable of all European primulas in the garden. I have grown it in a variety of positions, including on a trough and in an alpine bed at ground level, and I've possibly seen it at its best in a dry wall. It is quite indifferent to soil type and pH both in nature and in cultivation. It is at home on the Cottian granites and on the precipitous limestone of the Maritime Alps. It is often found on shady exposures but has no prej-

Primula 'Linda Pope'
Photo by Jim Jermyn.

udice against sunshine in the garden. In fact, some of my finest flowering clumps are in full sun in alpine troughs.

In nature, *Primula marginata* has a curious habit, found at altitudes from 800 to 3000 м. It prefers limestone on a mossy, grassy ledge on the north side of precipitous slopes or cliffs and rock fissures. I have found it at relatively high altitudes growing in rocky outcrops in full exposure. It produces strong, woody rhizomes of truncated stems hanging out of the rocks to almost 60 см in length. It is for this reason that certain cultivars are best grown vertically in a dry stone wall, where the chosen crevice will serve to hide the truncated mass of flowering stems.

Perhaps the highlight of this species is its foliage. But if one can locate a form with both excellent flowers and foliage, it is a winner! Jack Drake was recalling the first time he met up with the species. Whilst employed at Ingwersen's, he was seconded to a client's garden in Menton, southern France, to work and take photographs for Will Ingwersen. Mr. Will (as I like to refer to him) sent him up into the neighbouring mountains of the Col di Tenda to search for good forms of this primula. He pointed out that it was rare to find forms with both excellent

Classification of European primulas in the section *Auricula (Auriculastrum)*

From a taxonomic point of view, the most widely accepted subdivision was devised by Schott in 1851. His scheme set up seven subdivisions, putting similar species together. They are outlined here:

Eurauricula (closest to *auricula*)
   Primula auricula
   Primula palinuri
Brevibracteata (short bracts)
   Primula albenensis
   Primula carniolica
   Primula latifolia
   Primula marginata
Erythrodrosum (red glandular)
   Primula apennina
   Primula cottia
   Primula daonensis
   Primula grignensis
   Primula hirsuta
   Primula pedemontana
   Primula villosa

Arthritica (gouty)
   Primula clusiana
   Primula glaucescens
   Primula spectabilis
   Primula wulfeniana
Rhopsidium (shrub)
   Primula allionii
   Primula integrifolia
   Primula kitaibeliana
   Primula tyrolensis
Cyanopsis (blue appearance)
   Primula deorum
   Primula glutinosa
Chamaecallis (small and beautiful)
   Primula minima

flowers and attractive foliage—a point I must agree with. So off went Jack in search of his quarry. He returned with a number of excellent plants; what an eye he possessed. With a twinkle in his eye he told me that Mr. Will was astounded by the forms he delivered; some were large-flowered of good lavender-blue colour and superb foliage, exhibiting large, farinose, toothed leaves. The best of these forms was aptly named 'Drake's Form'.

The flowers are quite variable, and of the many cultivars I would implore the reader to be careful to choose the very best. From the rosettes of foliage spring 6 to 10 cm stems carrying an umbel of 2 to 20 individual flowers, perhaps up to 8 on average. The colour varies from a lavender-pink through bluish lavender to violet. The deposit of farina at the base of the throat suggests a white eye. Albinos are known in the wild, with a very fine cultivar, *Primula marginata* 'Casterino', displaying clean white flowers. The flowers of the species carry a strong mealy fragrance.

I recommend the following, a few of my favourite cultivars and hybrids: *Primula marginata* 'Beatrice Lascaris' is compact with pale blue flowers; 'Caerulea' AM 1980 is one of the best blue-flowering cultivars; 'Casterino' is pure white; 'Drake's Form' AM 1951 is a taller growing cultivar; 'Herb Dickson' is a fine dark blue; 'Laciniata' has an excellent cut-leaved habit; 'Napoleon' AM 1972 has clear blue flowers; and 'Shipton' has lilac-blue flowers.

Primula marginata 'Napoleon'
Photo by Margaret and Henry Taylor.

A number of hybrids are worthy of a place in the garden, and I will commence with the natural hybrids. I have already described the hybrid between *Primula allionii* and *P. marginata* named *P. ×meridiana*, yet there is another exquisite hybrid between *Primula marginata* and *P. latifolia* called *P. ×crucis*. This was first located in 1913 on the Col de la Croix and has more recently been found in the Mont Clapier region. The potential of this hybrid is very great, as it bears the habit of *P. latifolia* with more luxuriant clumps of foliage and solid umbels of purple-blue coloured flowers.

A number of hybrids are of uncertain origin, amongst which my favourites are the following: *Primula* 'Marven' has farinose foliage and the most striking violet-blue flowers and a white farinose eye. It is said to be a hybrid between

Primula 'Linda Pope'

P. marginata and *P. ×venusta*, but my own assertion is that it is a very fine form of *P. marginata*. 'Linda Pope' is a classic and will appear in nursery catalogues with the same frequency as Dvorak's Symphony No. 9, "From the New World", turns up in concert repertoires. It is an outstanding variety raised by a Mr. Pope of Birmingham, England. It received an FCC in 1967. The large toothed foliage is heavily farinose with large, mauve-blue flowers. This vigorous hybrid is a superb choice to plant into the cooler side of a dry stone wall. 'White Linda Pope' is an excellent, free-flowering seedling from the above with pure white blooms. I have found that this cultivar flowers over a long period through mid and late spring.

I cannot imagine a more multifaceted plant than *Primula marginata* and its hybrids. Despite their flowering in the spring months, the heavily farinose foliage is an added attraction the year-round. I have found that when growing the species and cultivars, their foliage colour can be significantly enhanced when given a generous top dressing of limestone chippings. They are also highly adaptable to their position in the garden.

A number of fine alpine species that I have not described can be found on a botanical or walking trip to the Maritime Alps, but I will conclude with an acaulis-type gentian that can be found only in this area.

The gentian in question is *Gentiana ligustica*, which I found growing at a low altitude of around 700 M at the base of limestone cliffs, home to *Primula allionii*. It was growing in grassy embankments and represents a perfectly distinct form of this acaulis group. It has a limited distribution in this region, extending down to the hills above Menton. It inhabits calcareous soils and is often found both on open sites and amongst deciduous woodland. In my experience, the foliage is broader than the vigorous *G. angustifolia* and produces a paler blue flower. It is undoubtedly a valuable addition for the rock garden or alpine bed.

Gentiana ligustica

When preparing to write this chapter, I was reminded to return to the pages of Farrer and reread the relevant chapters from *Among the Hills* (1911). I would strongly recommend any reader who is planning to visit the Maritime Alps to obtain a copy, for it is certainly one of the most enlightening reads on plant hunting I have ever come across. (Please ignore the references he makes to the hammer and chisel. We just have to remember that this type of plant collecting seemed acceptable at the time of his writing. It certainly is not so today.)

It has been fun recalling so many excellent alpine plants from this area and finding a place for them in the garden. What a formidable group of endemics. Which alpine garden can fail to find a home for at least one of these saxifrages, dianthus, primula, or a challenging viola? New ideas are always evolving with time and resources made available, so I will not be surprised to see many of the plants described making a greater impact amongst a wider group of gardeners.

Before I move on to the popular areas making up the body of the French Alps, I want to describe just a few plants from the Spanish Sierras, most notably the Sierra Nevada.

The Spanish Sierras

I now want to take readers on a hot and dusty journey to the south of Spain. In doing so, it is my intention to highlight a few species that merit a place in the alpine garden. Some of these will prove challenging, while others place little in the way of demands on the experienced gardener.

In the Central Sierras, some 120 KM west of Madrid, we can find some fine plants close to the slopes of Almanzor (2592 M). This mountain is part of the Sierra de Gredos (a range of mountains with jagged peaks, so typical of the topography associated with these elevations) and is home to a very beautiful alpine buttercup. *Ranunculus abnormis* is a tuberous-rooted perennial native to both Spain and Portugal. Below the Almanzor it makes a fine display in damp mountain turf, with linear foliage and large golden flowers reminiscent of an adonis on 18 to 20 CM stems, flowering at its best in mid to late June. I am very fond of this species, and nursery sales reflected its popularity; it blooms in the garden during the peak flowering period of mid to late spring. This unusual species enjoys a summer dormant period, when its foliage dies down. It is easy of cultivation and can be propagated by dividing up mature clumps during the autumn when it breaks into growth, or from seed sown as soon as the achenes are ripe. I would plant it between a few rocks on the raised bed and position it in full sun.

Moving south in Spain, two more ranges, or sierras, are deserving of close attention. The first is Sierra de Cazorla. The speciality from here is, not surprisingly, *Viola cazorlensis*, which can be found on a peak called Cabanas. On this limestone summit, we can find this true classic amongst the alpines of Europe, closely related to the Balkan *V. delphinantha* and *V. kosaninii*. The mountains here are subject to heavy winter rainfall and considerable snow cover, which rather belies a casual view we might have of this area. The viola can be found growing most commonly in shaded, rocky crevices at around 1500 M, sheltered from the searing summer heat but exposed to the cold in winter.

Such is the beauty of the flowers, that when plants become available from a skilled nurseryman I would snap them up. Many collectors of alpine treasures would automatically confine this beauty to the alpine house, possibly to tempt the judges to bestow rightful honours in its direction when exhibited. It received a richly deserved FCC from the RHS in 1981. A number of skilled growers have succeeded with *Viola cazorlensis* in vertical positions on tufa in the garden. It is important to plant established propagules (seedlings or well-rooted cuttings) early enough in the season to get them well-established before their first winter in the open. To succeed with this treasure will bring the grower a rich reward of small, needle-fine foliage rising from a woody base, with stunning, long-spurred flowers of a rich, dark carmine-pink. The effect of this glowing colour against the creamy white tufa will be truly spectacular.

Now to the tricky subject of propagation. I had better admit right away at having achieved no success on this front. Having spoken to one or two growers who have successfully propagated this viola, I would recommend first of all looking out for seed and sowing it as soon as it is collected. Knowing how this viola resents any root disturbance, it would be prudent to sow seeds individually into cellular pots, so that established seedlings can be pinched out and planted straight from the cells, rather than pricking them out and risking disaster. Cuttings are a tricky business, as the natural habit is for the plants to die back almost to ground level during the winter. Clearly, the soft wood cuttings must have established a strong root system before this takes place. Once again, I would root the cuttings into individual pots or a 7 CM deep cellular tray, and choose a mix containing plenty of perlite to aid root establishment.

Here, then, is a classic alpine plant that deserves every effort we can muster in order to enjoy the distinguished flowers. In nature it shares its location (but not habitat) with a beautiful dwarf narcissus, *Narcissus hedraeanthus*, with its short flower stalks appearing out of the soil at a low angle, giving the cream-coloured flowers an appearance of sitting on the ground.

In this region made up of steep limestone mountain and deep ravines, another choice and meritorious alpine plant can be found at around 1500 M. It is *Ranunculus gramineus*. Whilst running the nursery, it was my experience that this buttercup proved to be amongst the best selling of its race. It is often found growing amongst limestone rubble, wedged firmly between the grey rock. I have grown it successfully in an open, sunny alpine bed, where it provides height and colour with its large, glossy yellow flowers of 2 to 3 CM in diameter, carried on branching 30 CM stems above narrow, glaucous basal leaves.

A superior form with larger flowers was introduced by Alan Edwards in 1978 and named *Ranunculus gramineus* 'Pardal'. It is well worth looking out for. The species can easily be raised from seed, and any named forms may be divided during the dormant season.

A number of hybrids have been raised since the 1930s between *Ranunculus gramineus* and *R. amplexicaulis* which were named *R. ×arendsii*. This lemon-yellow flowered hybrid was never of great constitution until Elizabeth Strangman (formerly of Washfield Nursery, Kent) made the cross, using Edwards's superior clone *R. gramineus* 'Pardal'. The variable seedlings that make up this fine fertile strain (now correctly termed group) are called *R. ×arendsii* 'Moonlight'. They produce large, ivory-toned flowers. What fine garden plants each one of these buttercups has proved to be.

The second range of sierras, the Sierra Nevada, rising up above the celebrated city of Granada, is composed mainly of mica schist. Its highest peak is Mulhacén (3481 M), with another significant mountain, Pico de Veleta (3392 M). I will describe a few plants (most of which are endemics) found in this area that are well worth trying in a variety of spots in the garden. A visit to these mountains in late June may prove to be too early, and a trip in July may prove more rewarding, with the snows having receded. Most of the exciting plants are found in the true alpine band between 2500 and 3300 M.

At about 2000 M is an isolated limestone outcrop which is home to one of the world's most outstanding alpines, *Convolvulus boissieri*. Is it really that good? Yes, indeed, it is—forming tight cushions of silvery leaves with large pink or white flowers sitting right on top of the foliage. What could be more spectacular? In nature it forms great silver carpets, while in cultivation we would be more than happy with a neat cushion positioned either vertically or wedged at an angle between pieces of tufa rock in full sun. This classic alpine can be propagated from cuttings taken after flowering in late spring and early summer. Some winter protection with a pane of glass would be wise if we garden in a climate subject to mild, damp winters.

Growing side by side with the convolvulus is an excellent white-flowering rock rose, *Helianthemum apenninum*, which is such a useful summer flowerer for the rock garden. Closely associating with the convolvulus and the helianthemum is a plant found widespread on the open, sun-baked limestone of the sierras, the hedgehog broom, *Erinacea anthyllis*. I love this plant, and at the same time I resent its vicious spines. Beware when weeding and seeking out the seed! It forms a dome-shaped mound of rigid, spine-tipped stems producing many clusters of violet-blue pea flowers in late spring and early summer. It loves to be planted in between boulders of tufa in full sun. Look out for seed and employ a pair of long tweezers.

Convolvulus boissieri
Photo by Margaret and Henry Taylor.

Above this isolated limestone outcrop, the surrounding geology reverts to the more typical mica schist of this region. A very fine dwarf form of *Fritillaria lusitanica* is found here in the grassy undergrowth amongst junipers. With flowers on 10 CM tall stems, the flared bells are striped and flecked with green, brown, and gold. A fine addition for a sunny alpine border in our garden.

Growing on the cliffs and in schistose moraine at 3000 M is one of the treasures of the Sierra Nevada, *Chaenorhinum glareosum*. It is a perennial member of the family Scrophulariaceae, forming slender stolons in finely drained scree material. A lime-free, gritty mixture should suit this wonderful species, which produces short 10 to 15 CM stems carrying racemes of glowing red to violet flowers with a yellow palate. This treasure is best propagated from seed and positioned between rocks on a trough or raised bed.

Associating well with the foregoing is one of my own personal favourites amongst these local endemics. I have long been heralding forth the seed collections of *Leucanthemopsis radicans* made by Jim and Jenny Archibald. This short-lived perennial can easily be raised from seed. When grown in a lean, gritty, lime-free mixture, this little composite forms flat mats of wiry grey foliage covered with near stemless lemon-yellow daisies throughout the summer. It should be given pride of place at the edge of a trough, where it can tumble over the side and seed around its base.

On the summit of the Veleta is another outstanding daisy, *Erigeron frigidus*. Here the flowers are pressed down on the mat of foliage, but lower down the mountain the flower stems may attain to 10 CM. Each bloom will reach some 3 CM in diameter and is a beautiful lilac colour. How valuable a good alpine composite can prove to be when given a gritty mixture in full sun. Seed is the best means of increase.

A plant found growing in the same locality is that little member of the bell-flower family, Campanulaceae, *Jasione crispa* subsp. *amethystina*. It produces globose heads of pretty blue flowers on 10 CM stalks and is a welcome addition to a trough for early summer colour. These little tufted sheep's bits are also easily raised from seed.

In an adjacent valley, growing alongside a stream, one can find a very fine dwarf form of our own native marsh gentian, *Gentiana pneumonanthe* subsp. *depressa*. It is another example of a plant that when offered in a specialist seed list of species found in this region would be well worth choosing. Young plants can be positioned in a damp spot, perhaps amongst subjects such as *Parnassia palustris*, pinguicula, and *Primula deorum*. It forms upright, leafy shoots and a single 10 to 15 CM stem with a large, tubular blue flower in late summer.

Diligent search will reveal a few more treasures from these two peaks, the Veleta and Mulhacén. They include disjunct forms of *Androsace vandellii* and *Gentiana alpina*. Two other plants make up the cream of the crop, located at high altitudes. Just as the snows begin to recede at around 2500 to 3000 M in late June, the flowers of one of Europe's most choice buttercups are emerging. Growing in streamside snowmelt are multitudes of *Ranunculus acetosellifolius*; with glaucous, arrow-shaped foliage on short purplish stems, the cup-shaped white flowers are held singly. The overlapping segments are notched at the tip, and in its best large-flowered form, this proves to be a classic alpine buttercup. It is rather challenging to grow, in a similar vein to *R. glacialis*. A well-drained, humus-rich, acid soil that is not allowed to dry out during the short growing season is required. Soon after flowering, this species will go dormant, and care should be taken to collect the ripened seed and sow immediately.

Perhaps even more challenging to grow is my final choice, which hides under rocks in coarse scree, *Viola crassiuscula*. It is found above 2500 M, growing in schistose scree in scattered colonies with its tufts of caespitose foliage and miniature rounded flowers, a lovely lilac or cream colour. If seed can be obtained, young plants should be tucked in between lime-free rocks in a trough in a cool position. Care must be taken to ward off slug attacks on these alpine jewels.

This ends my foray into the southern sierras of Spain. With some understanding of the local terrain and climate, I hope that the reader will succeed with some of its treasures. They will need to be sought out from specialist nurseries and seed catalogues, but what a reward when success has been attained in the garden.

I will now return to the French Alps and describe some familiar plants from a well-trodden part of Europe.

The French Alps

I commence my journey through the French Alps in the west. In fact, a good starting point is southwest of Grenoble, in the western Dauphiné in the Vercors regional park. This is a limestone area with a number of classic alpine plants growing in close proximity. Associating together are *Allium narcissiflorum*, *Campanula alpestris*, *Ranunculus seguieri*, and *Primula auricula*, but it is the allium that I first of all wish to describe.

Allium narcissiflorum is undoubtedly the jewel within the race of European alliums. It cannot be confused (from a geographic point of view) with the closely related *A. insubricum*. The latter species has a narrow distribution confined to the Bergamasque Alps of northwestern Italy, between Lake Como and the Valli Giudicarie (northwest of Lake Garda). *Allium narcissiflorum* enjoys a wider distribution in the western French Alps, most notably from the foothills of the Dauphiné across to the Cottian Alps. It can be seen at its glorious best in the western Dauphiné around Vercors and the Pic de Gleize south of Grenoble.

Allium narcissiflorum

I have already stated that *Allium narcissiflorum* is closely related to *A. insubricum*, and until recently most plants offered in the U.K. as the former were in fact generally fine specimens of the latter. Subsequent seed collections made by the Archibalds and the Taylors of *A. narcissiflorum* from known geographic origin have ensured the true plant is now widely available.

I received a letter from the late Professor W. T. Stearn in September 1997, in which he stated: "In your interesting 1997–1998 catalogue you list *Allium narcissiflorum*. Personally, during 70 years of interest in the genus *Allium*, I have never seen this species in cultivation, although familiar with it in the herbarium." In his letter, he outlined the differences between the two species, and, yes, he was correct, for I, like many of my colleagues, was still offering the related species, *A. insubricum*. What a helpful letter that was.

Illustrations of the two species taken in the wild have rarely helped growers. Here is a simple description of *Allium narcissiflorum* and a little clarification of botanical differences between the two species. The bulbs of *A. narcissiflorum* are clustered on a short rhizome, with the outer tunics persisting as layers of parallel fibres. From five to eight flowers are held in the form of an umbel on 15 to 30 cm stems. Here is one of the distinguishing features: In *A. narcissiflorum*, the umbel is at first nodding, but later erect. With *A. insubricum*, the umbel is permanently nodding. The flower colour of the former is variable, but in its best form is a lovely sugar-pink.

In nature *Allium narcissiflorum* prefers to colonise loose, unstable, sunny limestone screes. When flowering, it is a spectacular sight, covering the hillsides with its soft pink hues in mid to late summer. It is an invaluable summer-flowering subject for a raised bed or rock garden. The best forms can be easily divided whilst dormant, but copious amounts of seed are also produced. Keep *A. narcissiflorum* well away from *A. insubricum* to preserve purity of stock.

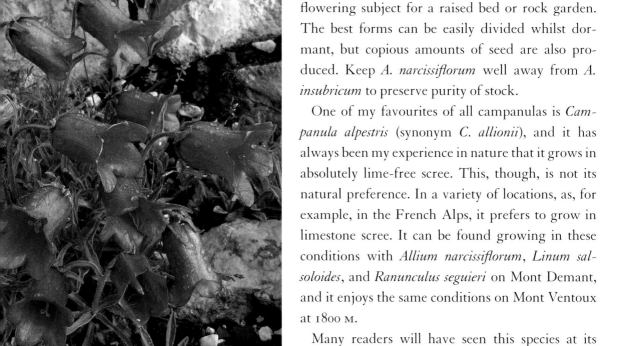

Campanula alpestris

One of my favourites of all campanulas is *Campanula alpestris* (synonym *C. allionii*), and it has always been my experience in nature that it grows in absolutely lime-free scree. This, though, is not its natural preference. In a variety of locations, as, for example, in the French Alps, it prefers to grow in limestone scree. It can be found growing in these conditions with *Allium narcissiflorum*, *Linum salsoloides*, and *Ranunculus seguieri* on Mont Demant, and it enjoys the same conditions on Mont Ventoux at 1800 m.

Many readers will have seen this species at its imperious best in the Graian and Cottian Alps, often frequenting mica schists and granitic formations. I have located fine specimens growing by the roadside on high passes, including the Col d'Izoard. I believe, though, that some of its finest forms are to

Campanula alpestris

be found on the limestone screes in the western French Alps, and it is perhaps from amongst these forms that a more permanent garden plant can be selected. This species would certainly be one of my first choices for a scree, trough, or raised bed.

But let me now describe *Campanula alpestris*, and I hope readers will understand why I give it such a special position. Nestling amongst the chosen scree material in the trough are rosettes of narrow, lanceolate, grey, hairy leaves. From each of these rosettes, short 3 to 4 cm stems carry a single (occasionally two) semierect flower. In its best forms, these flowers can be immense, reminiscent of Canterbury bells, in hues ranging from a slate blue and pale lavender to the most gorgeous satiny purple. There are albino forms as well. The campanula will race around the trough with its underground stolons clinging to the coolest haven of rock as well as the interior of the trough. It may be reproduced from seed or cuttings taken after flowering in early summer. It flowers in nature between June and August at altitudes of between 2000 and 2800 m. When collecting vegetative material, care should be taken to identify the nature of the rock on which it is growing. Clearly, some of the finest forms are to be found on

Campanula cenisia

limestone, although I am more familiar with superb variations growing on lime-free formations.

A number of alpine species that the keenest plant hunters will locate present the ultimate challenge to the gardener. I have, for example, had little personal success with certain Aretian androsaces, eritrichium, or the delightful *Campanula cenisia*. It is this latter bellflower that I wish to discuss, as it should prove to be one of the most exciting of all the European species from the French Alps. It has a wide distribution from the Cottian Alps across into the Swiss Alps, rising to high altitudes between 2000 and 3200 m.

It is often stated that in nature *Campanula cenisia* is a strict calcifuge. It certainly prefers to grow in shaly screes where the rock is of a slaty or flaky nature. I am not sure that these schistose rocks are necessarily devoid of lime, though, and this is another example of a plant whose main requirements relate to its aspect rather than the alkalinity of the chosen substrate. The plant produces a central taproot, from which radiates a mass of threadlike runners, reemerging more than 45 cm away in the form of a dense, wide tuffet of foliage. Neat rosettes are made up of small, rounded leaves from which arise short 2 to 5 cm stems, each carrying a rather shallow bell of a subtle shade of slate blue. A generous mat of flowers, at their best in late July and August in nature, is a sight to behold and one to photograph over and over again.

To reproduce this experience in the garden must surely be piloted in a trough. A cool root run is the first consideration, and given the tendency of this campanula to send out shallow radiating roots, these must be protected with a generous layer of slaty material and a position protected from the full heat of the day. To allow any sort of mollusc, whether it be a miniature slug or a larger relative, to come near a campanula will spell death. Possibly one overnight visit is sufficient to kill a plant. As with most campanulas, seed is the most satisfactory means of propagation. This is a challenge worth all the effort in our horticultural endeavours.

While I have often dedicated a trough to a single species, this is not going to prove the best choice in this case. Careful plant association will ensure a tasteful combination of flowers over a period of several months. Along with the campanula, I would recommend planting a selection of verna group gentians, a few

Dianthus glacialis, *Douglasia vitaliana* (synonym *Vitaliana primuliflora*), and *Primula hirsuta* in its best forms.

The French Alps are also home to the finest of all gentians in the acaulis group. It is *Gentiana angustifolia*, which has been the parent of some fine garden hybrids, too. I have grown *G. angustifolia* and some of its many forms over several decades now, and they have proved to be amongst the most reliable of all European alpine plants. I would place it amongst plants of the calibre of both *Dianthus pavonius* and *D. alpinus*, *Campanula pulla* and *C. alpestris* (synonym *C. allionii*), and *Primula marginata*, in terms of reliability.

Gentiana angustifolia

Unlike the closely related *Gentiana kochiana* and *G. clusii*, *G. angustifolia* is far from widespread in its distribution, occurring on limestone in the Alps of southeastern France and a station in Switzerland. It was described as early as 1787 by Dominique Villars (1745–1814) in his work *Histoire des Plantes de Dauphiné*. It is an inhabitant of subalpine meadows and copses and is often found thriving in fissures of rock, where it adapts as a true saxatile plant. It can also be located in large 60 CM wide patches on settled scree.

This adaptability in nature (where it ranges from 800 to 2000 M in altitude) is reflected in its good nature in the alpine garden. It can easily be distinguished from the other species within this section because of its linear to oblanceolate rosette leaves (or long, narrow leaves). The flowers are borne on a stem up to 7 CM in length, making them ideal for use as cut flowers. They are further distinct in that the calyx lobes stand out from the corolla tube. The flower colour is generally a vivid dark blue, and I am currently growing a free-flowering white variant, *Gentiana angustifolia* 'Alba', that complements the more normal blue-flowering species.

Some of the most outstanding cultivars amongst this group of gentian owe their primary parentage to *Gentiana angustifolia*. All of those I recommend to the reader produce deep blue flowers and are free-flowering, easy of culture, and straightforward to propagate. They include 'Belvedere', 'Frei', 'Krumrey', and 'Rannoch'. Both the species and cultivars are easily raised from cuttings taken after flowering from nonflowering shoots. Seed is also set in abundance and will produce a variable progeny; therefore, named forms cannot be propagated by this means and should be propagated only vegetatively.

These gentians can be planted in a sunny border containing an acid or limy soil and will prove utterly reliable. It is my view, though, that they look at their best when planted amongst limestone rocks, where their wide mats can run freely along with a selection of pulsatillas and fine forms of *Dianthus alpinus*.

The French Alps are also home to two species of gentian in the verna group which are well worth looking out for from a specialist nursery. They are *Gentiana rostanii* and *G. schleicheri*. The former is a very local species confined to the Cottian Alps and found in damp, marshy meadows at around 2000 to 2600 M. It is surely a geographic form of *G. bavarica*, which it closely resembles, with narrower and more pointed foliage and vibrant blue flowers. It is best grown amongst similar drought-intolerant species, such as pinguiculas, parnassia, and *Primula deorum*, in a soil mixture containing extra sphagnum moss to retain moisture. Seed should be saved and sown immediately to preserve a stock of this choice species.

Gentiana schleicheri is a rare species found growing in silicaceous rocks at around 2400 to 3000 M in the Mont Cenis group of mountains and in the Swiss Alps. It is an exquisite little cushion-forming plant, replacing the calcicole *G. terglouensis* of the Eastern Alps. This choice species forms a tufted habit with short, pointed, overlapping foliage. The deep blue flowers are borne singly and are almost stemless, sitting on the bold, cylindrical calyx. A special position for this plant positioned in between silicaceous, slaty rocks on a trough will suit best. It should be propagated from freshly sown seed.

A plant that associates well with these verna group gentians is *Alyssum serpylli-folium*, which some botanists will simply regard as a diminutive form of *A. alpestre*. In its finest forms, this variable species often associates with globularia, erysimum, and violas in shaly scree. This little member of the crucifer family forms a tight, tufted shrublet with grey leaves and racemes of golden-yellow flowers. Place it in full sun on a trough or raised bed, and it can be further raised from seed or cuttings.

It seems that each section of the Alps whose plants I describe provides one or more species of androsace. Whilst serving my apprenticeship on the Schachen Garden in the Bavarian Alps, I witnessed many fine examples of European alpine plants flowering at their best. Whilst this garden consists of a series of natural rock gardens within the true alpine zone, it is nevertheless partly contrived in its construction, and great skill was required to satisfy such a wide variety of plants. It was (during my period of tuition) in no small part due to the wisdom and experience of both Wilhelm Schacht and his son Dieter which ensured such success at this high altitude and also back at base in the Munich Botanic Garden.

Androsace pubescens

I well remember watching with joy as a well-established cushion of *Androsace pubescens* burst into flower, tucked into a vertical crevice of the endemic limestone on the Schachen.

This species has a fairly wide distribution from the Cottian Alps north to the Gran Paradiso and the Mont Blanc region. It occurs most commonly in calcareous shales and rubble slopes between 2800 to 3000 M. Experienced growers should succeed with this species out in the open, with the raised bed a fine home for the cushions, producing masses of white flowers. A cloche cover during the winter months will help protect the fairly open cushions of soft, green leaves from winter wet. Careful collection of seed will ensure a means of propagation.

Whilst botanising in the Cottian and Graian Alps, I often came across fine stands of both *Douglasia vitaliana* and *Petrocallis pyrenaica*, firm favourites of mine and easy of cultivation. These are both species that I like to be able to admire at close quarters. It is for this reason that I would plant them in a trough positioned in full sun. I have found that the petrocallis, a hearty member of the crucifer family, will thrive on either a limy soil or an acid one. All it asks is an open, gritty mixture, where it will produce wide mats or cushions made up of tiny rosettes, soon becoming hidden beneath a galaxy of soft-pink, fragrant flowers. It generally grows on granitic screes and is common around the Mont Cenis area growing with *Viola cenisia* and the douglasia.

A very fine white-flowering form of the petrocallis is occasionally offered under the name *Petrocallis pyrenaica* var. *leucantha*, which complements the type species. Both forms should be propagated by short, softwood cuttings taken after flowering. A cuttings mix of equal parts gritty sand and perlite produces an excellent root system for these alpine subjects.

Douglasia vitaliana (synonym *Vitaliana primuliflora*) is a somewhat variable species but in its best forms will prove to be an invaluable trough plant. Androsaces are closely related to primulas, and the two genera, along with dionysias, have much in common. Botanists have long been seeking to agree on a name for the species under discussion, as it seems to lie in no man's land. Although it shares many affinities with androsace, its flowers are heterostylous (that is, either pin-eyed or thrum-eyed), and therefore it is best fitted into a genus of its own.

Douglasia vitaliana is widely distributed in western Europe, stretching from the Pyrénées east to the Dolomites. It is found in fine form in the French Alps, often in scree and grit or in natural rock outcrops in alpine turf at around 2000 to 3000 M. Preferring lime-free formations, it forms wide mats of congested, silvery rosettes, spreading horizontally and rooting as it goes. The mats disappear under sheets of stemless citron-yellow flowers as soon as the snow melts.

Douglasia vitaliana

Petrocallis pyrenaica

It is perfectly floriferous and easily grown in the lowland garden, and fine forms have been given names. I would recommend the superior selection, *Douglasia vitaliana* var. *chionotricha* (synonym *Vitaliana primuliflora* var. *chionotricha*). It is an outstanding variant that was given to me by that excellent grower from the Czech Republic, Ota Vlasak. To propagate this late spring–flowering plant, I would detach rooted pieces from the cushion after flowering and pot them up into 7 CM pots prior to reestablishment and planting out.

From a genus containing more than 500 species, it is difficult to know how the taxonomist came up with a meaningful and logical process of classification. Well, violas are of great importance to the alpine gardener. Most of the species belonging to the section *Melanium* are real treasures in their native habitat, but many of them are challenging in the garden. One such species is *Viola calcarata*, sometimes known as the long-spurred pansy on account of its 8 to 15 MM spur. The first time I botanised on the Col de Mont Cenis, this pansy was at its floral peak in mid-July. It predominated in the alpine meadows and lawns, presenting itself in every possible shade from darkest violet, to mauve, yellow, cream, and white. Why, I wonder is this polymorphic species not seen more widely in gardens? I must admit to growing only its extreme eastern variant, *V. calcarata* subsp. *zoysii*, with its butter-yellow flowers. So spectacular are the flowers of this viola in these parts, at altitudes from 1500 to 2900 M, it should be a simple matter to obtain seed in order to introduce into gardens. At best, the flowers may reach 3 to 4 CM in diameter. Once we have raised fine colour forms, I do find it necessary to maintain them from seed or softwood cuttings, as they may suddenly collapse through exhaustion or due to a severe attack of greenfly (aphis). A well-drained spot on a sunny raised bed will suit admirably. My last word of advice for the more vigorous species of *Viola* is to attend to dead-heading of the flowers unless seed is to be saved. This also provides some respite for the plants.

Closely related to the foregoing is one of Europe's real aristocrats, *Viola cenisia*. Its specific name commemorates the area from which it is most prolific in nature. As well as the Mont Cenis area, it can be found farther south toward the Maritime Alps, and I have seen fine forms close to the Col d'Izoard. It is a true alpine plant often found in a band between 1800 and 2800 M. I have long been puzzled by the nature of the substrate in which it is often found growing. It is always seen at its best in a very loose material, which in my experience resembles a calcareous rock not dissimilar to a porous type of volcanic material. This may explain why the typical calcicole species *Anemone baldensis* is often located in close proximity to the viola. I am simply raising an awareness to study its natural habitat and pH of the substrate in which it is growing so that we might offer it more than a little hope in our gardens. Once again, I would favour a trough

Viola calcarata with *Geum montanum*

for this very special plant that flowers in early summer. In nature, it is dwarf in stature but creeps around in a loose, scree type of material with its frail clusters of dark green leaves. The flowers are rounder than *V. calcarata* and are a rich lilac-blue with a bright yellow eye.

There is something amusing about pansies and their flowers; it is as if they are smiling at us. I well remember first meeting up with the popular hybrid *Viola* 'Irish Molly', with its soft brown and yellow flowers. The late Bob Poland, who ran a nursery in Sussex, England, was showing me this cultivar whilst it was flowering in a sunny border and referred to it endearingly as "dirty-faced Molly". He meant no disrespect to the raiser but, rather, showed the amusing human side to these popular flowers.

Reginald Farrer referred to so many pansies as having "silly faces", but of *Viola cenisia*, he said, "You can see that it has a sense of humour and a waggish intelligence" (1911), owing to its beard and whiskers below the lower petal. I suspect that most alpine gardeners would be enthralled if they could bring their specimens of this viola to produce a flower, let alone the beard and whiskers!

My own experience would suggest that it is susceptible to extremes of water

Viola cenisia

management. In other words, overwater it at its peril and try not to let plants dry out. It should be given a cool but open position, and one should carefully save seed to ensure further stocks can be raised.

A plant often associating with *Saxifraga oppositifolia* and *Linaria alpina* in the Mont Cenis area is *Silene acaulis* subsp. *longiscapa*. I have seen wonderful forms of it growing in acidic shales with very large flowers on 2 to 3 CM stems. The flowers were almost reminiscent of a dwarf dianthus rather than the campion genus to which it belongs, with carmine-rose flowers. This is a first-class trough plant, producing a soft cushion made up of bright green tufts and flowering in the garden during late spring. The best forms of this variant can be easily raised from cuttings rooted into a mix of sand and perlite.

I have always been fond of columbines in the alpine garden. Those that are easier to cultivate are sometimes rather looked down upon; sad to say, I suspect I have been guilty of this practice. What is it about alpinists that we would prefer to look at a poor specimen of an aristocrat such as *Aquilegia jonesii* struggling away in a trough, rather than a fine stand of, say, *A. alpina* in a fine form? Well, I guess that it is all down to the lure of these challenging alpine plants. It's good, though, to strike a balance. So let me describe a favourite columbine, *A. alpina*. It is all too rarely offered in the trade, mainly because it is hard to trust the provenance of the stock on offer. If I could obtain seed of known origin, I would

Aquilegia alpina

relish the opportunity to raise plants and position them in relative isolation from other European species with which they may cross-pollinate. The 18 to 25 CM stems each carry a nodding, bright blue flower that associates well with the yellow flowers of *Geum montanum*.

There can be no doubting the importance of the European species of saxifrage in the garden. I have already described a few species of the section *Ligulatae*, or silvers, including those aristocrats, *Saxifraga longifolia* and *S. callosa*. Confined to a fairly small region in the southwestern Alps near the Franco-Italian frontier is a choice species, *S. valdensis*, which inhabits crevices in vertical rocks. It prefers either limestone or calcareous schist formations and generally chooses snow-free positions in full exposure. It will form large cushions made up of numerous, small, 1 to 3 CM diameter rosettes, tightly wedged in nature into a crevice by a single taproot.

Primula pedemontana

This is a choice plant deserving of our full attention, totally hardy and flowering, in my experience, only when given full light. The young plants are best wedged between limestone rocks or directly into a boulder of tufa and given full exposure. The 3 to 11 CM flowering stems are branched and carry a panicle of 6 to 12 pure white flowers during the late spring to early summer. A careful search through specialist alpine nursery catalogues will reveal the true plant, which is an excellent choice for a trough or raised bed. Once established, the hard nature of the rosettes will make vegetative propagation tricky. I would recommend saving seed to raise young plants, but care must be taken not to collect seed from plants positioned close to other related species if true-to-name progeny is required.

Wherever we may choose to travel in search of alpine plants in the European Alps, we will surely encounter a species of primula at some point in our excursion. In the French Alps, a number of species may be encountered; these include *Primula pedemontana*, *P. latifolia*, and *P. marginata*. When botanising in the areas around Mont Cenis and the Col d'Iseran, I recall fine stands of both *P. latifolia* and *P. pedemontana*, sometimes together. A fine spot to enjoy the latter is around the Col du Petit Mont Cenis, where the two species meet, and an eagle-eyed plantsperson may find the lovely hybrid *P. ×bowlesii*. *Primula pedemontana* belongs to the section *Auricula* (*Auriculastrum*) and the subsection *Erythrodrosum*.

Dr. Kress, formerly of the Munich Botanic Garden and a highly respected botanist, has published a most interesting paper with some modifications to the taxonomy of this subsection. As the above specific names are all well known amongst readers, I will retain them for the purpose of this book.

Primula pedemontana occurs in the Vanoise and Graian Alps and is easily distinguished by its foliage. Typical of this subsection is the effarinose foliage and the reddish glandular hair most pronounced on the leaf margins. *Primula pedemontana* has the most markedly shiny, dark green leaves and brick-red to dark red margins. Up to 16 flowers are held in an umbel on 3 to 12 CM stems and are a rich, deep pink, often with a white eye. In its best forms, this is a most attractive species, occurring from 1400 to 3000 M in altitude, generally growing in a peaty, humus-rich soil wedged in between rock fissures on silicate formations. I have found this plant in both vertical situations and on the level, and when choosing a site in the garden, I do not find that it is fussy as to position. It is worth emphasising that this species prefers a lime-free soil and should be given a humus-rich mixture in a cool position between rocks in a trough or raised bed.

When growing European primulas belonging to the section *Auricula* in pots, it is easy to divide plants on an annual basis to retain vigour and increase identical stock. When planted out, this may not be a practical proposition, and I would therefore recommend raising plants from seed. The progeny may well include hybrids if several closely related species are grown together. Some species of primula, when grown in a trough, will tend to run out of vigour and begin to form a woody crown and rootstock; at this point they should be lifted and divided after flowering or discarded in favour of young, seed-raised plant material. If this course of replenishing is carried out, the entire contents of the trough should be renewed with fresh soil. On no account should old and exhausted soil be reused, but rather discarded to the compost heap.

When plants are lifted for rejuvenation from a rock garden or raised bed, the same care and attention should be provided. Once the plant has been lifted with a generous amount of soil around the root ball, at least a further 15 CM (in depth) of soil should be removed and replaced with a fresh mixture. This could be made up of sterilised soil with added gritty sand and humus to suit the plant.

When established plants of primula are given a permanent position in a trough or raised bed and are happily growing between rocks, it may seem overly disruptive to lift and rejuvenate plants unless absolutely essential. In the interim period I would strongly recommend feeding plants frequently with a weak dilution of low-nitrogen tomato fertiliser during the growing season. This will lengthen their life in this unnatural environment.

A species of primula found in many parts of the European Alps is *Primula latifolia*. I once located a very fine form growing on the Col d'Iseran in close proximity to excellent examples of *Geum reptans*, *Ranunculus glacialis*, and *Eritrichium nanum*. The underlying soil here is predominantly of silicaceous nature and lime-free. I have also found this variable species in superior forms in the Swiss Engadine. Here, though, in the Graian and Cottian Alps, it often forms wide masses of woody rootstock.

The leaves of *Primula latifolia* are long and sticky in nature and support strong umbels on 5 to 20 CM stems, each bearing up to 20 flowers a glorious reddish violet to purple in colour. I have raised plants from commercial seed companies which produced disappointing flowers. I would therefore recommend that the reader choose plants in flower. In its best forms, this is a very fine species often

Primula latifolia

found at altitudes of 2200 to 2700 M, generally preferring the cooler side of a large boulder for protection. I have not found it to be fussy in the garden, but its vigorous nature demands a good depth of fertile soil in an open position in the rock garden or an alpine bed.

Primula latifolia belongs to the subsection *Brevibracteata* in the company of the species *P. carniolica* and *P. marginata*. Although it is possible to divide mature plants, I would leave them undisturbed and seek to raise superior flowering forms from seed. I will further mention *P. latifolia* when describing primulas found in the Swiss Alps, where it is once again located in some lovely forms.

In the French Alps and throughout Europe, the elder-flowered orchid, *Dactylorhiza sambucina*, may be found, often growing in rich colonies. My finest sightings were close to the Petit Mont Cenis. These consisted of both bright yellow-flowered forms along with purple ones. Experiencing turfy banks or hollows with hundreds of the short, dense spikes, a mass of yellow and purple, together with *Gentiana acaulis* and *Viola calcarata*, is a memorable sight. The species will grow quite happily in the open garden in a well-drained position and does not require the moist conditions in which it is so often found thriving in the wild.

From time to time, we alpinists will peruse seed catalogues during the darker winter months to decide which new species to experiment with. When searching through these lists, I am surely not alone in first of all venturing to place ticks beside the most choice species, only to find that I am already well over budget. Now to the painful job of reducing the numbers. Will I cross out some of the rarities or score out the more common ones? Sadly, it is often the rarities that remain on the order sheet. There are countless European alpine plants that we love to enthuse about in nature but rarely grow in our gardens. Amongst these species are the lovely scabious, *Scabiosa graminifolia*, and the striking yellow treacle-mustard, *Erysimum helveticum*. The scabious can be found at about 2000 M in the French Alps on stony, exposed limestone slopes, where it forms silvery cushions and lavender-coloured flower heads on 15 CM stems. It performs at its best in a sun-baked rock garden, flowering in the early summer months. It may

Dactylorhiza sambucina

Conservation and collection of wild plant material

A fairly touchy topic amongst horticulturists today surrounds the subject of conservation and the collecting of wild plant material. I say *touchy* because there is a wide variation of views on the matter. I have avoided devoting a single chapter to the subject but would rather raise isolated cases when appropriate. It is likely that of all the many plant families found in the European mountains, it is predominantly orchids whose rights of conservation have been most widely abused. It is not so many decades ago that responsible nurseries would receive during the dormant season large hampers of carefully packed plants collected in the wild, which would be potted up ready for the spring marketing season. Commonly seen amongst consignments were bare-rooted plants of the lady's slipper orchid *Cypripedium calceolus* and hepaticas.

This practice is mercifully now totally illegal, and even the digging up of bulbs from eastern Europe and Asia Minor, while still carried out, is more strictly controlled. A number of nurseries specialise in the growing of hardy European orchids and are supplying them as young plants raised from meristem or tissue culture as well as from seed. This is a positive move towards the conservation of these plants.

be propagated from seed. The foregoing species associates well with *Erysimum helveticum*, which is often listed in catalogues as *E. pumilum*. It is widespread in the Alps but often seen in the French and Swiss Alps, with its glowing yellow flowers. It forms neat tufts of foliage with 6 to 9 cm stems carrying fragrant yellow flowers. Both these plants require a sunny position and are indifferent to soil pH. Sometimes these simple plants provide the greatest of pleasure in the garden, and these two are well worth growing.

I will now conclude my journey through the French Alps and an in-depth discussion about growing some of its finest plants. I recently returned from a brief trip across lowland France, where I met a number of the local inhabitants, typically friendly and happy to discuss their most famous commodities. For sure we appreciate their wine, cheeses, and bread, yet on further reflection it is a land fairly complete in its attributes. A botanical trip to the French Alps, taking in the rich Mont Cenis along with the Cottian Alps, will further add to this feeling of completeness when one adds their botanical treasures to their culinary delights. If travel there is not feasible, imagine this scene: a gently sloping scree amassed with *Campanula alpestris* in very fine form, alpine turf awash with *Dianthus pavonius* in cherry-red, along with countless variations of colour displayed by the sumptuous *Viola calcarata*. All these treasures are growing amongst gentians, saxifrage, and soldanellas. A veritable banquet of plants, each

Erysimum helveticum

of which can be grown in the garden with less than a challenge to growers who apply the simple rules each alpine plant so richly deserves.

Such is the ease of travel within the European Alpine regions in this 21st century, that no sooner do we cross the French border than we meet a wealth of plants in both Switzerland and Italy, which are the subject of the next section.

The Swiss Alps

Having extolled the virtues of the French Alps, its populace, and its most favoured commodities, visitors to the mountains seem to have an even more special relationship with Switzerland. To many alpine gardeners the term *alpine* is synonymous with a trip to Wengen in the Bernese Oberland and lifting oneself up to the Eiger-Gletscher. From there the whole alpine panorama unfolds, paths leading through meadows adorned with gentians and pulsatillas. A rare sighting of *Cypripedium calceolus* in the open; higher up in the screes there are *Androsace alpina* and *A. helvetica* along with the exquisite *Eritrichium nanum* and

Alpine scene with cattle

Gentiana bavarica subsp. *imbricata*. Primulas, soldanellas, and alpine buttercups all vie for the best available pockets of soil. No wonder this was and still is the most visited country in Europe for alpine plants.

Many of us have been singularly motivated to try our hand at growing these plants simply by admiring their simplistic beauty in nature, here in Switzerland. I will describe plants from the three main areas in the Swiss Alps that best exemplify the awesome beauty of this country: the Bernese Oberland, Saas-Fee, and the Engadine. To some degree, the plants found in each of these areas are very similar, but each area also has some very distinct features for the plant hunter. It has been my experience in the Swiss Alps that the majority of the plants are calcifuge, with limestone a much rarer commodity than in the Eastern Alps. But there are calcareous substrates, and their evidence is immediately signalled by the presence of calcicole species such as *Anemone baldensis*, *Ranunculus seguieri*, *Dryas octopetala*, and *Saxifraga squarrosa*.

The seeming anomaly that sometimes puzzles the plant hunter—that of finding an apparent calcicole plant growing in what appears to be an acidic substrate beside calcifuge species—can be confusing, but certain plants provide a clear marker. I am quite certain that many alpine plants have learnt to adapt to their prevailing conditions and that it is the air quality, both around the aerial parts of the plant and its roots, that is far more significant than the pH of the soil. So there is a strong case for our not being too dogmatic about soil and rock types.

It is with this thought in mind that I will look at two of the most outstanding alpine plants which are closely related but to my knowledge have never met: *Ranunculus glacialis* and *R. seguieri*. Each one of us who has had the privilege of scaling high mountains in Europe during the peak flowering season will have personal high spots for the glacier buttercup. My own is undoubtedly the Diavolezza (2973 M) above the Bernina Pass in the Engadine. Here, *R. glacialis* has to be seen to be believed. As soon as the snow melts in late June and early July at these altitudes, the buttercup bursts into growth, showing first of all a few rather etiolated leaves, and then, within a few days, a full-blown clump of glistening, glabrous foliage cleft or deeply divided in habit. The flowers are variable in colour, held on branching stems, and at their best are enormous, round buttercups. Some are a glistening white, others cream to pink, and still more will display bright reddish flowers both in bud and when fully mature. This latter observation dispels the myth that the reddish colours are assumed only after fertilisation. It may be that in some areas plants change colour after pollination and subsequent fertilisation, but not amongst the plants I have studied. Once I have my eye in amongst this peerless of buttercups, it is hard to tear myself away. Each clump excites another photograph, and another, until the whole film is filled with *R. glacialis*. If we are lucky, a photograph may reveal a wonderful association of the buttercup, gentians, and *Androsace alpina* all together. Now that would be a fine challenge for us to reenact in a lowland garden.

That great Yorkshireman Farrer bluntly stated in *The English Rock Garden* (1919) that one simply could not grow this alpine buttercup without employing some sort of homemade moraine. Such a moraine as he was recommending involves running water through the roots of our glacier buttercup. I would suggest that such an elaborate system is not necessary. We need to create a deep (45 to 60 CM) alpine bed in the open garden made up of large, lime-free rocks and a freely drained soil consisting mainly of sharp sand and stones. It would be a simple matter to bury some leaky pipe around the perimeter of the bed and attach a water supply to the irrigation system. This should create an ideal habitat for not only the ranunculus but other calcifuge species used to growing in similar scree-type conditions in nature. Plants that would associate in this specialised environment would include *Geum reptans*, *Campanula excisa*, and *Ranunculus parnassifolius*.

Engadine, Switzerland

All alpine buttercups produce fruiting bodies in the form of achenes after flowering and subsequent fertilisation. These achenes can be rubbed away from their seating when ripe and sown either immediately in situ or into a John Innes type seed compost. The seed pots should be covered with 3 to 4 MM of coarse grit and plunged in sand. For any alpine gardener, the thrill of flowering plants of this highly specialised alpine buttercup would be regarded as a considerable feather in the cap.

I have recently had a close look at photographic evidence of a superb alpine buttercup growing in what appears to be a classic habitat for *Ranunculus glacialis*. The plants were located within view of the giant Matterhorn (4477 M),

Ranunculus glacialis

right on the border between Switzerland and Italy. On first sight, the plants resembled *R. glacialis*, but the foliage was heavily tomentose. A little bit of a puzzle. Across in eastern Europe, *Flora Europaea* (Tutin 1964) recognises a geographic form of *R. seguieri* subsp. *montenegrinus* with tomentose foliage. Could this be a disjunct form of the above plant growing in Switzerland? Who knows?

I have raised this puzzle because it adds to the fun of both identifying plants in the wild and determining how to grow them in our gardens. I have often come across *Ranunculus seguieri* in the Dolomites in its alkaline scree habitat, and when offered a similar substrate in the garden, on a raised bed or deep trough, it will perform well. It differs from *R. glacialis* in its slightly pubescent and glaucous foliage. The flowers are always a clean, white colour. It is a superb alpine species and deserving of our attention, never forgetting that it loves an alkaline soil.

Ranunculus glacialis forma *rosea*

Ranunculus glacialis, tomentose form
Photo by Ian Pryde.

Ranunculus seguieri
Photo by Jim Jermyn.

A classic scree plant that one often finds throughout the European Alps is the *Doronicum*, or leopards bane. In the Swiss Alps, I have seen some wonderful stands of *Doronicum grandiflorum* forming bold clumps, often on steep, unstable scree. It is a robust, herbaceous perennial member of Compositae. Once translated to the garden setting, it is too tall for the raised bed but will prove an invaluable addition to the rock garden with bold heart-shaped foliage, solid 15 to 30 CM stems, and luscious golden composite flowers. A fine clump will associate well with an underplanting of *Gentiana acaulis*, both flowering in the spring. Dormant plants can be lifted and divided to increase stock.

One of my own vivid botanical memories in the Engadine was the abundance of European primulas growing in absolute profusion, either in damp meadows or running along humus-rich rock crevices. In certain locations, three species—namely, *Primula hirsuta*, *P. integrifolia*, and *P. latifolia*—all meet together creating some lovely hybrids, some of which have proved to be fine garden plants.

When choosing a position in our garden for some of these primulas, it is important to be aware of their preferred habitat in nature. For example, *Primula integrifolia* is almost always found in abundant masses growing in damp alpine turf; rarely, if ever, is it found in rock outcrops or rock fissures. Yet, growing in close proximity, both *P. hirsuta* and *P. latifolia* prefer the latter rocky terrain. This may explain why many growers report poor results with *P. integrifolia*. It belongs to the subsection *Rhopsidium* and joins the company of *P. allionii*, *P. kitaibeliana*, and *P. tyrolensis*. It is a small but vigorous species and a hungry feeder, restricted to acid conditions in nature and requiring a moist position in full sun in cultivation. Although I have encountered many examples of this species, I have never spotted a white-flowering form. *Primula integrifolia* is generally located at an altitude of 2100 to 2600 M, where it enjoys wet, peaty conditions usually over silicaceous formations. It forms low mats of congested rosettes made up of short, obtuse effarinose leaves, producing short 1 to 3 CM stems bearing an umbel of up to three flowers of a bright magenta-pink to rose-lilac. The calyx can be tinged red, adding to the beauty of this species. In cultivation, along with a number of species in the auricula section, it can be shy-flowering. Regular feeding of plants during the growing season with a well-diluted tomato fertiliser should encourage flowering. Plant it on a raised bed in an acid, humus-rich, moisture-retentive mix and lift and divide clumps if they become tired and congested.

One of the greatest thrills provided in the Alps for me is to find a number of closely related primula species growing in close proximity. This leads to a rise in the adrenaline as a careful search reveals a number of hybrids. The initial excitement is raised with the discovery of a superb form, a winner we might say. This, though, can prove to be short-lived as a compatriot cries out, "Come over here!", as an even better example has been found. No wonder that when we translate this natural selection and hybrid development to horticulture, the plant breeder creating artificial F1 hybrids gains so much pleasure from the results. Nature very often creates the finest hybrids, and many of these have been collected as

Primula integrifolia

cuttings or rooted divisions and are now well established in our gardens.

A few years ago, Dieter Schacht and I spent an extremely fruitful time walking and botanising in the Swiss Engadine. In a number of locations we found the following species of primula growing in close proximity: *Primula integrifolia*, *P. latifolia*, and *P. hirsuta*. We chose to visit the area in the first week of July. It proved to be an opportune choice, with the snows just beginning to recede above 2500 м, while a number of subalpine species were still flowering.

Sadly, *Primula hirsuta* was long past flowering, having clearly produced a great display of flowers in early June, with seed capsules already swelling. It grows almost exclusively in crevices, mostly vertical but sometimes horizontal, preferring cliffs of silicate or volcanic formations. If often runs in rows with neat, effarinose rosettes of lax, sticky foliage. The flowers, in their best forms, are spectacular, held on short umbels up to 7 см in length with up to 17 flowers, more normally 3 to 5. The colour is variable, with bright magenta-pink predominating and an occasional white always proving exciting. The variation surrounding the shape and form of the flower is all-consuming; on one big boulder there may be large, open flowers a striking pink with a white eye, yet right beside it could be a horror with a narrower corolla of a dingy lilac. When choosing a plant for a trough or a prime position between rocks on a raised bed, care must be taken. There is simply no need to look at a poor selection. It is always best to buy a plant whilst flowering, or, when botanising in nature, to select a rooted side shoot of only the finest forms. These may later receive a name to preserve their identity and obtain an appropriate award from the RHS awards committee.

Despite the fact that we found no flowering plants of *Primula hirsuta* in the Engadine, we did locate many free-flowering hybrids of exceptional beauty. With *P. latifolia* flowering well in close proximity to the two aforementioned species, the following hybrids were clearly present: *P. ×berninae* (*P. latifolia* × *P. hirsuta*), *P. ×heerii* (*P. hirsuta* × *P. integrifolia*), and *P. ×muretiana* (*P. integrifolia* × *P. latifolia*). The question remained: with *P. hirsuta* flowering so many weeks earlier than the other two species, how had these marriages come about?

Primula hirsuta

Primula hirsuta

Well, to gardeners it really matters very little. Whatever the parentage, we can simply enjoy them. It is generally the case that, as a result of hybrid vigour, the resulting cross will prove to be a superior garden plant. As the plants are often sterile, they will of necessity have to be propagated vegetatively by division or by cuttings.

In the Engadine, most notably close to the Bernina Pass, these hybrids are quite spectacular. We tried to examine them and determine their exact parentage, but many of the plants displayed characteristics of each of the three parents. So we gave up and just enjoyed them—and that is exactly what we do in our gardens. The botanists and taxonomists demand order and accuracy, and rightly so; we all benefit from their lead. But let us not lose track of the more important simple pleasures each of these plants provides for both the plant hunter and the gardener, regardless of the name.

The hybrid primula that has made the most significant impact in horticulture is *Primula ×pubescens* (*P. auricula* × *P. hirsuta*). The natural cross is not to be confused with the nurseryman's *P. pubescens* hybrids, which are of long horticultural standing and are not always the product of just the two parents. They will have developed over a long process of artificial selection. Many of my favourite hybrids are from this type of selection, but first and foremost in my garden are plants created by natural selection, plants found originally in the wild.

Primula ×berninae

This particular hybrid is not commonly found in nature. *Primula hirsuta* is a calcifuge plant, preferring silicate formations. *Primula auricula* occurs almost exclusively on limestone. So when there is a meeting of the species at a limestone-silicate boundary, a wonderful marriage takes place. This arises in the Swiss Alps, most notably in the Bernese Oberland and the Valais region. It is generally a fertile hybrid, and because it is a cross between a pink and a yellow flowering species, the resulting plants display a vast range of colour forms, from white, yellow, pink, and purple, to brownish hues. One of my favourites from wild origin was found by the late Peggy Fell, who travelled widely in the Alps and located many superb forms and hybrids. When naming this plant given to me by her, I was keen to recognise her knowledge and sharp eyes with this outstanding find of *P. ×pubescens* 'Peggy Fell'. The plant has proved to be of fine constitution, producing large, almost stemless, deep reddish purple flowers.

One or two of my favourite man-made selections of *Primula ×pubescens* include 'Harlow Car', with flowers a lovely creamy pink colour, and 'The General', and in this selection the flowers are a rich velvety red with yellow, farinose eyes. Such is the vigour of these hybrids that they are best planted in an alpine bed. Be prepared to lift the clumps every three to four years and replant the strongest divisions up to 30 cm apart. A wonderful show can be created with a bed of mixed hybrids in association with pulsatillas, campanulas, and violas, to extend the flowering season.

I mentioned in my introduction that the very first alpine plant to make an impression on me was a soldanella, *Soldanella pusilla*. This species is widely distributed throughout the European Alps, but nowhere have I seen it growing more abundantly than in the Engadine. Within days of receding snows at truly alpine altitudes between 1800 and 3000 m, one finds damp, steep hollows still brown from the extended period of darkness under the snow. Frequently these habitats, when associated with an underlying lime-free soil, are home to carpets of newly emerging flowers of *S. pusilla*. The foliage is generally obscured by the flowers and assumes its normal appearance several weeks after flowering. In the garden, neat mats of tiny, orbiculate leaves form a deep green base for the short

Primula ×*pubescens* 'Peggy Fell'
Photo by Jim Jermyn.

2 to 8 cm stems, each carrying a nodding, campanulate flower—a perfect little fringed snowbell. The colour is the most exquisite pink to violet, and in its best forms it may be reddish pink. It is surely one of Europe's true alpine jewels and presents the gardener with just the one challenge: flowering it.

Growing the plant is straightforward in any freely drained, lime-free mixture in a sunny position. Most soldanellas produce their flowering buds the previous autumn, and these can be carefully located beneath the foliage. These buds are fodder for the marauding mollusc, and every effort should be made to keep slugs at bay. As I write this chapter, our region in Scotland has been beset with persistent squally showers, and these damp conditions are ideally suited to the slug population. Most of my soldanellas are planted in troughs, which, during the latter part of the season, I position in a cool, partly shaded spot. Careful examination during a damp spell will often provide evidence of a parade of little slugs around the base of the trough. This is the time to take action.

Soldanellas are also hungry feeders, and I would recommend feeding plants, particularly those positioned in a trough, with a low-nitrogen (tomato fertiliser) feed after flowering to help initiate flowering buds. To achieve a well-flowered plant of any soldanella is an achievement worthy of great praise and a memory for the alpine gardener. The simplest method of propagation is by simple divi-

Soldanella pusilla

sion after flowering, but never divide when the plants are undergoing stress.

One of the most sensational of all European alpine plants is *Androsace alpina*. I am sure many readers will agree with me that having located it for the first time in its native habitat, the experience remains indelibly printed in our memory. Although enjoying a widespread distribution in the Alps, it is always found on noncalcareous formations at altitudes between 2600 to 3300 M. My feeling is that it is a fussy plant with exacting requirements in nature, necessitating extra care and attention in cultivation. Having found a flat cushion or mat smothered with lovely rose-pink flowers spurs us on to try and grow it.

In the Engadine, as in the Bernese Oberland, it may be seen at its best thriving in grit and rubble on high, gently sloping scree. It is generally sparsely colonised, but once located there may be mats the size of an A4 sheet of paper (about 210 by 300 MM), completely smothered with exquisite pink flowers. Scrambling across stable scree, it is curious how, all of a sudden, we spot a well-established area of turf with patches of the androsace happily thriving in the decaying humus mixed with fine grits and rocks. It is rarely far from clumps of *Ranunculus glacialis* with *Geum reptans* and a few little rosettes dotted about with the vibrant blue flowers belonging to *Gentiana bavarica* subsp. *imbricata*. Oh, to repeat this perfectly natural association.

To state that growing this species in the garden is a challenge would be an understatement. It can be achieved with great care. Both the cushions and the underground root formation need masses of air movement. Here in east Scotland, we are frequently subjected to a meteorological phenomenon called a sea *haar* (a mist or fog coming off the North Sea). This spells disaster for many cushion plants as the high humidity surrounds the plant, suppressing free air movement and often promoting the outbreak of a fungal attack. For this reason, many alpine gardeners resort to growing their choicest plants in an alpine house and install extractor fans to ensure a constant provision of the very air movement these plants require.

Androsace alpina

So each of us must make a decision as to whether it is worth our endeavours to attempt growing such a species in the open garden. Excessive summer heat can also cause scorching and subsequent death, as could a miserable, damp winter without snow. I have a feeling that my marketing skills have just left me and I have lost another sale. But those of us who are made of sterner stuff persist, so we will plant our *Androsace alpina* in a trough, tucked in between slaty stones, incorporating a lime-free soil made up of a gritty sand mixed with soil and leaf mould. The plants should be covered with a cloche during the late autumn through the winter months. They must also be protected from an aphis attack during the summer.

The species forms a lax mat of foliage, sending out many adventitious roots, and it is from these rooted pieces that propagation can be carried out. To achieve a well-flowered, or even a partially flowered, cushion of this androsace should be deemed a great triumph. It is possible, however, and the experience of this accomplishment will rank highly. It is a gem of a plant, exhibiting such variation in the colour of flowers that raising plants from seed provides not only a sure way of establishing young plants, but ensuring some variation of flower colour.

Within one population of plants covering an area of perhaps just 1 sq. m, I noted flowers varying from soft apple-blossom pink to almost reddish hues.

I will never forget the thrill of a private slide show presented by my erstwhile employer in Munich, Herr Sebastian Seidl, who once kindly showed a colleague and me pictures of a trip he made to the Pennine Alps. He ran through a number of his wonderful slides, with classics such as pulsatilla and primula featuring strongly. Then came this picture of a cushion-forming plant tucked into a rock crevice, covered with cherry-red flowers. "What on earth is that?" I asked. He had a loud, infectious laugh and waited for our further response. We were stunned, quite simply stunned. Here was an awesome example of the beauty of this particular androsace. Never before, nor since, have I seen such an extreme colour form. Not surprisingly, he said he would always keep his location a secret. What a treasure. I have always been greatly indebted to him for allowing me to work in the Munich Botanic Garden. He was a strict but fair employer and eventually allowed me the greatest privilege by agreeing to my working in their affiliated alpine garden, the Schachen, for the ten-week period during which the garden was open to the public. This natural alpine garden provides an invaluable source of seed for distribution, at the same time enabling the staff to obtain vital research into the successful cultivation of a wide range of species.

The Bernese Oberland is home to two other species of androsace, including *Androsace helvetica* and *A. obtusifolia*, both of which hybridise with *A. alpina*. I will discuss the cultivation requirements for *A. helvetica* when I reach the Austrian Alps, but the variable hybrid *A.* ×*heeri* (*A. helvetica* × *A. alpina*) is occasionally offered in nursery catalogues. It is typically intermediate between the two parents, with the leaf rosettes and the cushions of a more lax nature than those of *A. helvetica*. The flowers are generally a pale pink or white. It is an ideal choice for a trough and will prove easier than both parents. The same is true of *A.* ×*aretioides* (*A. alpina* × *A. obtusifolia*), which is not uncommon in the wild. It forms a loose mat from which arise short umbels of two to three flowers with attractive pink flowers. It resembles the species *A. hedraeantha* from eastern Europe.

If we had to make just one choice, one ultimate choice made from all the Aretian androsaces, it might be made from either *Androsace alpina*, *A. helvetica*, or *A. vandellii*. Having experienced the late Duncan Lowe's skill as a cultivator, both in the open garden and in pots, it would have to be the last of the trio. Duncan was quite simply the master grower of androsaces, and his raised beds with self-sown plants of this androsace was perhaps, for me, the pinnacle of his cultivation skills. I have never seen them better grown in cultivation and would propose that his method be the benchmark to which we gardeners can all aspire.

Androsace vandellii has enjoyed at least four specific names over the years, including one that describes it well, *A. argentea*. This name, though no longer valid, refers to the wonderful silver sheen of its cushion of foliage. Duncan Lowe rated this species so highly because of its "abundance of flowers, the fine symmetry of its cushion, a good resistance to pests and diseases, and a strong determination to stay in character" (Lowe 1995). What more could we ask? He further went on to say that "it alone is the androsace that can actually be grown bigger and flower better in cultivation than in the wild". By his standards, I would agree. Let's see what we can do.

Androsace vandellii is widely distributed in nature, suggesting that it is a very old species, found in the Alps, the Pyrénées, the Spanish Sierra Nevada, and on a few stations in the Dolomites. This androsace, in contrast to the beautiful *A. alpina*, is truly saxatile (a plant especially adapted to growing in rock fissures), growing only on granite cliffs either in a shaded niche or in full sun. The one proviso is that the roots must find a dependable source of moisture. This single requirement can prove a great challenge for us in the garden. How often do we need to create a cool environment, in full exposure yet with a constant provision of air and moisture at the roots? Add to this challenge the searing summer temperatures realised by the location of many readers' gardens.

Because of the silvery, tomentose nature of the cushions, it is important to state that once established, these cushions resent overhead watering or subjection to rainfall if grown on the level. This does not mean they must be confined to an

Androsace vandellii

alpine house—on the contrary, *Androsace vandellii* can be grown on a raised bed but with semipermanent cover provided by a movable artificial PVC frame. I would direct the reader to chapter 9, which includes advice on creating and planting a raised bed. I will, though, isolate a well-tried growing mixture that consists of, by volume, one part leaf mould to two parts of lime-free, gritty sand.

The flowers of *Androsace vandellii* are borne singly, one to three to a rosette, and are purest white with a yellow throat. A well-flowered cushion flowering in a protected trough or raised bed should be a pinnacle of an alpine gardener's achievements. This species, as with its close relatives, is easily raised from seed.

A plant that never fails to amuse and enchant when I come across it is *Sempervivum arachnoideum*. It runs down through humus-filled crevices in sunny positions, with its clusters of small rosettes covered with a web of woolly, interwoven hairs. The flowers are a bright reddish pink, and a volcanic boulder pitted with holes is the ideal spot for this popular alpine. Similar in habit, *S. montanum* is more robust but once again a thoroughly amenable plant in the garden.

Before concluding with plants found in the Swiss Alps that we should endeavour to try out in our gardens, I will highlight two highly desirable alpine plants: *Saxifraga* ×*kochii* and *Campanula excisa*. The saxifrage is widely distributed in the Alps, predominantly in Switzerland and Austria. It is the natural hybrid between *S. oppositifolia* and *S. biflora*. In its best forms, it is a lovely cushion-forming plant best cultivated in a trough or raised bed. The recently raised hybrid from the same parentage, *S.* ×*kochii* 'Firebrand', raised by Don Peace, is worth looking out for. I will accord *S. oppositifolia* more deserved attention when discussing its merits from the Austrian Alps. *Saxifraga biflora* as a species would rarely merit a place in the garden owing to its short-lived nature occurring as a snowmelt plant in high acidic screes. A trip to Zermatt in the Valais region is a classic area for choice species, being dominated by the mighty Matterhorn. *Saxifraga* ×*kochii* and its parents associate with such treasures as *Campanula cenisia*, *Androsace vandellii*, and *Pulsatilla halleri*. The hybrid forms a neat cushion of crowded leaves with reddish-purple flowers. I have found it prefers a slightly cooler position tucked in between acidic rocks. Cloche cover is advisable during the dormant season. The best forms of this hybrid should be propagated by cuttings taken after flowering.

The first time I came across *Campanula excisa* was at the famous alpine plant nursery (sadly, no longer in existence) at Broadwell in the Cotswolds, England. It was Joe Elliott's nursery, and he employed a highly skilled nursery manager, Ralph Haywood, who was a master propagator and grower of rare alpine plants, in particular many campanulas. To experience the immaculate order so typical of their nursery, with neat rows of perfectly formed campanulas as well as many

Sempervivum montanum

other genera, grown in little clay pots, was an unforgettable experience. Sadly, neither Joe nor Ralph are
still living, but their legacy and countless raisings are
still thriving.

I was surprised to meet up with such fine plants of
Campanula excisa (a strict calcifuge). The underlying soil at Broadwell (typically Cotswold) was
highly calcareous, and in the main calcicoles thrived
there. But I should have realised their ingenuity and
adaptability to rise to any such challenge. The campanula under discussion is offered only by specialist
nurseries, although it presents little of a challenge to
the grower. It is definitely lime-hating and is seen at
its best at glacier level around 2200 m in altitude, on
the northern and southern slopes of Monte Rosa
(4633 m). Here, beside the streambeds, the plant
forms wide mats with its fragile, lance-shaped
foliage and curious, violet-blue, narrow-tubed bells
with five-folded lobes and a punched-out hole at the
base of each segment. Its requirements are exacting

Sempervivum arachnoideum

in my experience, but is no more demanding than its close relative, *C. alpestris*.

It was when reading Farrer's 1919 epic, *The English Rock Garden*, that I noted his experience in successfully growing *Campanula excisa* exclusively in pure, washed river sand. This makes a lot of sense, since the species is a glacial scree-loving plant creeping by underground stolons. I would avoid introducing any humus into the mixture, but this lean mixture must be topped with a generous layer of gravel, and plants should be kept well watered during the growing season. Seed-raised plants establish better than divisions, but should the reader encounter neat little flowering specimens, such as I found at Joe Elliott's legendary nursery, you will fall for them immediately. I wish you the best of luck with the curiously beautiful perforate bellflower.

The Valais is geologically rich in gneiss and schists, and Saas-Fee must be one of the richest floral centres in the Alps. The Matterhorn is close by, along with an array of choicest alpine plants. It is true that some of these species are challenging to grow in the garden, but most are well within reach of both the beginner and the seasoned gardener. Each time I return to the Alps, I feel highly motivated to search out new plants from nurseries to augment my own garden. A careful search may need to be undertaken, but they are available, and how rewarding each of these Swiss endemics will prove to be.

The native human population has a rare commodity that stretches way beyond their bank vaults and their expertise with clock and watchmaking. It even stretches beyond their delicious Lindt chocolate bars; it is their unique alpine scenery and flora, a veritable heritage that has given pleasure to multitudes of visitors and motivated many to grow their very first alpine plants.

The Italian Alps

It may surprise some readers to learn that Italy is very much a mountainous country. These mountains fall into two large groups: the Alps bounding the north and west of the Lombardy Plain, and the Apennines running north and south along the entire Italian peninsula. Such is the significance of the Italian Dolomites (which forms part of the Alps), its flora, and its impact on the alpine garden, that I will describe its flora along with the closely connected Julian Alps in a separate chapter.

The Italian Alps form Italy's frontiers with France, Switzerland, Austria, and the former Yugoslavia. They are more or less a continuous chain with a break in the Lake District that Italy shares with Switzerland. The flora is very varied, with areas supporting a staunchly calcifuge flora, while others feature some of the most celebrated of all lime-loving species.

The Matterhorn

I will commence in the west with the magnificent Gran Paradiso massif (4061 M), the highest mountain wholly in Italy. This is an area prominent with its reddish gneiss rock formation supporting a correspondingly rich flora. *Primula pedemontana* is abundant here, along with a favourite pulsatilla. Of all the members of the buttercup family, I invariably come back to the pasque flower as one of my staunch favourites. I think its all-round qualities, ease of culture, and joyful reminders that spring has returned again endears them to so many of us. *Pulsatilla halleri* is not only an exciting find in nature, but it represents one of the finest and most long-lived of the genus for the garden. It is found in the Gran Paradiso region at altitudes up to 2800 M. Those plants located in the true alpine band will be of dwarfer stature than the specimens found lower down. Although plants located in these parts prefer a lime-free substrate, it does not appear to be fussy as to soil type in the garden. The basal leaves of this species are more distinctly lanate or woolly, but the foliage is barely visible at flowering. In the best forms, the flowers can be enormous, dark violet, nodding goblets—one of spring's greatest joys.

Throughout the Alps, including the Gran Paradiso and Pennine Alps, a number of dwarf species of phyteuma occur. The miniature rampions are surely one of the most endearing of all alpines, with their little globular heads of clawlike, congested, blue corolla lobes. Most of the species are calcifuge and occur on stony mountain pastures, screes, and in rock crevices. In the Alps, they tend to flower well into July and August, in common with other members of the campanula family. As a result of this later flowering, we may find when botanising in these parts that the little tufts of foliage are just breaking into growth with the empty seed capsules still remaining from the previous year. A number of species are worth looking out for in seed lists, including two that belong to the Italian Alps: *Phyteuma humile* and *P. globulariifolium*. Both are an excellent choice for a trough, to provide late summer colour. Plants should be tucked in between acidic rocks in a sunny position. Once plants have become established, they should be left well alone and can be propagated only from seed. Each of the closely related species has bright blue flowers.

Lower down, altitudinally speaking, in the alpine meadows, the taller growing species of gentian will stand out prominently. We may frequently find the stately specimens of *Gentiana lutea* often assuming heights at flowering of up to 150 CM. Much dwarfer is *G. punctata*, more refined in every way but preferring a lime-free substrate. In the region covered here, two further species may be found which I would like to see cultivated more often in our gardens. A calcifuge species of great beauty is *G. purpurea*, with clusters of upright purple bells formed in the base of the upper leaves. It is a tall-growing plant of architectural

Pulsatilla halleri subsp. *halleri*

beauty, producing flowering stems in excess of 45 CM. Closely related, but preferring an akaline soil, is *G. pannonica*; it differs from the foregoing with deeper
purple flowers with red-black spots. Both are deserving of a place in the rock
garden or a bed where their taller stature and broad, ribbed foliage can be
appreciated. When raised from seed, patience is necessary; up to five years will
be required prior to flowering. This is a waiting game well worth enduring for
such fine summer-flowering representatives of this famous genus.

The Lake District region of the Italian Alps stretches from Lake Maggiore
and Lake Lugano in the west beyond Lake Como toward Lake Garda in the
east. The flora within this area is both varied and distinguished.

Very much at the distinguished end is a rare androsace found only on a few
mountain summits close to Lake Como at altitudes of 1800 to 2600 M. *Androsace
brevis* is closely related to *A. wulfeniana* from the Eastern Alps, and although rarely
offered, it may become available from a specialist nursery. On no account should
material be collected from its very localised habitat. It forms small caespitose cushions made up of rounded rosettes with single reddish flowers on 10 MM stems.
When encouraged to flower, it is a rewarding species best planted in a vertical

crevice supported by noncalcareous stones and afforded winter protection. As with related species, this spring-flowering plant should be propagated from seed.

The Lake District is also home to some further choice alpine species, including *Allium insubricum*, *Campanula raineri*, *Saxifraga vandellii* and *S. cotyledon*, and *Primula albenensis*, *P. cottia*, and *P. grignensis*. What a set of plants!

I described *Allium narcissiflorum* and extolled its virtue as a garden plant when describing species from the French Alps. The closely related species more commonly available in nurseries is *A. insubricum*. It is an easy, free-flowering plant, and all it asks is a freely drained soil and a sunny position. It forms a deciduous clump of short rhizomes and 15 to 30 cm stems carrying a permanently nodding umbel of purple-pink flowers in late spring to early summer. Plenty of seed is set, which can be either collected for subsequent sowing or left to allow plants to self-seed. Both of the related species represent a pinnacle in European terms of floristic beauty from amongst this large genus.

Of all the choice members of truly alpine campanula, *Campanula raineri* will rank as perhaps the finest of all. Farrer stated, "It occupies but an infinitesimal space in the world's wide expanse. For this, the most sensational perhaps of our European Alpine Bells, is confined to the upper limestones of the Bergamask mountains about the Italian Lakes" (1919). Yes, he certainly loved this species, as I do. I wonder how many times he used the superlative to describe his choicest species. I wonder, too, how often I applaud a "favourite" plant. Perhaps it is like our own children—they are all favourites but not accorded favouritism. In reality, a favourite plant *is* the superlative, the most liked, but I have already broken this rule over and over again.

This campanula is an absolute lime-lover, most frequently found occupying horizontal crevices, filling every chink and cranny with its fine, long runners. It prefers to grow in cooler exposures, and although occupying the same stations as the choice *Saxifraga vandellii*, *Campanula raineri* is found in the more sunny exposures. Where found in nature, *C. raineri* flowers late, well into August, but here in Scotland it will be flowering much earlier—in early July (midsummer). The first sign of life is heralded by its tufts of ash-grey, little, rhomboidal-shaped leaves. But beware! Just as we watch with excitement as the new foliage reemerges, so do the resident population of slugs. How these loathsome molluscs communicate, I have no notion of an idea, but they seem to amass together from the local community to attack all members of Campanulaceae. They first of all seem to identify the label with the most expensive price tag. They then proceed, in a matter of hours, to devour all the visible foliage. It is therefore of paramount importance to lay a protective barrier of slug pellets (safely away from the attention of birds) to combat the little horrors.

Allium insubricum

Campanula raineri

I have planted *Campanula raineri* in a trough in the company of a few saxifrages and a *Daphne ×hendersonii*, positioned beside the front door of our house. Here I can defeat the attentions of any aggressor and readily enjoy the close crowd of immense, china-blue, upturned cups. Returning to Farrer, he adds, "The flowers are a waxy-smooth texture and a radiant charm of serene and unconquerable beauty impossible to express." He managed pretty well with his description, and in the garden, *C. raineri* is easily pleased in a trough or raised bed. Give it a cool position and allow it to run amongst small pieces (3 to 5 sq. cm) of limestone. Plants growing happily will set seed, the best means of propagation, without disturbing the mother plants.

I have already related how closely allied the campanula is to *Saxifraga vandellii* in terms of habitat, with the two often sharing the same limestone boulders. The saxifrage comes into the same category, relative to rareness, as the androsace first described, *Androsace brevis*. Both are local and rarely offered in specialist catalogues. But when they are available, I would recommend their purchase if an appropriate position can be provided. *Saxifraga vandellii* was first discovered on the Corni di Canzo, northwest of Lecco, northern Italy, in 1763 by D. Vandelli, whose name the species commemorates. I have found it growing on limestone cliffs near to the Passo di Croce Domini, where it forms tight cushions of sharply pointed leaves. At flowering time in June, it can be seen at its glorious best, with its short 4 to 6 cm flowering stems densely covered with glandular hairs topped by a compact cyme of three to six perfectly formed white flowers. It is most closely related to the equally beautiful but more widespread *S. burseriana*. My first inclination would be to plant this rare species on a boulder of tufa, as described in chapter 9. Having established a tight cushion on a piece of tufa, *S. vandellii* will be quite impossible to propagate vegetatively, and seed should therefore be saved to replenish stocks.

Fortunately, there are no challenges with the culture of my next choice of saxifrage from this region of the Alps. *Saxifraga cotyledon* is generally located within the subalpine vegetation zone at an altitude of around 1500 m. This species inhabits silicaceous rocks in vertical positions. I have not found it to be in any way fussy as to position or soil type in the garden. Seed-raised stock and nursery-grown specimens can be difficult to verify, as it is apt to hybridise with the geographically widespread *S. paniculata*. It can be recognised, though, by the broad, regular, and finely toothed leaves that separate it from its closest allies, *S. hostii* and *S. paniculata*. From these it also differs with its panicle carrying more numerous flowers, which occupy at least half the length of the flowering stem. It usually consists of a large rosette (up to 7 to 12 cm in diameter at flowering size), accompanied by smaller daughter rosettes which are joined by short runners to the parent rosette. In its best forms, the red pigments or spotting within the flowers can be spectacular, the most exaggerated being *S.* 'Southside Seedling'.

In recent years, the status of strain within the nomenclature of plants has ceased to be recognised by the International Code of Nomenclature for Cultivated Plants. This is to be regretted in the case of some plants, including certain species of hellebores which set copious amounts of seed, resulting in considerable variation. The latest recommendation is to give group status to such a variable species and append a cultivar name for plants of notable merit. I will now reassign this saxifrage to *Saxifraga* Southside Group and recommend that the reader select a favourite form. Once the selection has been made and planted in

Saxifraga vandellii

the chosen position, allow room for the long and arching (up to 70 CM) branched panicle of flowers. They flow down with great character. The plants should be vegetatively propagated from cuttings. Seed-raised stock will vary and certainly differ from the parent plant. Once the flowering rosette has performed, it will die, with subsequent side rosettes taking up the mantel. It should not be described as a monocarpic species, but it is certainly a noble one, including its more well-known group variants. It should prove to be a prominent plant in the garden, flowering through early summer and into midsummer.

Primulas feature strongly in this area of the Italian Alps, and there is evidence of a significant early development in these parts. I have already written about the virtues of the widespread and variable species *Primula hirsuta*. It has long been known that a rather desirable form of the species exists on a limestone sub-strate in a number of locations to the east of Lago Maggiore. It occurs on dolomitic (calcareous rock) cliffs, often shaded by beech trees just below the alpine zone. It was described in 1988 as a distinct species, *P. grignensis* with its *locus classicus* (type habitat) in the Grigna Meridionale (the Como Province, Italy). My own personal feeling is that this whole subsection (*Erythrodrosum*) of primula deserves a closer study, involving both taxonomists and horticulturists, to determine further their status. There is clearly a great deal of variation within a geographic population of plants. Should material of this species become available, one needs to remember only that it is uncharacteristically a calcicole plant and will thrive when positioned between pieces of limestone on a trough in dappled shade. It displays a diminutive habit with a neat umbel of rose-pink flowers.

Another plant belonging to the same subsection of primula is again sitting uneasily either as *Primula villosa* subsp. *cottia* or as a good species *P. cottia*. As I have already mentioned, Dr. Kress, the now retired botanist formerly of the Munich Botanic Garden, carried out much work on this illustrious group of plants. To help him with his studies, a well-stocked nursery frame was filled with perfectly grown plants of each member of this important subsection on which he was focusing. Each was carefully labelled with its proposed name and origin. Whilst discussing this collection of plants with the then curator of alpines, Dieter Schacht, we contemplated the results of removing every label and hiding them from Dr. Kress. Now, not wishing to aggrieve his already poor heart condition, I suspect my position would have been immediately terminated if found to be the culprit. But the question was, would he be able to rename them? I doubt it. In fact, if the plants were mixed up, it is unlikely that many of them could be separated from one another—the point being that we may well be looking at perhaps just one or two highly variable species. In reality, we have at least five, and possibly another two, to add to the list.

So where does *Primula cottia* fit into the picture, and does it really matter at all to the gardener? I doubt it matters, as I generally found that my nursery customers looked first and foremost at the specimen, not at the name. If *P. cottia* belongs to *P. villosa*, which is a native of the Austrian Alps, this form is 550 km disjunct from its parent. *Primula cottia* is found growing on a mountain named Chalansa, in northwestern Italy, amongst schistose rock at around 2800 m. It thrives in nature on a southwest exposure, growing in humus-filled ledges. It is now well established in gardens and presents the grower with no problems. It forms compact clumps of hirsute foliage similar to *P. hirsuta*, and, on short 2 cm tall stems, an umbel of three to four brightly coloured rose-pink flowers are produced. Mature, congested clumps can be lifted and divided after flowering and either potted up or replanted in a fresh acidic soil.

It is significant that even in the 20th century, European plant species new to science were discovered and introduced to gardens. It is of no surprise to me, considering the many inhospitable and remote mountain ranges that exist in Europe (unlikely to attract the attention of either walkers or botanists), that new species should be discovered, including those of the well-known genus *Primula*.

Primula cottia
Photo by Margaret and Henry Taylor.

Primula albenensis
Photo by Margaret and Henry Taylor.

A plant I am growing in a trough and which is proving a valuable new addition to my collection is *P. albenensis*. This was first described by Dr. Kress in 1981, and a paper on the species was written by Banfi and Ferlighetti in 1993. It is a pretty species, resembling a perfectly created hybrid between *P. auricula* and *P. marginata*. Found growing on the slopes of Mount Alben at around 2000 M, northeast of Bergamo, Italy, it is conspicuous for the amount of farina displayed on its aerial parts. This is also my experience when it is cultivated.

Fritz Kummert of Graz and Henry and Margaret Taylor of Invergowrie, Scotland, have located the species in nature, and they note that it grows in humus-holding cracks in cliffs, sometimes under overhangs of dolomite rock. The colour of the flower, while variable, generally ranges between blue and violet-blue, with a white form also known in the wild. What a thrill to be able to introduce a completely new European species to our gardens in the closing years of the 20th century. In nature, *Primula albenensis* grows in close proximity to *Saxifraga vandellii* and *Rhodothamnus chamaecistus*, with *P. auricula* growing nearby on sunny cliffs.

As a garden plant, it has settled down well and recently received the coveted AM from the RHS. It should be allowed to settle down in a trough and left well alone, with seed providing the best means of reproduction.

Continuing east on our journey toward Lake Garda, we meet the Ortles group northwest of the Alpi Orobie. At this point, the flora of the Eastern Alps begins to assert itself. One of the outstanding alpine buttercups, *Ranunculus parnassifolius*, occurs here on limestone formations. I described it earlier in its magnificent pink-flowering form, *R. parnassifolius* 'Nuria', from the eastern Pyrénées. Here in northwestern Italy, it is found in its classic form with dark green, oval to heart-shaped leaves. The flowers here are pure white, and in its best developments are large and open, held on 6 to 10 CM stems often up to five per stem. Because of its variability in form, plants should be selected in flower from a reputable nursery. It is a vigorous and deep-rooting plant and therefore requires a rich, well-drained soil mixture, and the type species thrives amongst pieces of limestone. It can be propagated from freshly sown seed or by division.

I will now continue by describing plants from the very rich area either side of that most romantic of lakes, Lago di Garda. I had the privilege of working on the eastern shores of this lake whilst helping to set up a nursery in Bardolino. This unique opportunity afforded me the extra chance of exploring the surrounding mountains during my free time. In the main, this area supports a calcicole flora that has the feel of an extension to the Dolomites. There are, though, pockets of silicaceous rock formations which immediately strike the plant hunter, as, for example, on the Passo di Croce Domini. Here the rolling

Ranunculus parnassifolius

contours support rich meadows with *Anemone narcissiflora*, dotted with *Fritillaria tubiformis* and wide clumps of *Primula glaucescens*, suggesting a calcareous substrate.

A few kilometres away, and the colour of the soil changes to a reddish brown, the rock is a shining siliceous material, and a new primula appears amongst the calcifuge *Soldanella pusilla*; it is *Primula daonensis*. Another kilometre along the military track and the scene changes back to the greyish limestone, but this time dampish meadows are aglow with splendid forms of *Primula spectabilis* fighting for space with the simple but effective *Ranunculus bilobus*. Such an area demonstrates the diversity of plants that can be found in the European Alps without exerting oneself greatly or being exposed to any danger.

In fact, imagine the scene as I left my workplace on the side of Lake Garda, driving around the north end towards the smaller lake, Lago di Idro. I arrived at the village of Anfo and as the early evening approached, I drove my resourceful little Volkswagen Beetle up and up, circumnavigating many hairpin bends.

Anemone narcissiflora with *Fritillaria tubiformis*

It was early June and I was meeting more and more snow at the side of the track. Would I eventually make it to the Passo di Croce Domini? The scenery changed as I passed steep walls of limestone, many of which were flecked with shades of reddish purple—but more of *Daphne petraea* later. I became nervous as the oil well of my Beetle kept grating against the unyielding lumps of limestone I was endeavouring to avoid. I had reached the pass now and felt hungry and ready to make a pit stop. The ambient temperature had also changed dramatically. I was aware that the grassy meadows would make an ideal spot to pitch my tent. I parked up and stretched my arms, weary after all the extreme steering movements, and surveyed the scene. As many a reader will know, it is the clean air, the smell of fragrant flowers, the peace, and the sound of finches annoyed by my intrusion. But there was one terrible thing missing: I had no one to share all this with.

Nevertheless, I settled down and chose a level spot for my tent. The problem was finding 3 to 4 sq. m free of primulas and buttercups. When this close to nature, one creates a great respect and awe for the whole arrangement in these surroundings. The views can be spectacular, and such an experience fuels a desire to try and recapture a little of this landscape and its flora in our own gardens. The smallest of troughs can provide just such a miniature landscape. I am sure not to be alone in collecting a handful of manageable stones when walking in a favourite landscape or habitat and utilising them in the garden on returning home.

Having given the reader a little foretaste of this wonderful part of Italy, let me now look a little closer at some of the plants which we ought to be growing ourselves.

Whether we are botanising in the high mountains to the west of Lake Garda or in the area I have just described, one cannot fail to appreciate the beauty of the primulas growing so luxuriantly in these parts. Of those that grow on calcareous formations, perhaps one of the most spectacular, is a cliff dweller, *Primula auricula* var. *albocincta*, seen as its best in the Monte Baldo range and on Monte Tremalzo. The type species is variable in habit, but here it displays one of its most distinct forms, with heavily farinose, truncated stocks wedged into vertical crevices. The plants are larger than normal, with huge floppy leaves, and at flowering time produce long peduncles up to 25 CM in length, with umbels of 5 to 20 bright yellow flowers. I have found this form to be an excellent garden plant. It is not fussy as to position or its demands regarding soil pH. All it asks is a sunny, well-drained position and space to perform. I have it planted in an alpine bed positioned between pieces of dolomitic limestone. It does not spread greatly but sets plenty of seed that may produce a variable offspring when planted in close proximity to closely related primula species with which it will wish to form a marriage.

One of the most spectacular of primulas in nature, owing to its superabundance and beauty of flower, is *Primula spectabilis*. A walk along the grassy ridges of Monte Caplone in early June will reward the plant hunter with sheets of its matted rosettes interspersed with *Gentiana clusii*, the dainty waving stems of pale blue–flowering *Linum austriacum*, and *Ranunculus bilobus*. The primula forms dense clusters of sticky rosettes, very broad and curling back at the tip. For this reason, it cannot be confused with its cousins in the subsection *Arthritica*, *P. clusiana*, *P. glaucescens*, and *P. wulfeniana*. The flowers will commence as the snow melts in May and June, producing a distinct purplish peduncle or stem rising up to 10 CM with an umbel of up to five huge flowers of a rich, warm, rosy red. Such is their beauty in nature that I lament at my inability to reenact this floral charm in the garden. I have no problem cultivating the plant, but I still have to master the skill of flowering it successfully. It is certainly a rich feeder. It resents drying out completely and requires full sun. I can provide all of these requirements as well as additional pieces of dolomite rock to please it well. I will not give up. I must add, unless one plans to raise plants from wild-collected seed, that such is its variability in flower that I would recommend buying plants in flower.

Of lesser beauty in my experience, but somewhat easier to please, is *Primula glaucescens*. It is also a calcicole plant that I have found growing in great masses amongst the oxlip, *P. elatior*, on earthy banks at an altitude of around 2400 M. In these parts of northern Italy, *P. glaucescens* cannot be confused with its geographically disjunct relatives in the Eastern Alps. It produces stout rhizomes with persistent remains of withered foliage near the apex and has strong, fleshy roots. The leaves are stiff, leathery, and sharply pointed with 12 to 15 CM stems carrying an umbel of up to six flowers. The colour varies from pinkish red to lilac, and for some reason I seem to have missed out on the better forms. At its best it is quite lovely, easy of culture, and will happily flower. The vigorous clumps should be lifted and divided every three to five years, thus rejuvenating tired plants. An alpine bed or rock garden will suit this species admirably.

Not surprisingly, in a number of locations this species meets up with the pre-

Primula spectabilis

viously described *Primula spectabilis*, and where this occurs hybrids can be spotted, but only if a plant exceeds the virtues of its parents does it really merit a place in our gardens. Such a hybrid carries the name *P. ×carueli* (*P. glaucescens* × *P. spectabilis*) and is intermediate between the parents.

Concluding the fine and varied selection of primula from this part of Italy, I will describe the calcifuge species, *Primula daonensis*. Belonging to the subsection *Erythrodrosum*, it is very easy to identify in its own unique surroundings of siliceous and granitic formations. It does not tend to form large clumps of foliage but rather single to multirosettes of downy, sticky leaves with orange to red glandular hairs. Short 2 to 8 cm stems hold an umbel of three to six flowers of good colours, a rose to magenta-crimson often with a white eye. I have planted this species in a trough along with other calcifuge plants where it will perform well. It is not a vigorous plant and will not outgrow its position. Seed is set in abundance and provides the most practical means of reproduction. All these primulas flower during the mid to late spring months in the garden, and I would always recommend choosing a number of later flowering subjects to accompany them on the trough or alpine bed.

Never far away from the primulas in nature is an utterly simple but somehow

Ranunculus alpestris

enchanting little buttercup, *Ranunculus bilobus*. Throughout the Alps, white-flowering alpine buttercups can be encountered as an indicator of the snow's recent departure. The most commonly found species is *R. alpestris*, then here-abouts it is *R. bilobus*, but farther east two even more closely related species may be identified: *R. crenatus* and *R. traunfellneri*. The foliage of each of these species is a glowing, glossy, deep green in colour; it is simply their shape that varies slightly and separates the geographic forms. In the case of *R. bilobus*, it does not display the tricleft, deciduous leaves of *R. alpestris*, but rather has rounded, kid-ney-shaped leaves delicately scalloped at the margins. The flowers are dainty, pure white buttercups on 3 to 6 cm stems. As with each of these related species, *R. bilobus* is easy to grow in a variety of positions. It requires good light and plenty of moisture in a humus-rich soil. Clumps can be lifted and divided after flowering, or the freshly collected seed can be sown to raise new stock.

True alpine specialists often have eyes for saxatile plants or species adapted to growing in rock fissures. I can relate only my own experience of meeting up with plants of this category. Plants fitting into this genre that can be found around these lakes in northeastern Italy include *Daphne petraea*, *Saxifraga tombeanensis*, and *Physoplexis comosa*. What a trio of classic alpine species.

It is perhaps brought home to me more forcibly as I write this chapter how
fortunate I was to live and work on the side of Lake Garda. I would often
take the first ferry in the morning from Torri del Benaco on the eastern shore of
the lake, across to Maderno. I then drove along the lake, rising up above the
well-arranged lemon groves, and took a route through fields of maize. These
led toward the thick pine woods that signalled a sudden change of landscape as
the awesome cliffs of limestone towered above me. Such were the treasures
awaiting my arrival that I often sped through the cooler woods, but on occasion
I would pause and enjoy the specialised flora that abounds at these lower subalpine levels.

A great joy is to pull up at the edge of the pine woods and explore the deep
needles mixed with soil that accumulates amongst the deep and hidden boulders
of limestone. In early spring there are fine clumps of *Helleborus niger* in the
clearings, but from June onwards a moment of real excitement is to find *Cyclamen purpurascens* (formerly *C. europaeum*) as it appears in scattered colonies under
the pine trees and mixed deciduous species. It is not confined to shady places, but
occasionally plants will be found growing in more exposed, sunnier aspects,
especially in rock crevices.

The foliage can be spectacular, kidney-shaped to heart-shaped, with the
colour varying from a dull green to pale green with silvery markings or almost
pure silvery hues. The leaves are more or less evergreen, but the flowers are the
real highlight. The colour varies from rose-pink to carmine with an occasional
white. For me, the greatest thrill is the rich fragrance emitted, which further
enhances the species as a first-class summer-flowering garden plant. It is easy of
culture, enjoying a cool, semi-shaded spot with good, loamy soil. I would recommend the reader incorporate plenty of leaf mould and if possible some limestone
rubble. The tubers should be deeply buried at planting. I have found *Cyclamen
purpurascens* to be perfectly hardy, and although this species does not seed as pro-
lifically as *C. hederifolium* or *C. coum*, plants will appear from self-dispersal of
seed. This is a rewarding plant, and once appreciated may well cause the grower
to catch the bug and seek new forms. Beware!

Returning to the car, I would begin to climb up through *Laburnum alpinum*
and *Amelanchier ovalis*, flowering profusely in June. The roof of the car would
be brushing against the descending branches laden with yellow racemes of
laburnum. The smooth, military tracks dating back to the last war began to
deteriorate. My altimeter was rising up above 1500 m toward 1800 m and higher.
I stopped for a moment at the side of the road, knowing that I was unlikely to
create a traffic jam, and surveyed the scene. There was a delicious fragrance that
could only belong to a member of the genus *Daphne*.

Cyclamen purpurascens

Cyclamen purpurascens

The first time I set my eyes on *Daphne petraea*, I just stopped, looking in awe at this floral wonder of the Alps. It is so rare, confined only to these limestone precipices, and yet the gnarled little shrublets hanging from those frightful cliffs look as if they have been there forever. Who amongst earthlings could hazard a guess at their age? I dared to move and approach these perfect domes of flower and then buried my nose in that unique floral fragrance. Few smells come close to this experience, with perhaps the exception of its close cousin, *D. cneorum*.

From time to time I enjoy an amble down my namesake's street in London, more famous for is tailors and shirt outlets, yet a few steps into the inner sanctum of Messrs. Floris, and their wonderful fragrances remind me of Monte Tremalzo. From Jermyn Street, London, back to Italy and the daphne—an alpine wonder of the world. When he first found the plant, Farrer rather lost the plot, to quote a modern idiom: "At the moment I had no

Daphne petraea
Photo by Jim Jermyn.

inclination to wisdom of any sort; my brain felt dissolved into an icy liquid somewhere in the pit of my stomach. The little warm hollow was filled with a silence so complete that it seemed as if the Earth-mother herself was sharing in the solemnity of the moment" (1919). Like me, he was rather happy and quite in awe.

Fortunately for the alpine gardener, there is no reason to be fearful of its culture. At long last growers in the United States, Canada, and Europe can purchase this daphne either on its own roots or propagated by grafting. I will personally always choose a plant that has been raised from a cutting. I am more confident of it lasting longer and performing more closely to its true character than a plant that is half Chinese and half European. Where should one plant this treasure? Either between pieces of tufa rock or actually directly planted into a boulder of this material. The method of planting is described in chapter 9, but with care, the grower can enjoy many years of pleasure as the little plant increases in size.

Daphne petraea forms tight little evergreen shrublets with tiny, dark green oval leaves. The flowers, in heads of two or three, are huge, open, rosy pink trumpets so typical of this famous genus. A very rare white form is now available at a suitably high price, but who would balk at such a beauty that has the potential of lifelong pleasure compared with an expensive wine that disappears with the second course of a good meal?

Having stated my own preference for plants propagated on their own roots, I must provide an alternative view. There is no doubt that grafted plants will flower more profusely and at an earlier age, but of course they will not produce suckers from the scion. A number of fine cultivars are available from specialist nurseries. In the U.K., we are fortunate to have Robin White, ably supported by his wife, Sue, who have supplied a wonderful array of daphnes through their nursery in Hampshire, England—Blackthorn Nursery. *Daphne petraea* cultivars include the following: 'Grandiflora' is an outstanding cultivar, perhaps the most commonly grown, with large, open flowers of an intense pink. 'Michelle' is a clone introduced by Henry and Margaret Taylor which is proving to be more vigorous, with a similar flower to the foregoing. 'Tremalzo' will prove to be one of the choicest of forms with pure white flowers.

As already noted, one of the great thrills for the plant hunter is to find a number of closely related species of the same genus growing in close proximity. On these mountains to the west of Lake Garda, as well as finding *Daphne petraea*, specimens of *D. cneorum* and *D. striata* are close by. While I was working in northern Italy in 1977–78, I often found these species but concentrated my search for *D. petraea*. At times I found huge mats hanging off the limestone boulders, often up to 1 M across. At that time, I knew little of the natural hybrid between *D. cneorum* and *D. petraea*, called *D. ×hendersonii*. The history of this hybrid goes back to 1930, when two gentlemen were botanising here. W. Scott Henderson and Sir Arthur Hill found the hybrid. It was not until 1981 that this most meritorious of hybrids reached cultivation in gardens. The hybrid combines all the qualities of both parents and has proved to be an excellent, fully hardy alpine plant for the open garden. It is easily rooted from cuttings and therefore does not need to be grafted. It is best of all planted in full sun in a deep, well-drained soil, looking superb when positioned between limestone boulders. There are, though, clones that are suitable for a trough or planting at the edge of a wall or raised bed to allow their semiprostrate habit to cascade down.

Daphne petraea 'Michelle'
Photo by Margaret and Henry Taylor.

I will recommend a few *Daphne ×hendersonii* clones that will reward the grower. All of them produce a compact, evergreen shrublet with glossy, dark green leaves and warm pink to reddish flowers held in a terminal inflorescence. To give the reader an idea of the space a mature plant of this hybrid may eventually assume, the measurements are provided. 'Appleblossom' was introduced by Henry and Margaret Taylor, with an open habit, 45 CM wide by 15 CM high; 'Blackthorn Rose' is 45 CM by 20 to 30 CM; 'Ernst Hauser' is a vigorous clone, 60 CM by 30 CM; 'Marion White' is a pure white-flowering clone, 45 CM by 30 CM; and 'Rosebud', introduced by Henry and Margaret Taylor, is 45 CM by 20 CM. Each of these clones will flower in mid to late spring, followed by a second flush in mid to late summer.

As to the maladies that can affect daphnes, I feel I can speak from bitter experience. I know of no pest damage in the open garden, but I have firsthand experience of the disease known simply as die-back. It is often fatal and is caused by an infection, most commonly botrytis. The initial cause is often manifest on young plants still seeking to establish themselves in the garden. Dead blossoms remaining on the plants trapped by the new growth and proving susceptible to fungal attack are often affected. As a plant matures, a mat of decaying leaves and flowers can accumulate at the base of the plant, again attracting a fungal attack. Overhanging foliage from neighbouring plants during a prolonged damp spell can trigger a fungal attack. I have a nasty feeling that each of these circumstances has affected my plants of daphne, with disastrous consequences.

The best remedy is good hygiene, a practice we really must pay attention to if we are to succeed with the choicest of alpine plants. Another control is to soak plants with a systemic fungicide during the late summer.

Propagation is easily carried out by striking semiripe cuttings, and once rooted the soft growth should be pinched out. Before potting them up, I would always leave the rooted cuttings carefully shaded from the fiercest of sunlight until growth commences the following spring.

Daphne ×hendersonii, along with its modern cultivars, must surely be one of the success stories of modern horticulture and reflects the success of eagle-eyed plantsfolk both in the field and with the hybridists' paintbrush.

When botanising in the Monte Caplone locality to the west of Lake Garda, the harsh limestone faces are home not only to *Daphne petraea* and *Primula auricula* var. *albocincta*, but also a rare and choice saxifrage, a member of the section *Porphyrion*, subsection *Kabschia*: *Saxifraga tombeanensis*.

The botanist Boissier, who collected it in October 1864, was the first to recognise it as a distinct species. Prior to that it was thought to be a form of *Saxifraga diapensioides*. *Saxifraga tombeanensis* forms the tightest of cushions with very little in the way of calcareous incrustation, preferring more shaded, vertical limestone rocks between 1200 and 2000 м. The flowering stems are 3 to 7 см in length, with one to four pure white flowers held in a cyme. A well-flowered cushion is a wonderful sight. The best way to reenact nature's performance is to plant small cushions directly in a boulder of tufa to flower in the spring. Choose a cooler position out of direct sunlight and save seed to replenish stocks.

One of the most curious and exquisite of all European alpine plants is found growing on the limestone cliffs beside *Daphne petraea* and lower down nearer sea level. It is the devil's claw, *Physoplexis comosa*. The species now belongs to a monotypic genus, having long been known as *Phyteuma comosum*. I often take a while to conform to changes in nomenclature thrust upon me by the taxonomist, but here is one that sits easily owing to its extreme uniqueness.

This is a species totally faithful to a limestone cliff face. It is found here and farther eastward in the Dolomites. The plant, a member of the campanula family, forms a robust, fat, and waxy, yellowish orange rootstock that moulds itself into soilless crevices and crannies drawing nourishment from the dolomitic limestone and any available minerals and moisture from which it can draw. It is by no means confined to cool or shady positions, but it generally prefers them. I know of a location right beside a busy road at just a few hundred metres above sea level where the plants are growing in a sunny aspect and are showing flowers of a deep reddish colour, which may well reflect the position in which they are growing.

The foliage typically extends to about 10 см, but when growing in dense shade it may be much longer. It is kidney-shaped and roughly toothed but varies considerably from being grey with a fine down to smooth and glossy. The flowers come up in dense heads on stems up to 5 см. They are very unusual but quite wonderful, producing a bunch of long-tubed, claw-shaped, deep pink to pale blue flowers. There is really only one way to grow this most coveted of plants in the open garden, unless any reader possesses a naturally occurring limestone cliff in their property. *Physoplexis comosa* loves to be grown directly into a boulder of tufa. It is best positioned away from the blazing sun and should establish well, flowering during the early summer months. It sets plenty of seed that can, with care, produce fine young plants. In nature, at altitudes of 1800 м and upwards, it rarely flowers before the end of July, but when seen at its best, this will prove to be an unforgettable experience. Since it is a member of Campanulaceae, great care should be taken to combat an attack of slugs that, not surprisingly, recognise its superior value to the owner.

Moving away from these distinguished saxatile plants, I will now introduce a striking member of the family Caryophyllaceae, *Silene elisabetha*. I have found it

Physoplexis comosa

Physoplexis comosa
Photo by Jim Jermyn.

flowering in early August in fierce, white limestone rubble and in fissures upon large boulders. It, too, produces a long taproot that penetrates deep into the limestone substrate. When flowering, it stands out like a belisha beacon with its enormous ragged, flopping petals of rosy crimson. It is a striking sight against the white limestone, where the long, narrow leaves form a rosette emanating from the rootstock. As with other campions and catchflys, it produces plenty of seed, and I have planted it amongst small pieces of limestone along with *Campanula raineri* in a trough. The two plants associate well in the garden, flowering in late summer.

Often growing in the limestone waste accumulating at the edge of a mountain track is one of the loveliest of alpine pansies, *Viola dubyana*. It is a fine, summer-flowering species native only to the limestone mountains of northern Italy between Grigna and Monte Baldo. It loves to seed around in the fragmented debris, forming a tuft of dark green foliage with deep violet to purple flowers with a yellowish white central spot. It is often found in nature flowering from May to July. Another species which slugs just love, it should be planted in a raised position on a trough or raised bed and allowed to seed about in its rather unfussy way.

Viola dubyana

Geranium argenteum

My final choices from this rich locality are across the waters of Lake Garda above the eastern shores, where a series of high mountains rise with no particular distinct summit. The range is known as Monte Baldo, with Cima Valdritta (2218 м) the highest peak. Two plants amongst many grow on these mountains—one an endemic—and seriously merit our inclusion in a collection of European alpine plants: *Geranium argenteum* and *Callianthemum kernerianum*. The geranium is quite beautiful, and, as its name suggests, it is notable for its lovely silvery, downy foliage. This great asset, to which can be added the most spectacular of soft-pink flowers, makes for a complete and easy alpine plant. *Geranium argenteum* grows in the grassy lawns along the crests of Monte Baldo amongst a mass of golden buttercups and pale blue *Myosotis alpestris*. I found exquisite plants tucked in crevices of limestone as well as wide clumps competing with *Carex baldensis* and other grasses.

Geranium argenteum will reward the gardener with lax tufts of silvery foliage and months of glistening pink flowers. I would recommend a meagre diet to encourage dwarfness. It should be positioned in fullest sun, and seed can be saved if the gardener has the patience. It should be kept away from *G. cinereum* and *G. subcaulescens* if purity of offspring is so desired. But what a lovely plant it will prove to be.

Not far away from the geranium are the pretty rosettes of *Jovibarba allionii* running along humus-filled rock crevices. The many and varied houseleeks are such fun and in this case produce globular rosettes of hairy, yellow-green incurved leaves, which, when exposed to full sun, assume a lovely pink colour. The flowers are yellow. It is a great trough plant and easily propagated from cuttings.

A fitting conclusion to this part of the Italian Alps is to describe a very special member of the buttercup family, Ranunculaceae: *Callianthemum kernerianum*. It is restricted to growing in short turf and limestone rubble, principally along the summit spine of Monte Baldo. There are, though, a few localised occurrences in the Valli Giudicarie at 1400 to 2000 M. It shares its habitat with *Gentiana clusii*, *Primula spectabilis*, and *Ranunculus bilobus* and flowers during early June or July as soon as the snows recede. It closely resembles its cousin *C. anemonoides* from Austria, forming lovely glaucous, deeply divided foliage that generally appears after flowering. The flowers are 2 to 3 CM in diameter and are either white or

Jovibarba allionii

Callianthemum kernerianum

very pale pink with a central boss of green with orange nectaries. It is easy of culture, demanding a deep organic soil, freely drained and preferably, but not necessarily, of a calcareous pH. In the garden, the buds form during the late winter and early spring and do not seem to be prone to the vagaries of the winter. It performs well on a raised bed, and to facilitate seed collection after flowering, great care should be taken to watch the green seed heads (follicles) and gently tease them away. When they fall away into the awaiting seed envelope or egg cup, they are immediately ready for sowing. I would recommend sowing onto a John Innes type seed compost or another loam-based mix, and then covering with a thin layer of compost and chick grit, plunging the pot in a sand frame. Germination may take place the following spring or erratically over the next few years. I always leave the seedlings to mature for one year or more, giving them frequent low-nitrogen liquid feeds. When it comes to planting, wash out (this involves soaking the root ball in water until the compost falls away) the pot of seedlings, as they resent root disturbance, and then single out the young plants for either potting or planting out.

This is a rewarding plant, for it flowers very early in the garden, sometimes catching me by surprise. An old plant will produce many hundreds of flowers and steal the show, as indeed pan-grown plants do on the literal show benches. It demands full sun and a deep root run. That is basically all and fittingly concludes this rich locality in northern Italy.

It is my view that most of the plants covered so far in this chapter are pretty easy of cultivation but, my goodness, it certainly helps actually to see where and how these plants grow in nature before attempting to recreate a special position for them in the garden. Europe has become more easily accessible in recent decades, and having lived and worked here, I can thoroughly recommend this part of Italy, where the range of fruit, the ice cream, and the pizzas are simply sensational and more than complement the lakes and the endemic flora.

Before moving to the Dolomites and the Austrian Alps, I will describe a few plants from the Apennine Mountains.

The Apennines

The Apennine chain of mountains runs down the length of the Italian peninsula, reaching 2912 M in the Gran Sasso, the highest peak in the Abruzzi mountains in the middle of the chain.

Italy as a country has one of the greatest diversities of alpine plants in all Europe. The area I have already covered and the Dolomites (to follow) are widely botanised, but little has been written about the botanically rich area within the Apennine chain. I recall speaking to a number of plant hunters about their experiences in this region, but more recently the expert Czech grower, Dr. Vojtěch Holubec, has recorded some exciting finds in the Majella and Gran Sasso mountains. Both mountains come under national park status and amazingly contain over a third of Italy's total flora. Both mountains are composed of limestone, and dolomite features strongly.

A number of alpine species are found here which are of great importance both botanically and horticulturally, and a number are deserving of more attention. But prior to rising up to high elevations, I want to write about a spring-flowering cyclamen species that can be found in deciduous or coniferous woodlands in the Apennine Mountains. It is not a species of high altitudes and is rarely found above 500 M. I remember listening to the late Will Ingwersen recounting a thrilling experience from these parts. A friend had taken him to visit a special wooded area, and as he approached he admired the woodland floor dotted with the magenta and deep-pink flowers of *Cyclamen repandum*. As well as mentioning the striking colour of the flower, he spoke of the sweet scent emitted by them

Cyclamen repandum

along with the beautifully marked foliage. It is a species I have found to be perfectly hardy here in Scotland, but slow to establish. Flowering-size corms will bloom here from April through May in the open garden and should be planted around deciduous trees and shrubs about 9 cm deep in a freely drained soil rich in leaf mould. Once established, seed will set and be distributed by ants. This is an excellent choice to add to a bed associating with hepatica, wild primroses, and other shade-loving species.

A plant that has been thoroughly confused in U.K. gardens for many decades is *Gentiana dinarica*. A member of the acaulis group, this is strictly a calcicole plant with a restricted distribution in the Balkans and in central Italy. It represents one of the finest species within this popular group, and close to Prati di Tivo (in the Abruzzi mountains), it colonises the alpine turf overlying the limestone at about 2000 m. It appears in the thousands, flowering soon after the snows have departed in May and June with striking dark blue trumpets.

Once stock can be sourced of known geographic origin, this rarely offered species will prove to be one of the best species of acaulis-type gentian for the garden. It is still grown in continental botanic gardens and forms wide mats of typically elliptical to lanceolate foliage. Once clumps have established in the garden, they should be divided after flowering and rejuvenated in fresh soil. I have not found it germinates easily from seed, so vegetative means of propagation are more reliable.

A genus that deserves more attention with some attractive species is *Globularia*. They certainly feature more abundantly in the eastern European mountains. One I would recommend the reader search for is *G. meridionalis*, which thrives on the Apennine limestones at altitudes around 2000 m. It forms prostrate mats of evergreen, dark green, linear leaves and short 2 to 4 cm stems bearing large, globular sky-blue flowers. This species, along with its cousins, is an easy alpine plant, demanding full sun and a position allowing the mat of foliage to spill over the edge of a rock or wall. It is spring-flowering and would associate well with another plant found in these parts, the variable *Alyssum cuneifolium*. The globularia can be propagated from cuttings, often found with roots, or from seed.

Gentiana dinarica

Somewhat disjunct from the main area of the Apennines on which I have been concentrating, around the Gran Sasso and Majella mountains, is an area in the northern Apennines close to Monte Vecchio. Here is the classic location for one of Europe's most attractive primulas of the subsection *Erythrodrosum*, *Primula apennina*. It is generally found in nature inhabiting rock fissures and pockets of humus on cliff ledges on sandstone rock faces. Its geographic location separates it conclusively from its closest cousins, while it forms its characteristic foliage covered with orange-brown glands so prevalent in this subsection. Magenta-pink flowers are held in an umbel and make this an attractive species for the collector of auricula-type species. Once obtained, it prefers a lime-free soil tucked in between pieces of sandstone and is readily multiplied by seed.

One of the foremost treasures growing in the higher alpine reaches of these mountains, at around 2400 M, is the very best form of our beloved edelweiss, *Leontopodium alpinum* subsp. *nivale*. Here it thrives amongst crevices and crannies in the limestone pavement as well as in humus-rich pockets on the limestone terraces. It associates in nature with the moss campion, *Silene acaulis*, which is a perfect foil for the edelweiss. Many alpine gardeners and plantsfolk have been critical of the forms of *L. alpinum* available in the trade. Too often they have proved to be rather course in habit with elongated flowering stems and small flowers. The subspecies *nivale* is quite simply the best form and in my view the only one I have grown that really remains dwarf in stature. It grows well in a trough but must not be allowed to become waterlogged. It can also be planted directly into a boulder of tufa, but it does associate well in the garden, as in nature, with *Silene acaulis*, with its tight cushions and bright pink flowers. Even out of flower, this edelweiss has the most wonderful silver, downy foliage nestling in a tight tuft, followed by short 2 to 5 CM stems, each with a huge edelweiss flower. It will produce self-sown seedlings that should be allowed to establish randomly amongst its close associates.

One of the most popular of spring-flowering alpine plants for a trough is *Douglasia vitaliana* (synonym *Vitaliana primuliflora*), which in most of its European locations is strictly calcifuge. Here, in amongst the weathered limestones of the Majella, is perhaps the best form of all, *Vitaliana primuliflora* subsp. *praetutiana* (synonym *Douglasia vitaliana* subsp. *praetutiana*), growing alongside a very fine form of *Androsace villosa*. How well the two would associate on a trough, the vitaliana/douglasia with its glowing yellow flowers over lax cushions, and the white-flowering androsace. I have not found this douglasia form to be at all fussy about soil pH, but it does require an open, sunny, well-drained position. I have never raised this form or the type species from seed, but it is easily propagated from cuttings. It is a rewarding alpine plant, unique in its section, with bright yellow flowers, and it ranks very highly amongst alpine gardeners.

Another high alpine species that would associate well with the douglasia in a trough is *Gentiana orbicularis*, found growing in the same locality. It is a member of the verna group of gentians, and although very closely related to *G. brachyphylla*, it is easily identified because of its preference for a limestone substrate. It is distributed widely at altitudes of 2000 to 2800 M in the Alps, and here in the Apennines it can form large cushions. The flowers are a striking, deep blue on short stems with very attractive orbiculate foliage. It is a real gem for a trough but will need to be sought out diligently to find the true plant. Once captured, it can be multiplied from freshly sown seed.

If ever there was an alpine plant for which I will diligently search, my final choice from these rather special mountains fits the bill. If the reader has a taste for the diverse members of the buttercup family, Ranunculaceae, and believes that the already described *Ranunculus parnassifolius* found in the Pyrénées and Cantabrian Mountains is desirable, what about an almost stemless adonis with typically golden-yellow flowers? Well, here amongst the highest habitats for plant life in the Majella, between 2500 and 2700 м, where the snows do not recede until June, is one of the most elusive treasures, *Adonis distorta*. I say *elusive* because little has been written or known about this species until our attention was drawn to it by Vojtěch Holubec. It is found in a scree habitat, much as the Pyrenean species *A. pyrenaica* prefers. But here it nestles between pieces of limestone and tufts of grass, forming cushions of deep green, incised (deeply cut) foliage, dotted with huge golden flowers. If any of us are lucky enough to source growing plants or freshly collected seed of this species, I have no doubt it would like to be planted in a deep soil with added limestone rubble. It would surely associate well with the closely related calcicoles, *Callianthemum kernerianum* and *Campanula raineri*.

Continuing my search for some of the most attractive of European alpine species, it is so rewarding to encounter newly introduced or recently described plants. Surely some more are still awaiting our attention, but meanwhile the many well-established plants which are easily obtained provide the backbone of our chosen species for the garden.

For many readers, central Italy is perhaps most notable for its famous cities of Rome and Florence. These in turn are also famous for their Frascati and Chianti wines, respectively. But I hope to have raised the profile of the little known Italian treasure, the Apennine mountains, home to a number of outstanding alpine garden plants.

View toward the Schachen Garden

6: The Eastern Alps

The Austrian and Bavarian Alps

Many of us who have visited Austria and southern Germany have been affected by the warmth and friendliness of the people there. Nowhere is this more evident than in the mountains, where one can immediately recognise their endemic population by a "*Gruss Gott*" greeting as we meet on an alpine path or enter a mountain hut for some sustenance.

Within this chapter, I will include the Bavarian Alps, really an extension of the Austrian Alps. This part of southern Germany is home to an important alpine garden, the Schachen Garden, in which many horticulturists have learned the rudiments of serious alpine gardening and which is the source of many of the fine photographs contained within this book.

Some readers may be surprised at the number of pictures included within these pages that appear to illustrate alpine plants in their native habitat. They may contend that showing a perfect picture of an alpine plant in nature is misleading to the lowland gardener. I do not believe this is the case; rather, here is an opportunity for readers who have not yet had the privilege of encountering these plants in the wild to catch a glimpse of their natural representation. It serves as a lead to which we may aspire in our quest to grow the particular plant, in character, in our own garden. Let's not allow an obvious challenge to prevent us from trial and error. Many disappointments have spurred me on to eventual success. Reading about a particular plant's natural requirements and viewing a picture of the plant at its best will, I hope, provide a further catalyst for our endeavours. I also wish to point out that the pictures within this volume, most notably those of both Wilhelm and Dieter Schacht, are taken not only by professional photographers but by artists in their field. I have watched and admired Dieter's photography on many occasions, and although he does not waste time,

Dieter Schacht photographing in Engadine, Switzerland
Photo by Jim Jermyn.

he does take great care with each picture's composition. The results you can see for yourself in the many photographs used throughout this book. Let's also not forget their work in growing these European alpine species in the Schachen Garden.

Although much of the Schachen Garden is a natural outcrop of limestone rock garden, the concept of any garden is contrived and artificial. Young plants have to be nurtured to withstand a period of drought and to cope with the changing climate, to mention just two challenges facing the horticulturist. The Schachen Alpine Garden, which is host to many of the alpines pictured in this book, is very much a garden, and we can all learn from the experience and trials of the gardeners responsible for its care and culture.

Many parts of the Bavarian Alps support a calcicole flora, yet as we consider the main part of the chapter about the plants of Austria, a much broader picture emerges. From a botanical point of view, Austria can be regarded as an eastward extension of Switzerland. The main alpine chain continues eastward in a series of great blocks—the Oetztaler Alps, the Hohe Tauern, and the Niedere Tauern—until we reach the lower altitude of the Schneeberg mountains. Austria extends for some 217 km, but because of the high alpine passes and tunnels, it seems much more than this as we make our journey to enjoy its rich flora.

The greater part of these mountains supports a calcifuge flora often found thriving in a silicaceous or mica schist substrate. There are, though, calcareous mountains supporting a very different selection of plants, and once again this clear differentiation of substrate must guide us as we prepare a home for our chosen plant in the garden.

The Hohe Tauern is perhaps the richest area in the Austrian Alps and home to many lovely plants we will attempt to grow in our gardens. It reaches across parts of three provinces: Tyrol, Salzburg, and Carinthia. Much of the area is designated as a national park and includes the nation's highest mountain, the Grossglockner (3798 m). Austria's Hohe Tauern is home to a number of saxifrages that are of great horticultural significance. The area is particularly rich in members of the subsection *Oppositifolia*, with the best known of the species being *Saxifraga oppositifolia* itself.

Few of us have not enjoyed growing this species and a number of its fine variations at some time or another. There seem to be a concentration of related species and forms in these parts, where many of them choose to grow in loose gravel and in natural rock crevices on schistose formations. The species *Saxifraga oppositifolia* can be found in two quite distinct forms: *S. oppositifolia* subsp. *oppositifolia* and *S. oppositifolia* subsp. *blepharophylla*. So how do they differentiate in nature? First of all, the former is the most common and widespread geographically, occurring in the mountains of Scotland and represented in gardens by some outstanding cultivars. These include the very fine, free-flowering *S. oppositifolia* 'Theoden', which would be my first choice for its sheer flower power. Any one of these chosen cultivars produce a prostrate mat with trailing stems covered with small, unstalked, opposite leaves of a bluish green colour, often lime-encrusted. The almost stemless flowers are large and frequently open up to 20 MM in diameter. In the case of 'Theoden', they are a rich rose-purple.

Saxifraga oppositifolia

When any of the most vigorous cultivars are planted out, they must be given a cool position out of direct sunlight and in a lean mixture. I do not believe that the soil pH is at all significant, as the type species appears to grow on both calcareous and acidic formations. When planted in a rich mixture, plants will lose their true character and expand quickly to form large mats of woody stems, but it is my experience that they generally become exhausted after about two years and need to be replaced. I love to grow these saxifrages in a cool position away from the exposure of early afternoon sun and position them so that they can fall over the edge of a trough or run down between rocks. The pure white-flowering cultivar, *Saxifraga oppositifolia* 'Corrie Fee', is also an outstanding one. They can all be propagated successfully by cuttings taken after the new growth has ripened. A rooting mixture of sand and perlite is recommended.

The Hohe Tauern is home to a very fine form of the *Saxifraga oppositifolia* subsp. *blepharophylla*. To the casual plantsperson, the botanical differences

Saxifraga oppositifolia subsp. *rudolphiana*

between the subspecies are minimal, but on closer inspection it will be noted that in this one the hairs on the leaf margin continue all the way to the rounded apex, whereas in the type species these hairs stop short of the apex. Yes, a minor point, but this is a very fine variation, and when available in a free-flowering form, *S. oppositifolia* subsp. *blepharophylla* will prove a most valuable addition for the garden.

The next variation I want to describe has often been regarded as a good species. It is certainly the most extreme of all the forms in terms of its habit. *Saxifraga oppositifolia* subsp. *rudolphiana* will rank as one of Europe's choicest alpine plants, and when seen at its floral best will vie with any of the best dionysias. When botanising on the Grossglockner Pass in July 2004, specimens of this saxifrage which I was so eagerly seeking were covered for longer than usual with a blanket of snow. This very distinct subspecies is identified by its tiny, almost microscopic, leaves and very hard cushions or mats. The flowers in this instance are fairly uniform, a deep reddish purple. It grows on schistose outcrops and loose gravel at an altitude of around 2500 м. Now to the challenge presented by this subspecies: how to grow it in the garden. I have succeeded in pleasing it sufficiently only to coax it to form a neat cushion of foliage. A label close by proved that this was the case to any skeptics, but could I flower it? No, and I have still not succeeded! This does not mean that it is in any way less deserving of our continued trials, but if we are being reasonable I would direct the reader to its more reliable cousins as the sensible choice for the garden. If the reader can make his or her way to these parts of Austria and the season is spot on in terms of the time of flowering, a treat is in store.

Another species within this subsection is the easily cultivated *Saxifraga retusa*. The specific epithet means slightly notched at the tip, but I have failed to identify this feature either in the leaf or petal tips. It is, though, a fine species for a trough, forming a tight mat of shiny green leaves and a mass of purplish red flowers in clusters of two or three. This attractive plant flourishes on a trough or raised bed, but I would always try and position it in such a way that it can fall down between pieces of lime-free stones.

It is certainly the case with all these saxifrages that drought is their main enemy. Despite their growing in schistose gravel or a cleft in a cliff or boulder in nature, their roots can find moisture. At the other extreme, they also resent an excess of winter wet, and I would strongly recommend a winter cloche cover for these species.

Growing in a similar habitat but often confined to the windswept ridges in open positions, where it does not compete with the meadow flora, is *Dianthus glacialis*. This observation is perhaps significant, because I have found that despite it being easily raised from seed and forming tight little cushions on a trough of an acidic, gritty substrate, longevity is not a feature of this species. Young plants should be planted in an open position between flat stones on a raised bed in an acidic, shaly gravel mix, where the tight cushions will flower profusely. The flowers, on 15 to 18 mm stems, are an intense pink with serrated petals and are borne freely above a tight cushion of bright green, linear leaves. Self-sown seedlings should be allowed to establish and perpetuate the flowering sequence.

Belonging to the same family, Caryophyllaceae, is an attractive alpine soapwort, *Saponaria pumilio*. It, too, frequents the summit gravels of the Hohe Tauern but is equally satisfied when tightly wedged between vast slabs of weather-riven granite in the southern Dolomites. It is fiercely calcifuge, forming shiny domes and mats the size of a football. These great lucent domes emanate from just one central taproot, which, along with their lateral roots, will search out cool depths in either sharp grit, rock, or blackest humus. In the Hohe Tauern, the flower buds are often visible by mid-July but seldom open fully until early August. The pale to deep pink flowers sit on dark red, baggy, and sticky calyces.

Dianthus glacialis

This is a lovely, late-flowering species for the raised bed, where it should be wedged between stones in an acidic mixture. It can be raised from seed and has been parent to a couple of outstanding garden hybrids that are deserving of inclusion in our alpine plant collection. They are *Saponaria* ×*olivana* and *S*. 'Bressingham Hybrid'. The first is a hybrid between *S. pumilio* and *S. caespitosa*. It forms a more open and lax cushion than *S. pumilio* and makes a first-class plant to position at the edge of a sunny wall or perimeter of a raised bed. Here it will produce a mass of radiating stems, clothed with large, apple blossom–pink flowers in profusion during the summer months. It is a sterile hybrid and must therefore be propagated by stem cuttings that root easily when taken after flowering.

The vibrant, deep pink–flowering hybrid, 'Bressingham Hybrid', is a cross between *Saponaria oxymoides* and *S*. ×*olivana*. This one produces wide, red-stemmed mats with soft, hairy leaves. The tip of each stem terminates in a cluster of deepest pink flowers in late spring to early summer. As with the previous hybrid, stem cuttings will provide a ready means of reproduction.

A plant I have grown very fond of as a result of many high alpine encounters

Saponaria ×olivana

is *Gentiana bavarica* subsp. *imbricata*. This member of the verna group is often found associating with the white-flowering form (so typical of the Eastern Alps) of *Androsace alpina* and *Ranunculus glacialis* in the Hohe Tauern. It is an alpine plant in its truest term, occurring at 2400 to 3000 m. It is characteristically free-flowering, forming a tight, congested cushion with almost circular leaves set so closely together as to resemble tiles on a roof. It is this description and its insistence on a lime-free substrate that differentiates it from its closest relatives. Its neat tuft of lime-green foliage covered with the deepest blue flowers is a sight to behold in late spring. If a nursery-grown specimen is located, it should be given pride of place and have its beauty admired. It is best propagated from freshly sown seed collected as soon as the fat capsules have swollen to maturity.

We all love to grow *Gentiana verna* in its most widely available form in commerce, and it is simple and relatively unfussy of culture. This high alpine subspecies of the Bavarian gentian demands more care and attention. It should be tucked in between shaly pieces of schistose rock and given pride of position in a trough. In order to promote free-flowering, it should be positioned in full sun. I

Gentiana bavarica subsp. *imbricata*

have found to my cost that during a long, dry spell during the summer months it must not be allowed to dry out completely.

If I may take the reader to lower elevations, there are two spring-flowering alpine plants for which we must attempt to find a home in our gardens. The first is *Callianthemum anemonoides* that favours alkaline soils in the Austrian Alps, where it is found growing amongst rocky terrain within the subalpine zone. It is rarely found above 1500 M and sometimes considerably lower, frequenting open clearings amongst pine woods. This species is closely related to its Italian cousin, *C. kernerianum*, and if the two are planted together in the garden there is little to differentiate them. All that this glorious member of the buttercup family requires is a rich, deep, gritty loam. It greatly appreciates a generous topping of up to 10 CM of gravel, through which it can push its early flowers. They nestle together in a huddle, resembling anything but a buttercup or a member of Ranunculaceae.

When working at the Munich Botanic Garden, I first encountered this outstanding *Callianthemum anemonoides* positioned between large boulders of limestone on the rock garden. I will never forget watching the flowers, reminiscent of dahlia buds, opening up before the emerging foliage to reveal large, creamy

Watering during the growing season

On the subject of watering, I would like to counsel the reader to pay careful attention to the best time of day to carry out this essential practice. Most plants, when undergoing their cycle of growth, are experiencing significant stress during the hottest part of the day. Some species, most notably saxatile plants, have adapted to cope with periods of drought through hirsute foliage or glaucous leaves to hold on to their own moisture reserves. Others do not cope as well. It is in these cases that I would water thoroughly at the coolest part of the day—just before I go to bed at night or first thing in the morning. Care should be taken, though, not to overwater species such as *Leontopodium alpinum* subsp. *nivale* and certain Aretian androsaces. I have been responsible for killing both plants in this category through overwatering, and at the other extreme neglecting the watering of *Gentiana verna* subsp. *oschtenica*. It can be so annoying when we know what a plant needs and still forget to apply these obvious requirements.

Gentiana verna

pink, many rayed, composite-looking flowers. Years later, when running Edrom Nurseries, I exhibited a mature clump of this species (which had been presented to me on my departure from Munich) in an orange box at a Scottish

Callianthemum anemonoides in cultivation
Photo by Klaus Patzner.

Rock Garden Club Stirling Show in early March. During judging, I left the vicinity of the show hall and later returned to commence selling to the public. I noticed, to my amazement, a large certificate stating that the plant had won the Forrest Medal (awarded to the best plant in the show)—much to the chagrin of one or two dedicated amateurs, whose prize plants had been beaten by this upstart of a professional (not planned, I can assure readers). One of them approached me, saying, "So when are you going to offer this scruffy daisy then?" I replied, "When I have succeeded in bulking up stock of this lovely buttercup". Like me, all those years ago, he was surprised to know that he was looking at a little-known member of the buttercup family. Wilhelm Schacht introduced this plant to the Munich Botanic Garden from its native Austria, and it has now become widely available in commerce since this early introduction. It received an FCC in 1992.

As with its close cousin, *Callianthemum kernerianum*, *C. anemonoides* can easily be cultivated, and stocks should be replenished from seed, collected, and handled in the same manner as was described for the Italian species.

The most rewarding of all the subalpine snowbells in terms of culture is *Soldanella montana*, as it will form a large clump up to 15 cm across. It inhabits pine woods at altitudes around 1600 m in Austria and seems quite unfussy about soil pH in cultivation. The vigorous clumps consist of rounded, leathery, deep green leaves, with the margins slightly scalloped. The flowers open in late spring and typically resemble fringed bells, in this case a pleasing purple colour held on 15 CM stems. An excellent form of this species raised at Jack Drake's Nursery was awarded an FCC and represents a vigorous, free-flowering clone. The species is easily propagated either from seed or from division of the clumps after flowering and should be much more widely grown.

The Austrian Alps are home to a number of primulas belonging to the section *Auricula*. Nowhere in my experience is the type species for this section, *Primula auricula*, better represented than in the limestones of upper and lower Austria. I described the heavily farinose form from the locality around Lake Garda, *P. auricula* var. *albocincta*, and the typical form of this species is equally virtuous but often lacking the meal, or farina.

More local, though, is the beautiful calcicole species *Primula clusiana*, belonging to the subsection *Arthritica*. As with most species of European primulas, it is variable in flower quality and is represented in gardens by a very fine form given the cultivar name *P. clusiana* 'Murray-Lyon', which is both free-flowering and vigorous in habit. The species belongs

Soldanella montana

Primula auricula

Primula auricula

to the northern calcareous Alps of Austria and a few stations in the Bavarian Alps of southeast Germany. It is sufficiently separated from its close relative found farther east, *P. wulfeniana*, and is usually located above the treeline between 1800 and 2500 M. It prefers short turf or moist rock fissures and is capable of assuming large, dense colonies where it forms a stout rhizome with fleshy rosettes of pointed, glossy green leaves. The flowers, which appear in spring, are a bright rose-pink colour and held in an umbel of up to four flowers on 5 to 10 CM stems.

Primula clusiana is easily grown in a moisture-retentive soil and does not seem to demand a calcareous substrate in the garden. I have not yet found that my own seed-raised stock produce the finest of flower colours, so I have tended to retain the cultivar *P. clusiana* 'Murray-Lyon', which must be propagated vegetatively. It would be helpful to raise fresh stock of this species, but only the best forms should be retained. Some authorities have suggested that the clone 'Murray-Lyon' is a hybrid between *P. clusiana* and *P. minima*. I do not share this view, but the hybrid does occur throughout the range of *P. clusiana* when it meets up with *P. minima* and is named *P. ×intermedia*. This hybrid is represented in the Schachen Garden by a very fine form, and it is this one which I am currently growing. Both Farrer and Will Ingwersen rated this cross as one of the best of all natural European primula hybrids. I would agree.

It produces larger, more oval-pointed leaves, retaining the fine teeth of *Primula minima*. The flowers are very much intermediate between the two parents, large and carmine-pink, and held in a short umbel of two flowers. It is a free-flowering hybrid that will vary according to the form collected, but it grows happily in my alpine bed in a well-drained, moisture-retentive soil in full sun. It is a sterile clone and should be lifted every three or four years and divided to replenish stocks.

Perhaps a baker's dozen or so European alpine species can be regarded as the *crème de la crème*. Into this category comes—somewhere near the top in terms of the impression it makes in nature—*Androsace helvetica*. I have met up with this species in a number of locations in the Alps, most notably in the Dolomites, but a colleague of mine, Klaus Patzner, has provided a collage of stunning photographs, which he recorded quite masterfully in upper Austria.

Androsace helvetica
Photos by Klaus Patzner.

When I first set my eyes on this species, I was not prepared for its beauty and was totally taken aback by the perfection displayed with the glistening ash-green tomentose domes seemingly fastened to the limestone cliffs. These cushions are studded with sessile flowers of milky white with golden eyes. A well-flowered cushion seen in nature is a stunning experience and can leave the lucky onlooker quite spellbound.

It prefers calcareous rocks and a sunny exposure, while some of the cushions will be used to a lengthy snow cover, with others left hopelessly exposed to the year-round weathers. Yet their final behaviour seems no different. I once asked Duncan Lowe what he thought about its cultivation before purchasing plants myself. He stated that much depended on the selection of seedlings. Here was some sound advice, for he was advising me to raise a batch of seedlings and choose only the strongest and fittest for onward cultivation.

There is no doubt that having closely inspected the tomentose nature of the cushions, somewhat similar to the equally challenging *Eritrichium nanum*, *Androsace helvetica* is going to resent any form of top watering. It certainly will grow when wedged between limestone in full exposure to light but only when it is protected by an overhang of rock. A boulder of tufa would also make an ideal home in a similar position, but in both of these artificial locations the cushions must be fully protected from the weather during the late autumn and winter months. Many readers will undoubtedly play safe and employ the services of an alpine house plunge bed. This very special androsace is worth all our endeavours but is also an example of a plant to seek out in its native habitat, to enjoy and savour the photographic experience over and over again.

Moving farther east into the Eisenhut group at the eastern end of the Hohe Tauern, there are a number of plants for which we would do well to find a home. Still with an eye on androsaces, a wonderful species inhabits the imposing Eisenhut (2441 M) itself, growing on the windswept ridge in fissures of weathered shale. *Androsace wulfeniana* produces fairly tight cushions which are bright green this time and more sparsely flowered but glowing with flowers of deepest pink with a yellow eye. Having climbed to truly alpine elevations, it is always exhilarating to find a plant of this calibre at its very best. This was my experience during the past summer whilst botanising in Austria. Once we had

Androsace wulfeniana

found the pristine flowering cushions, the only negative comment related to the lack of natural light, blue sky, and the odd puff of cloud. How unreasonable can we plantsfolk be!

Translating this species to the garden concept is further challenging—and requires the very best of luck. It is demanding of a lime-free, gravelly mixture with plenty of air both around the cushion and its roots. Thin slithers of shaly material should be placed carefully under the edge of the cushions and a cloche cover is essential during the dormant season. Careful collection of seed can be carried out to initiate a means of propagation.

Growing in close proximity to the androsace is another primula of the section *Auricula*. It is the last of the subsection *Erythrodrosum* to be described and is surely one of the most virtuous of the group, *Primula villosa*, flowering in late spring. I was able to admire its flowers at an altitude of around 1900 to 2100 M near to the Turracher Höhe in the Nockberge National Park. It displays all the features so typical of its subsection with a neat rhizome with sticky, green leaves with the characteristic reddish glandular hairs on both surfaces. An umbel of up to eight flowers is held on a stem 3 to 10 CM in length; these are a bright magenta-rose to soft pink, often with a white eye. In nature, the plants are equally at home wedged into humus-filled crevices of silaceous rock or growing in stony alpine turf. It is therefore advisable to choose a lime-free mixture for this species and position it between rocks on a raised bed in full sun. The rosettes are slow to develop into clumps and therefore seed is a better means of increase.

For me, the greatest thrill in this part of Austria is provided by two pulsatillas, one which is widely distributed in the Alps, *Pulsatilla vernalis*, and the other which is rarely seen but deserving of just as many plaudits as the former. *Pulsatilla alba* is little known in horticulture and is often confused with *P. alpina* (synonym *P. alpina* subsp. *alpina*). In fact, the former has been named *P. alpina* subsp. *austriaca* in some current literature. So familiar are plantsfolk with the tall, robust-growing *P. alpina* subsp. *alpina*, which prefers (but not exclusively) an alkaline soil, that the Austrian species stands out distinctly. It has another disjunct occurrence in the Apennine Mountains,

Primula villosa
Photo by Jim Jermyn.

Pulsatilla vernalis

Pulsatilla alba

but is seen at its best in the Nockberge and the Sextener Dolomites. *Pulsatilla alba* is much dwarfer in stature, rarely exceeding 15 cm in height, forming large clumps of beautifully divided foliage and masses of perfectly formed, glistening white flowers, often with a blue reverse to the petals. The impression, when traversing a stony meadow amidst many hundreds of these pulsatillas staking their claim along with carpets of *Loiseleuria procumbens*, *Primula minima*, and *Primula glutinosa*, is quite stunning. It is my experience that this species prefers a lime-free substrate, but there may be exceptions as with most pulsatillas. Whilst searching for new plants amongst great colonies of this pulsatilla, our party located a stunning lemon-yellow variant of the species; this, too was of mouthwatering beauty. We each reflected, though, later in the day that the species is rarely ever seen in gardens. I certainly know that established clumps of the species thrive in the garden of Alan Furness of Hexham, northern England, but I have yet to encounter it in a plant catalogue.

Freshly collected seed should provide the best means of raising plants, and there can be no valid reason for it proving tricky of culture. Once established, clumps of these true alpine pulsatillas should not be disturbed but allowed to expand, whereupon they will set copious amounts of seed which must be sown as soon as it is collected. What makes this species so outstanding amongst its peers is that in nature it is clump-forming, whereas most of its relatives are generally found in vast numbers consisting of solitary plants.

This observation is often the case with the lady of the snow, which ranks as one of the most desirable of all alpine plants. *Pulsatilla vernalis* enjoys a wide distribution and is so named because of its early flowering, as soon as the snows recede. This fact has frustrated me on many occasions, none more so than this previous season when I was botanising in Austria. The finite timing of a trip to the Alps is such that whatever dates one chooses, there is a good chance of missing the pulsatillas but gaining the alpine primulas or enjoying the lower meadows and missing out on the higher alpines. The last two years (2003 and 2004) in the European Alps have contrasted strongly in terms of snow cover, and as we experience further extremes in our climate change, we will just have to be adaptable once we arrive at our destination.

We began our ascent of a popular mountain in the Sextener Dolomites, passing steep, grassy meadows simply sheeted with *Pulsatilla vernalis* just beginning to lose flowers and pass on to the shaggy seed heads. The multitudes of single plants displayed no further colour, and we simply reflected on what might have been a few weeks earlier. As we still saw evidence of unmelted snows, we questioned whether it would have been possible to ascend the mountain to enjoy these pulsatillas when they were at their best. What is it, though, that makes *P. vernalis* so desirable? For me it is its dwarf stature, short stems of 5 to 10 CM, each supporting a great goblet staring up at the sun, white as an opalescent pearl within and the outside a mix of gold and violet silk. Some flowers have a pinkish sheen. When waiting for the sun to shine on them they are sullen, nodding goblets, yet they transform dramatically with light and open up to the onlooker.

Pulsatilla vernalis

In the garden they present no difficulties but demand an open position with a deep, well-drained soil mixture. I would recommend planting this pulsatilla, like its relatives the adonis and callianthemum, with a generous topping of up to 10 CM of gravel. This provision will help to deter rotting at the neck so often caused by an attack of slugs that enjoy nestling around the old and decaying foliage at the base of the plants.

A working mill, Defereggen Tal, Austria

Another asset that makes this pulsatilla, along with all its related species, so special are the seed heads which follow flowering. These seeds provide the only practical means of propagation, and as the floppy heads mature, a careful tug will prise the seeds away and into a bag ready for immediate sowing. I generally lay the seed quite haphazardly and thickly on top of the levelled compost in the seed pot or tray, allowing at least 2 cm of space below the top of the container. I then sieve about 5 to 10 mm of seed compost on top of the seed, above which I will add the same amount of chick grit. The pots are then carefully labelled, placed in a tray of water until soaked, and then plunged in sand. The seedlings may germinate quickly, but I prefer to allow them to go dormant during the winter and then single out and pot them up the following spring. If the pot of congested seedlings is allowed to sit too long, the roots will become so inter-twined that severe losses will occur at the time of potting. It is for this reason that some growers choose to handle the seedlings soon after germination when the first true leaves have established. Either way, care must be taken to protect the seedlings from excessive sunlight during the first summer. Seedlings of *Pulsatilla vernalis* usually commence flowering in the second season.

Closely related to the pulsatillas is another member of the buttercup family, *Callianthemum coriandrifolium*, which is found in robust form in the Austrian

Callianthemum coriandrifolium

Campanula alpina

Dianthus sylvestris

Alps. It is easily distinguished from its European cousins *C. anemonoides* and *C. kernerianum*, with its more lush, deeply cut, branching foliage and pure white flowers. It is less compact than the other two species but certainly deserves a place in a deep, organic, lime-free soil. Although fairly widely distributed in the Alps, it is a true alpine and is found in fine form in the Hohe Tauern. Clumps should be left undisturbed, and freshly sown seed is the best means of reproduction.

A plant that I have always found enchanting both in its native Eastern Alps and in the garden is *Campanula alpina*. Sadly, it is seldom seen in gardens or offered in the specialist catalogues. In many ways it resembles a miniature expression of the bearded bellflower, *C. barbata*. It is a dwarf taprooting species which loves to occupy the alpine turf along with *Soldanella pusilla*, *Pulsatilla alba*, and *Primula minima*. It may not be strictly calcifuge, but I would recommend a lime-free substrate for its cultivation. It is summer-flowering, producing a 5 to 10 CM stem with numerous slate-blue flowers hanging like a graceful fountain of blossom. Each bell displays a pretty fringe of hairs. This choice species should be planted in a gritty, lean mixture to encourage it to perform for several years. It is neither monocarpic nor biennial, but it has a tendency to exhaust itself to death. It sets copious amounts of seed and is a valuable addition to the raised bed or rock garden.

Many members of the pink family are deserving of a place in the alpine garden, but few of us are prepared to experiment with the lesser known species. Although in 2004 I was a little too early for the flowers of *Dianthus sylvestris*, I was made aware of the charming qualities of this species whilst botanising in the Nockberge. It loves to seed into crevices on limestone boulders, where its short, arching stems, clothed with its vibrant carmine-pink flowers, arrest the passerby. It is from these dwarfer manifestations that I would choose plants for the garden and position them at the edge of a trough or raised bed. Here, the arching stems of vibrant pink can be fully appreciated during early summer. Further stocks can be raised from seed.

I will conclude my description of the Austrian flora by moving farther east to the Schneeberg group of mountains within sight of that great city, Vienna.

Here are some more alpine treasures that deserve a prominent position in the garden. Summer colour in the alpine garden is always a priority with such a concentration of species flowering during the spring months. Generally speaking, *Campanula* is a genus we can rely on with this in mind. Another of my especial favourites is *C. pulla*, occupying a restricted area of distribution in eastern Austria. As Farrer rightly described this species, "It is the imperial glory of the alpine section" (1919). Although a calcicole in nature, *C. pulla* is not concerned at all about the soil type in cultivation, and I wish only to advise the reader to

Campanula pulla

employ some caution to apply the brakes owing to its ability to expand rapidly from its roots. Position it between deep boulders of limestone and allow it to fill a decent patch, where it will send out its thready rootlets and appear with bright green, glossy leaves, from which arise a myriad of shining bells, a glorious violet satin. Dwarf in habit, it contrasts wonderfully during the summer months with yellow-flowering potentillas and can easily be reduced in dimensions and rejuvenated from simple division. I found a beautiful pure white-flowering form when visiting Josef Holzbecher's wonderfully stocked nursery in Brno, Czech Republic. *Campanula pulla* 'Alba' is a valuable addition to augment the purple type species.

Another campanula I have come to enjoy more and more is the monocarpic species *Campanula thyrsoides*. Although widespread throughout the Alps, it is often found in very fine forms in eastern Austria. It inhabits the upper meadows and is immediately recognised by its tall, thick, 30 CM spikes adorned with many erect, straw-yellow bells during the summer. The flowers are fragrant, and their colour is a pleasing diversion from the characteristic blue of the race. It forms a stout rosette of narrow leaves and replenishes itself from an abundance of seed. It is too tall for a raised bed but associates well in an alpine bed or rock garden.

Gentiana pumila

Of the specialities found here in the east, one of the choicest is a little member of the verna group of gentians, *Gentiana pumila*. It is generally found between an altitudinal band of 1600 to 2500 M, where it grows in short turf and stony places. It is a calcicole, often accompanied by *Primula clusiana*, *Dryas octopetala*, and *Androsace villosa*. This species forms little tufts with rosettes of linear foliage and short 3 to 8 CM stems, each bearing a dark blue verna-type flower. It is not difficult to please in a trough consisting of a calcareous mixture, positioned in full sun. Freshly sown seed will enable growers to replenish stocks.

An alpine buttercup of some merit that closely resembles the Italian *Ranunculus bilobus* is *R. crenatus*, native to the Eastern Alps. In its best forms it produces large, white flowers during the late spring and can be determined by its toothed, heart-shaped leaves. As with all buttercups, the mature clumps can be divided after flowering or propagated by seed sown as soon as it is collected.

Closely related to both *Soldanella pusilla* and *S. minima* is a local endemic, *S. austriaca*, which is perhaps the most desirable of all soldanellas. It displays pink to lilac fringed flowers with additional stripes of a deeper colour. Neat little clumps of orbiculate leaves can be divided up after flowering, or seed can be saved. What an enchanting group of plants are the soldanellas.

The previous species is perhaps as local as the next alpine treasure, *Viola alpina*, which is found in the easternmost Austrian Alps and again in the Carpathians. It is particularly at home on the Schneeberg, where it grows between limestone rubble at higher elevations of 2000 M or lower down in the alpine turf, where it associates with *Campanula alpina* and *Soldanella austriaca*. It is a precious little viola, with dark blue flowers with a creamy white centre. It will grow well on a trough, associating with species such as *Campanula raineri* and *Primula auricula* in a mixture containing a calcareous soil with pieces of limestone incorporated to provide an additional cool root run. As with other choice species of viola, seed must be saved on a regular basis and can be sown either in situ or in pots for a later redistribution.

My final choice involves one of the best known of all alpine plants, *Dianthus alpinus*. Some readers will pronounce it as the most precious of its race. I am torn

Viola alpina

for my favourite between this variable species, the exquisitely marked flowers of *D. callizonus* from Romania, or the vibrant show created by *D. pavonius*. A difficult one! The real forte of this species is its ease of culture; despite it being a calcicole plant, it is quite happy growing in an acid soil and will reward its grower with a sheet of flowers on an annual basis with the minimum of effort employed. During July and August it creates a lovely display of various shades of pink in nature and adorns the high alpine turf of the Wiener Schneeberg from 1500 to 2000 M.

All this species asks is uncluttered space in a well-drained soil, where it forms wide, luscious mats of emerald green. The flowers are immense, often up to 3 CM in diameter, rounded with overlapping petals and typically rose-crimson in colour. The greatest fun possible is raising this species from seed

Dianthus alpinus

and selecting favourite colours as they come into flower. The variation is considerable, with some flowers more deeply fringed, some with showy peacock eyes of purple, and others a soft pink or even white. It is my view that seed-raised plants are generally of a stronger constitution than those raised from cuttings. But once a clone has been selected and named, subsequent propagation has to be of a vegetative nature to maintain purity of stock. The most popular cultivars include *Dianthus alpinus* 'Adonis', an old cultivar apparently found by Farrer in its native habitat, with flowers opening salmon-pink and fading to white. I have now lost my stock but it may still prevail. *Dianthus alpinus* 'Joan's Blood' has deep crimson-purple flowers, and *D. alpinus* 'Millstream Salmon' has attractive salmon-pink flowers. Each one of these cultivars will add to the abundant range of flower colours that can be raised from home-collected seed. This form of gardening takes the fun of growing alpine plants to a new dimension and reminds us of the far-reaching possibilities that nature offers.

As we close the book on this richly diverse country of Austria, I think we can better appreciate that it is not only the pride of classical music that emanates from its illustrious citizens, but their whole heritage provided by its long chain of mountains. It is from this great range of mountains that both tourism and we gardeners have greatly benefited. No doubt we will continue to do so for many millennia.

The Dolomites

I have now reached the part of the Alps with which I am most familiar and to which I have become particularly attached. It is an alpine region in northeastern Italy that meets up with the Austrian and former Yugoslavian frontiers. The alpine scenery created by the unique formation of these mountains is truly spectacular. Having led a number of botanical tours to the Dolomites, I know that when married couples have joined me, where the wife is the keen plantswoman, the husband has never been bored owing to his being totally immersed in the scenery, pretty villages, and the endemic people along with their mouth-watering fares, grappas, and cappuccinos. This is an area that appears to be lacking in nothing a visitor could wish for.

The distinctive geology of the Dolomites is also what makes this area so special. I should explain very briefly that the term *dolomite* refers to a crystalline magnesian limestone. Many of the best known mountain ranges here, or *Grupe*, form great pinnacles and castellations with both vertical and horizontal cleavages. From a botanical point of view, it is significant to mention that a number of clearly defined mountains are composed of hard granite or silicaceous formations supporting a calcifuge flora. The real fun is created when the typical

Weisshorn, Italy

dolomite meets up with the granite or volcanic intrusions, often separated by a narrow valley. It is fascinating how both the calcareous and calcifuge floras suddenly apply their brakes and rarely meet in the middle. It is when we are armed with the rudiments of this geological theory that we can make accurate conclusions as to the correct identity of our favourite plants. Once we have made these observations in the field, we are also well placed to translate the fundamental requirements of each plant to our garden's constraints or adapt accordingly.

Owing to the significance of its geological makeup, the Dolomites comprises the richest flora of the Alps and is deserving of being further subdivided into the main ecological zones to help readers identify the requirements of its most desirable species.

The coniferous and wooded zone

I am an advocate, wherever possible, of making full use of the lifts available to walkers, raising them from the subalpine zone (which ranges here roughly from 1800 to 2400 m) up to the higher levels. Yet, countering this view, one of the finest experiences is setting off early in the morning and ascending on foot through the wooded zone in our quest for the higher alpines.

The peace and solitude that accompanies the hiker as this easy ascent is made is quite therapeutic. The first part often involves ambling horizontally through the lower meadows and then, following a mountain stream, the gentle ascent commences. The wooded zone generally comprises pine, juniper, or birch, and each one of these plant types becomes dwarfer in stature as we gain height. Underneath the pine trees I always keep my eyes fixed in amongst the broken twigs and rotting pine needles for a sign of plant activity. My favourite species at this level is the single-flowered wintergreen, *Moneses uniflora* (also a rare Scottish native), but here in the Dolomites it runs about freely in full or dappled shade, with its large orbicular leaves. From each rosette of leaves springs one single stem, 6 to 9 cm in length, holding the most perfectly formed, nodding, wide-open cup of purest white with a protruding style. On closer examination,

Clematis alpina

there is still more beauty than I have described, with the venation of the petals. Armed with a flash camera, the evidence can be preserved but the plant left well alone. When material becomes available, I have only achieved success when planting it amongst an ancient rotting tree stump, where its threadlike roots so typical of Pyrolaceae will receive the rightful protection they desire. A challenge!

Running around in similar conditions is a plant we need not fuss over in our garden, *Linnaea borealis*, the lovely twin flower, whose Latin name commemorates the Swedish father of botany, Carl Linnaeus. This spreading member of the honeysuckle family, Caprifoliaceae, forms evergreen mats of slender stems and small, oval leaves. The flowers are most attractive and are held in pairs consisting of pendant bells a lovely pale pink in colour on short 9 CM stalks. It loves to be planted in acidic dappled shade in the garden and forms a perfect carpet of foliage under which to plant a variety of early-flowering bulbs that will contrast with the pink flowers in late spring. It can be propagated from cuttings.

As we gain a bit more altitude and the sunlight begins to make a more significant penetration, so the flora changes. Lower shrubs will become the natural support for the scrambling *Clematis alpina* (synonym *Atragene alpina*), a deciduous shrub that loves to climb to a modest height of about 2 M. A careful observation of the most attractive flowers reveals large blue to violet petals with striking, white petallike staminodes within. This species is popular in gardens, and my recommendation is to plant *C. alpina* 'Frances Rivis', which has the purest of blue flowers with the fine white inner staminodes, and allow it to scramble over an old stump as a foil for taller plants around it.

A number of attractive plants occupy the subalpine turf and grow at the edge of the paths. *Polygala chamaebuxus* is just such a species, a mat-forming perennial seldom without a flower at any time of the year. The shrubby milkwort loves to run around with its subterraneous stolons amongst stony turf, producing shiny, oval, leathery leaves and attractive pea flowers with a yellow and white keel. The form *P. chamaebuxus* var. *purpurea* has a

Polygala chamaebuxus
Photo by Jim Jermyn.

Cypripedium calceolus

yellow keel and purple wings. Both are invaluable garden plants and flower profusely throughout the growing season and beyond. They are best positioned in a cool wall, where the compact, shrubby growth can tumble down, and what a fine association they provide with a mixture of dwarfer ferns and either ramonda or haberleas planted in close proximity.

One of the highlights of walking through the wooded, subalpine zone is to enter the classic habitat for the lady's slipper orchid, *Cypripedium calceolus*. Having left the coniferous zone, the terrain often levels out as juniper bushes and deciduous scrub join together and establish themselves in the long since dried-up stony river beds, giving evidence of a previous period of ice or water movement. This habitat, with an underplanting of *Erica carnea*, is the ideal spot to commence a careful search for the orchid.

At one time, these plants were dug up and collected for the commercial market. Fortunately, this is now outlawed, and it is only the browsing cattle brought up from lower elevations at the time of flowering that threaten all but the plants carefully protected under a vicious canopy of *Pinus mugo* and *Juniperus communis*. In the summer of 2004 Dieter Schacht directed me to a particularly rich habitat that supported a large number of the orchids just beginning to peak and pass their best. Some of the clumps carried seven to eight flowers, while others were single, but any example of this outstanding orchid at its absolute best is a sight to stop anyone in his tracks.

The lady's slipper orchid is surprisingly easy to grow in the garden, particularly for those who garden on an alkaline soil. It prefers dappled shade and loves to be planted at the base of a tree or shrubs. The natural soil should be given a few bucketfuls of both fresh and well-rotted pine needles (not spruce or larch) to encourage the mycorhizal properties so vital for the success of the plants. At no time should the soil be overly compacted, and established clumps should be left undisturbed to provide the annual delight when the brown and yellow lady's slippers, along with their twisted petals, adorn themselves. For those of us who have a naturally acidic soil, I would recommend adding a dusting of dolomite dust to the soil along with some small lumps of limestone to accompany the additional pine litter. A high price may well be paid for the initial plants purchased, but what a thrill it is to reenact one of nature's great surprises.

The alpine meadow

A visit to the Dolomites during June or July is never complete without enjoying a walk through the Alpi di Siusi (Seiser Alm) above the bustling village of Ortisei (St. Ulrich). This is described by some writers as the most extensive alpine meadow in the Alps. It is very impressive. A fine time to enjoy this experience is the middle to end of June or early July. Thereafter, the farming community will have applied their scythes to the herbage, ready for storage and as fodder for the cattle.

An initial look at these meadows prior to traversing them is enlightening.

Alpi di Siusi (Seiser Alm)
Photo by Ian Pryde.

Rich alpine meadows

Survey the scene, the changing colours, and then proceed, remaining wherever possible on the well-trodden paths. Each contour provides a new association of plants. Predominant in the flora are myriads of orchids, leguminous plants (providing vital nitrogen-fixing properties), composites, campanulas, and vibrant lilies. The fragrances are quite outstanding, with the powerful fragrance of *Trifolium alpinum* joining forces with the fragrant orchids, *Gymnadenia conopsea* and *G. odoratissima*; the sensual scent of vanilla orchids, *Nigritella nigra* and *N. rubra*; as well as the creeping shrublets of *Daphne cneorum*, never far away from the more open, alpine turfy meadows they often inhabit.

I will highlight a few species that typify the flora found in this particular location and that is duplicated in other parts of the Dolomites. To replicate this type of feature in the garden is possible, but it is a highly exacting project. I have no experience of creating such a meadow garden and further advice may be sought prior to embarking on such a project. I have, though, planted many of these species in a mixed alpine bed and allowed them to intermix, seed around, and provide a vivid reminder of their homeland.

A common feature of these meadows is the delightful association of the bearded bellflower, *Campanula barbata*, with its 20 to 30 CM stems and many pale blue hanging bells flowering amongst the single-stemmed arnica. The rich golden-yellow daisies are produced on solitary 20 to 30 CM stems, and this

Campanula barbata in an alpine meadow

Lilium martagon

Lilium bulbiferum

combination works extremely well in the garden. *Arnica montana* should be allowed to seed about with the campanula.

Announcing themselves as beacons of solid stature are two lilies sometimes found in large numbers but more normally in smaller colonies. *Lilium bulbiferum* is a spectacular plant, easily grown in the garden and a firm reminder of its fire-red blaze of colour in nature. Each of the tall 30 to 45 CM stems produce up to five terminal upturned flowers of a vivid orange colour. At the base of each of the leaves are little black bulbils that can be collected and planted out as a means of propagation.

The martagon lily, *Lilium martagon*, may not be quite so spectacular in nature but, once again, always arrests our attention when we find a perfectly formed head of flowers untouched by the hungry cattle. Tall, red-mottled stems bear a loose cluster of pink to purplish Turk's caps with darker spots within. A few clumps of both these lily species, planted carefully in the garden so as not to clash with gentler tones, will provide a pleasant reminder of those rich alpine meadows in nature. A number of fine varieties and cultivars of the martagon lily are worth seeking out, and a firm favourite of mine is the white variant, *L. martagon* var. *album*.

I am always a little wary of introducing invasive members of the daisy family (Compositae) to the garden. If a genuine meadow garden is created, where the whole balance between grasses and flowering plants is controlled, what a wonderful part these composites play. I once became so keen on our own local weed, fox and cubs (*Hieracium aurantiacum*), that I planted some. I rather suspect that it will be with me, and in places it ought not to be, forever—pretty, but dangerous. Yet when meandering through the Alpi di Siusi, there is much variety from, for example, *Crepis aurea* with its wonderful orange blooms; *Hypochoeris uniflora*, the giant catsear, standing out with solitary tall stems, each holding a large yellow daisy; or in shorter grasses the more dainty clumps of mauve to violet-blue daisies belonging to *Aster alpinus*. Each merits a place in our alpine garden, but care must be taken to exercise their restraint.

I have not yet managed to create the right balance to maintain plants of the pea family, Leguminosae, according to their true character. I have no doubt they are obtaining too high a level of nutrition in my garden soil and losing their way as a result. Let me choose a few species to try out, intermixed with any of the associated plants described in this section. I think the inclusion of these species is humorous and also lessens the pressure brought to bear on gardeners whose normal goal is to grow only the rarer species. The kidney vetch, *Anthyllis vulneraria*, with its rounded clusters of golden-yellow flowers, is very showy. A little more challenging is the alpine milk-vetch, *Astragalus alpinus*, displaying whitish to pale violet flowers. If only to try and rekindle memories of the strong meadow fragrances, I do try and maintain plants of the alpine clover, *Trifolium alpinum*. It makes such a show, whether in longer grass or alpine turf in nature, with its large, deep pink to purplish clover flowers. A number of rampions will add character to our meadow garden, typified by their dense globular heads or spikes in various shades of blue. The round-headed rampion, *Phyteuma orbiculare*, is a favourite of mine, with deep blue, globular heads on 30 CM stems.

More challenging to grow but certainly not impossible are the semiparasitic louseworts. This is a large genus of plants with many fine European species, some with vibrant reddish purple flowers and others with tall spikes of yellow. My advice is simply to try a number of *Pedicularis* species on the basis of trial and error. It may be that a few mosses or grasses will provide the right relationship to trigger success. One of the most attractive is *P. verticillata*, well worth a try, with its purplish red flowers, or the dwarfer *P. kerneri* with bright red flowers.

Two tall-growing gentians merit a position in the garden, whether it is a meadow garden or a more formal rock garden. The first is the celebrated *Gentiana lutea*, which is certainly the giant of the race, with solid stems that can ascend up to 1 M. The basal leaves are large and bluish green. In the axils of the upper leaves are clusters of yellow flowers. It is a stately plant and deserving of a position if the grower can wait patiently for it to assume its normal stature.

Less imposing than the foregoing is the attractive *Gentiana punctata*, which, despite conforming to an alpine meadow habitat, prefers to grow in shorter turf, sometimes in large colonies in nature. With similar foliage to *G. lutea*, the 30 to 45 CM stems are topped with clusters of the most enchanting orange-yellow, purple-spotted upright bells. Both gentians form deep taproots, with those of the former the source of a rather bitter Enzian schnapps, which certainly warms the inner chambers of one's body when knocked back in a oner!

The meadow garden, however contrived or imperfect in its balance of species, will bring colour through the later months in the season. Most of the plants outlined, with the exception of the orchids and louseworts, are easily raised from seed and can be allowed to self-sow in the garden. The Dolomites is not only home to a rich array of true alpine plants, but its meadow flora ranks highly, too. Perhaps a taste of this diverse range will instil confidence in the reader to experiment with a few of them.

Marshes and streamsides

On the hillsides and within the snow valleys are damp, marshy areas, and within these habitats a careful search will reveal some of the loveliest of alpine flowers. I will now describe a few which are deserving of an appropriate, moisture-retentive position in our gardens.

Much has been written about the concerns surrounding the conservation of wetlands in the U.K., and one of its primary commodities, sphagnum moss. This is a natural material that, while in need of preservation, does present gardeners with an invaluable property which, when incorporated into a naturally damp soil, will support most of the plants I am about to describe. This moss is now being farmed, or grown commercially, and one should have no qualm of conscience when obtaining it from such a source. I know of no natural material that retains moisture in the way that sphagnum moss does. As long as it is living moss that we incorporate into the garden, perhaps in a naturally damp hollow or at the edge of a permanently running streamside, then it should thrive and support an interesting flora.

A damp alpine meadow in the Dolomites often reveals a varied flora, and there is no finer sight than a vast meadow of *Trollius europaeus*, the globe flower. On closer inspection, one finds a number of plants growing alongside but shorter in stature. *Trollius europaeus* is easily grown in the garden and less demanding of boggy conditions than some other marsh species. It produces 30 cm stems with several terminal flowers which are immense, almost spherical, made up of ten incurving, golden-yellow sepals. The flowers have a subtle fragrance more pronounced when encountered in a vast colony on a warm day. Once planted and established in the garden, it flowers in the late spring to early summer and can be increased from seed which does not need to be sown fresh.

Primula farinosa

A plant which generally associates with the globe flower in damp meadows is *Primula farinosa*. Though it is widely distributed in Europe, it is surprising that for such an attractive plant it is seen so sparingly in gardens. It has a tendency to be short-lived when planted in a well-drained raised bed or alpine bed. It needs to associate with kindred species and be planted in a damp, humus-rich mixture. Here it will seed about and maintain itself without concern to the grower. It is our own British native bird's-eye primrose producing neat tufts of farinose rosettes and short 8 to 12 CM stems bearing umbels of bright pink, yellow-eyed flowers. In nature, throughout a colony of pink-flowering plants, I have often found a white one, and if seed is available of such a form it, too, would be a valuable introduction.

Flowering later in the season, sometimes well into late summer, is a personal favourite from this marshy habitat. Another British native, the grass of Parnassus, *Parnassia palustris*, can easily be raised from seed and will establish fine colonies in a damp bed with added sphagnum in the garden. From small tufts of heart-shaped leaves rise stems up to 20 CM, with large, solitary white flowers with transparent veining. It is a superb species, with flowers somewhat reminiscent of the little woodlander, *Moneses uniflora*.

I wish to describe two more species that will present growers with more of a challenge, but with care and the correct environment, both should be given a try. *Gentiana bavarica* is easily identified from its close relatives within the verna group of gentians. First of all, it alone inhabits marshlands and boggy situations, where it produces a rosette of rounded, lime-green leaves and 10 CM stems clothed further with overlapping leaves. The solitary terminal flowers are of the most vivid, deep blue, attracting immediate attention from even a casual walker. I once spotted a fine clump of the species on an alpine embankment in the Swiss Engadine and thought it was surprising to see it in such an open position. On closer inspection, the habitat revealed a little rivulet racing down and through the gentian's roots. It has definite demands, and these should be acceded to in the garden, where I would plant it in a damp pocket with added sphagnum moss.

In the Dolomites, it is often found growing with plants of the enchanting little alpine butterwort, *Pinguicula alpina*. The butterworts are members of the family Lentibulariaceae, containing a range of insectivorous perennial species. *Pinguicula alpina* produces neat little sticky rosettes of lance-shaped, yellow-green leaves with short 4 to 6 CM stems carrying pretty little white flowers and pronounced yellow spots in the throat. During the dormant season, the rosette reverts to minute overwintering resting buds, which, when grown in sphagnum moss, will receive the required protection. If not, I have found it advisable to press them gently into damp, humus-rich soil or cover them with a modest layer

Gentiana bavarica

of gritty sand for protection. The butterworts are fun to grow with the care and attention they deserve.

This type of niche gardening may seem of little significance, but such a specialised environment could support a varied flora to include species from other parts of Europe and would likely include a few more primulas, including *Primula deorum* and further species of pinguicula.

Alpine turf and acidic screes

It is from this particular habitat that many of our favourite Dolomitic species emanate, although it is the classic calcicole species that often take centre stage.

I have generally chosen to make a holiday base at the upper end of the Val Gardena (Grödner Thal) in the village of Selva (Wolkenstein). Continue up on a southerly course, and we arrive at the Sella Pass. Here we can enjoy wonderful views of the imposing Langkofel group. Surrounding this famous mountain is the richest of alpine turf supporting a wide range of species. The underlying soil is of rich, reddish brown consistency, and I am not sure that the pH is as significant as its richness.

The first plants to strike the visitor with awe are, for me, the finest clumps of *Pulsatilla alpina* subsp. *apiifolia*, seen at their best here at the end of June. This

Langkofel group (Sasso Lungo)
Photo by Jim Jermyn.

Pulsatilla alpina

golden-yellow–flowered subspecies is widespread in the Alps, generally preferring an acid soil. It is variable in the depth of colour, but here in the Dolomites it is to be seen at its very best.

Although I am currently growing fine clumps of this pulsatilla in a rich alpine bed, I am never satisfied with the depth of flower colour, but perhaps the poor air quality and light intensity plays some part in this, too. It flowers later than the lowland pulsatillas and is often at its best in early summer in gardens. Established clumps should not be disturbed, as plentiful seed can be sown from the ripened, fluffy seed heads.

If *Pulsatilla alpina* subsp. *apiifolia* has a preference for acidic soils, then the type species *P. alpina* has a leaning towards a calcareous substrate. The latter is certainly not fussy as to soil pH in the garden and is undoubtedly a first-class garden plant. It resembles the foregoing with bold tufts of ferny foliage and tall 20 to 45 CM stems displaying large, snow white, often blue-backed flowers. Farrer felt that this species was the "great king and glory of the race, covering all the hills with blobs of snow" (1919). Who could argue with him? It is a great plant, and both the type species along with its yellow-flowering subspecies warrant a prominent position in the garden.

Closely related and also found in this habitat of shorter alpine turf is *Anemone narcissiflora*. It is an abundant species and quite indifferent to soil pH both in nature and in the garden. The attractive palmately lobed foliage is a wonderful foil for the 30 CM stems, carrying an umbel of up to eight large, white flowers often flushed pink below. Established clumps look particularly well when planted amongst blue-flowered columbines such as *Aquilegia alpina* or *A. pyrenaica*. It is easily raised from seed but can take up to three years to flower thereafter.

Another member of the section *Farinosae* of primula is found in the acidic turf often growing with *Primula minima* and *Soldanella pusilla*; it is *P. halleri*, with attractive, one-sided umbels with up to 12 bright pink flowers on 10 to 15 CM stems. The farinose foliage is similar to *P. farinosa* and it is easily grown in a humus-rich mixture in an alpine bed.

Abounding in the acid turf and rocky slopes is the ubiquitous alpenrose, *Rhododendron ferrugineum*. This evergreen shrub often forms dense thickets, with its deep green leaves, reddish scaly beneath. When seen at their floral peak, the hillsides come alive with the generous clusters of deep pinkish red flowers. Neither this calcifuge species nor its close relative, the lime-loving *R. hirsutum*, are often planted in the rock garden, perhaps owing to their more illustrious Himalayan cousins taking pride of place. This is a pity, as they both offer much to enhance our gardens with their flowers and foliage.

Anemone narcissiflora

The high alpine turf is home to two little androsaces, *Androsace obtusifolia* and *A. chamaejasme*. They are both very similar in character, popping up in the short grass, with fluffy rosettes of rather silvery pointed leaves. The flowers of both species are held in umbels of up to eight flowers with a yellow eye on 3 to 6 CM scapes. Neither species is fussy in the garden relative to soil pH, but both require a freely drained position in full sun. They often associate with either *Gentiana verna* or *G. brachyphylla* in nature, and what a fine combination they would make on a trough. Abundant seed is set and provides the best means of propagation.

I have always felt that the verna group gentians are best planted in a trough, and I well recall my first encounter with an entire trough planted with *Gentiana verna*. This trough was positioned in a prominent spot by which all of Jack

Upper treeline with *Rhododendron ferrugineum*

Drake's Nursery customers passed on their way to the shop. How prudent! This type of gardening in miniature is most effective, and during the weeks of spring when the gentian was flowering, most customers availed themselves of a few more pots of *G. verna*. Sound marketing, I felt, and a practice I continued when I took over Edrom Nurseries.

Gentiana verna is met with frequently in the alpine turf associating with alpine potentillas, daphnes, and a whole host of exciting species. When leading botanical parties to the Dolomites, questions have often arisen as to the true identity of species within this group of gentians. All this adds to the fun, but identification is generally made the easier with an understanding of the prevalent rock type and the altitude. It seems indifferent to soil pH and is a plant of the lower alpine turf, whereas *G. brachyphylla* is a calcifuge species of higher altitudes, sometimes found growing at altitudes of 3500 M. Whereas the foliage of *G. verna* is bright green, the leaves of *G. brachyphylla* are bluish green and more rounded to diamond shaped. It is a wee miniature and when offered in the nursery trade can easily be identified. I would love to create a dedicated trough for this species and enjoy the striking, deep blue flowers on short 3 CM stems. *Gentiana brachyphylla* will prove more of a challenge than the widely available *G. verna*, but what a thrill to master such a challenge.

The high point for me when visiting the Dolomites is to venture into the Monzoni Thal above the Pellegrino Pass to the south of the Marmolada (3342 M).

Gentiana verna ×*pumila*
Photo by Jim Jermyn.

Gentiana brachyphylla

Farrer dedicates a whole chapter to this lovely valley in his superb book, *The Dolomites*, first published in 1913. I am always keen to locate two primulas here, and Farrer's first glimpse of them is worth repeating: "For suddenly one is upon the igneous substratum again, with the result that all the moor is spread with a veil of violet by the incalculable multitudes of *Primula glutinosa* sprouting in rich heads of purple from its neat little tuffets over every ridge, bank and level of the turf. Many of its hills it shares with *P. minima*, which here on the Monzoni Thal gives rise to a whole series of hybrids." He is totally accurate in his description here, and how often I yearn to return to witness this wonderful sight, seen at its best in the latter half of June.

Belonging to the subsection *Cyanopsis*, *Primula glutinosa* presents a challenge to the alpine gardener and is rarely seen in cultivation. Let me paint a broader picture of its behaviour in nature, and then maybe we can better understand how to translate these requirements to the garden. It is most definitely a calcifuge species of the higher alpine pastures and rocky terrain—most notably on silicate formations. In nature, it favours slopes where the winter snow lies deep.

Primula glutinosa
Photo by Jim Jermyn.

Like its close cousin, *P. deorum* from Bulgaria, it is deep rooted and enjoys plenty of moisture at the root along with the fresh air it obtains in nature. Interconnect all these factors and the reader will better understand why we face a challenge—but a challenge is not an insurmountable hurdle! So let us proceed.

I would advocate a specialised deep trough or raised bed incorporating an acid soil rich in peaty humus. A number of large pieces of silaceous rock should be buried in the soil to at least half their depth. When planting my propagules of *Primula glutinosa*, seed-raised by preference, I would add some finely chopped live sphagnum to aid the retention of moisture around the roots. I would then position the trough so as to receive good light but not full sun, water well and continuously on appropriate occasions during the growing season, and then stand back and hope for the best. The clumps of leathery foliage emanate from a stout rootstock and are somewhat sticky, and they should not be lifted but rather left well alone. The flowers are borne on an umbel of up to eight in number and are dark purplish blue in colour with a wonderful fragrance that is hard to describe. I will leave that to Farrer, who states, "And not only are they grateful to the eye almost beyond any other of their kind, but they are no less pleasant to the nose, exhaling a delicious clean warm sweetness" (1919). Plants set plentiful seed in nature and once established in the garden should do the same, thus providing a means of replenishment.

Although I am certain of this species' true identity, for it can be found by the acre in absolute purity, nevertheless one can guarantee, most notably in the Monzoni Thal, that within a few hundred metres there will be countless mats of *Primula minima*. I also adore this primula; it demands respect and closer inspection, for it varies greatly, and I hope Dieter Schacht's photograph here conveys this special beauty that it promises in nature and yet so often defies to reproduce in the garden.

Primula minima

Primula minima belongs to its own subsection, *Chamaecallis*, and is widely distributed in the eastern half of the Alps at altitudes of 1700 to 2700 M. It is essentially calcifuge but not exclusively so; when found on limestone it is growing in humus-rich, acid soils above the underlying rock. This species is totally different in habit to *P. glutinosa*, in that it favours humus-rich, sparse meadow and often forms large mats. In silicate regions it is generally found in gritty terrain and occasionally in rock fissures. Its roots are not as far-reaching as *P. glutinosa*. It forms branching rhizomes with crowded rosettes made up of shiny, deep green, cuneate (wedge-shaped), deeply toothed summer leaves. Whilst dormant, the rosette is small and compact. The single flowers are large, 1.5 to 3.0 CM in diameter, and held on a 2 to 8 MM peduncle, a rich rosy-red colour.

Now to its cultivation. I had better come clean at once and admit that I have never succeeded in flowering *Primula minima* with more than the occasional flower. It grows well in my acid soil, and, intriguingly, the white-flowering form, *P. minima* var. *alba* does flower quite well. A friend who runs a nursery garden at higher altitude in the northeast of Scotland, Fred Carrie of the Tough Alpine Nursery, has succeeded with pure stock of *P. minima*, so I suspect that since he renders no super solution to its culture, a lack of clean air movement may be my problem. I will not give up. It is easily grown on a trough or raised bed in a gritty, acid, humus-rich mixture. Another recommendation from growers seeking to flower it well is to apply a high-potash liquid feed at various times during the growing season. A proprietory feed of, for example, Phostrogen (in the U.K.) 10:10:27 is worth trying. On this occasion, I will not recommend propagating this primula from seed, as we first need to flower it, but it can easily be lifted and teased apart both to rejuvenate and increase stocks.

Where *Primula glutinosa* and *P. minima* meet, the most wonderful hybrids can be found. In my view, they rank highly, along with the Bernina Pass primula hybrids in the Swiss Engadine, as the finest in Europe. These hybrids found so freely in the Monzoni Thal consist of large-flowered minimas with two flowers per stem, glutinosa-type flowers on 7 cm stems with the reddish pink flowers of minima, and glutinosa-type stems with wide-open minima-type flowers. Each one varies still further, and it is my experience that these hybrids, when brought into cultivation as rooted cuttings or side shoots, will grow and flower more reliably. Some of these natural hybrids have been accorded names. I see no valid reason for this, as the infinite variations are too great. For the sake of horticultural order, one of the named hybrids has long been cultivated, which is *P.* ×*floerkeana* and its white-flowering form, *P.* ×*floerkeana* var. *alba*. This hybrid is close to *P. minima*, with a short peduncle of two flowers a rich rose-pink colour.

On siliceous rocky formations, *Primula minima* is often growing amongst *Loiseleuria procumbens*, the creeping azalea. This little evergreen, mat-forming member of the heather family, Ericaceae, is also shy flowering in the garden but worth every effort to force it into doing so. In nature, the mats may stretch for a metre hidden by minute clusters of pale to deep pink flowers. This year I found a pure white form, but it won few plaudits from my compatriots! It roots along as it goes and will happily perform in a cool position on a trough, and it can be chopped up at will to replenish stock.

The acid shales and gravels are also home to a happy little spreading plant that presents no problem for the alpine gardener except to control its movements. It is *Linaria alpina*, the alpine toadflax, which runs around with trailing stems with tufts of whorled, blue-grey leaves and violet and orange toadflax flowers in racemes all summer. It should be allowed to self-seed in an alpine bed and can easily be rooted out when it becomes a nuisance.

Either side of the wide Monzoni Thal are cliffs and rocky outcrops with supporting scree and moraines flowing down toward the valley. On the one side are the white rocks of dolomite, while on the other are shining igneous formations with large granite boulders supporting a fascinating flora. Amongst these blocks of granite, the aggregate varies in size from a small shed to some pieces as big as an apple box. The scree is stable but is sufficiently isolated to be virtually free of humus or soil-filled pockets. What a surprise, then, on my first visit when I found great waving coppices of *Geum reptans* rooting down between these boulders and leaping around with long, red, strawberrylike runners. The pinnate foliage is attractive and fernlike, but what of the flowers? They more than match the magnificence of the clumps of foliage, with their huge yellow blooms

Geum reptans
Photo by Ian Pryde.

held on 15 CM stems, followed by equally attractive seed heads made up of waving, rose-pink pin cushions. This jewel of an alpine plant, the best of its race of mountain avens, must be given space. It is a staunch calcifuge and requires a deep, rich, perfectly drained mixture in fullest sun. Once it has settled down in the garden amongst pieces of granite, seed can be saved to perpetuate stock.

The geum is often growing beside *Ranunculus glacialis* here in the Monzoni Thal. Close by is an arête with steep cliffs of granite, upon which is growing the ultimate of alpine treasures that makes this area even more special. Glacial boulders as well as the cliffs are studded with the blue flowers of the king of the Alps, *Eritrichium nanum*. It has even seeded down amongst the gravels eroded away from the glistening rocks above. It was therefore a very satisfying feeling as I sat contentedly with friends amongst the most glorious of alpine plants right at my very feet. Why, then, if it is so prolific here is it so hard to please in the garden? Let me add a few more details relative to its habitat in nature. It begins to appear at altitudes over 2400 M and up to 3500 M. At these altitudes, the air is thin and clean, the light is intense, and the snow cover generally stretches from late September or October until mid-June to early July. So here are a few characteristics of the alpine territory we cannot recreate in our low-level gardens.

The often tight cushions or small, crowded mats consist of dark green tomentose leaves, and as soon as I encounter such a cushion I acknowledge alarm

Eritrichium nanum
Photo by Jim Jermyn.

bells—winter wet, sea haars, just one incidence of fungal attack, and away it goes. More about the flowers. A colony of flowering cushions on a dark, rocky outcrop is simply a blue blaze, an intense colour just occasionally hinting at turquoise and totally covering the foliage. Each flower has a centre of yellow that fades to orange as the bloom matures. No matter how many times we return to the Alps, we never tire of the pristine beauty of the king of the Alps.

I have raised plants from seed and they soon form neat little cushions; all seems to be going quite well. I have then planted them onto a trough tucked in between pieces of granite. A few flowers then appear on tired-looking, lax cushions. They are not the real colour at all, and one can tell that the cushion is about to die.

One day perhaps someone will discover the key not only to growing this plant but also to flowering it according to its true character, with all the vibrancy it shows here in the Dolomites. Growers have tried cultivating the European eritrichium for more than 100 years and failed. I doubt if we are meant to succeed with it, and for this reason I am more than satisfied with a trip to the Alps—and when I'm too old to manage this, then I will happily enjoy the photographic record or watch slides or DVD presentations. The king of the Alps should be admired and never touched.

Limestone scree and rock crevices

Perhaps the classic Dolomite habitat is the characteristic calcareous scree, boulder crevices, and turfy terrain. There are a number of these archetypal locations, of which the Schlern and Langkofel are two wonderful spots to visit at the end of June through July and August. This seems a long season, but to embrace the earlier snowmelt soldanellas and gentians, as well as the later-flowering campanulas, an extended break is necessary!

Another recommended area to visit early in the season is the Rolle Pass under the wary watch of the pinnacled Pala group, where a number of exciting species are found. In early to mid-June, under the Cimon della Pala (3184 м), an open glacial valley is strewn with enormous boulders comprising dolomite limestone

Soldanella pusilla × alpina

Soldanella alpina

Soldanella alpina

Soldanella minima

interspersed with finer material and humus-filled pockets between the moraine. As soon as the snows begin to recede, clumps of soldanella either force their way through the remaining patches of snow or advance farther in the muddy soil, still awaiting the regeneration of the grassy herbage. *Soldanella alpina* is certainly the most commonly encountered species in the Alps. Hereabouts it forms modest clumps of leathery, rounded leaves with short 9 CM stems carrying wide, fringed bells of a lovely rosy purple. This species is easily grown in a calcareous soil, wedged between stones on a raised bed. It does not spread widely but forms a solid tuft in cultivation, and it is best perpetuated from freshly sown seed.

The most eye-catching of all soldanellas is very much at home in pockets of humus within this limestone scree; it is *Soldanella minima*. A closer inspection of this specialised habitat reveals some hidden activity. Beneath the surface rocks and running through the searching root system is a channel of melting snow-water that provides a regular supply of water and a cool root run during the early part of its growing cycle. This is hard to reenact at home, but fortunately the soldanella can be flowered in a dedicated trough.

This one can immediately be differentiated from the calcifuge *Soldanella pusilla* by its thickish dark green leaves, without the prominent veining of *S. pusilla*. *Soldanella minima* generally has whitish to the faintest of pink flowers, whereas *S. pusilla* flowers are a rich rose-pink in colour. In nature, the flowering period can commence in May and last to July, whereas in my garden it commences at the end of April and extends into May. I grow it in a little round trough that is now filled with shining green, rounded foliage. Because the trough is both shallow and only 25 CM in diameter, I am careful not to allow the plants to dry out during the growing season. I am also aware that within this tight mat of growth and root system there is competition for nutrients; therefore, a weak feed of liquid tomato fertiliser is given at irregular intervals during the growing season. The soil is humus-rich and intermixed with small pieces of limestone. I believe that in order to mirror the dormant season these species experience whilst under a blanket of snow, they are best kept on the dry side from the late autumn through to early spring. A careful watch should be kept for slugs that will actively seek to devour the embryonic flower buds which are barely visible, tucked down in amongst the foliage during the dormant season.

The reward for all this care is a trough with a myriad of little white flowers on 4 to 9 CM stems that will capture the attention of all one's friends. This is one of the perennial joys of the alpine garden.

Further species abound in this grey, calcareous habitat. Splashes of yellow and white greet the walker as numerous clumps of alpine poppies colonise any gravel or sloping scree, with two subspecies predominating. The yellow-flower-

Papaver alpinum subsp. *rhaeticum*

Papaver alpinum subsp. *sendtneri*

Papaver alpinum subsp. *rhaeticum*

ing form is *Papaver alpinum* subsp. *rhaeticum*, while the white one is *P. alpinum* subsp. *sendtneri*. They appear to demand no form of humus at all in the limestone rubble and seed about without any special needs, apart from the acute drainage they so desire. In the garden, I find that all alpine poppies, regardless of their name or provenance, enjoy any freely drained, sunny aspect. If planted

Silene acaulis

in a raised bed, they will invariably seed into the path beneath and alert the grower as to where *they* wish to grow.

Amidst the wide clumps of alpine sneezewort (*Achillea oxyloba*) and silvery milfoil (*A. clavennae*), with their abundant white daisies, are broad, rosy pink sheets of *Silene acaulis*, with near stemless flowers over tight cushions. It loves to grow between stable limestone boulders and produces a wonderful show when wedged between ancient, weathered limestone pavement. The extensive mats of foliage can be lifted up as they fan out over the rock mass. I have often felt that in order to encourage flowering, it is well worth attempting to reenact this situation in the garden by positioning our plants of *S. acaulis* at the edge of a raised bed, for example. This way, the mat will spread over the perimeter wall and benefit from the extra radiant heat that is stored in the rock, thus seemingly enhancing the flowering. This is also true of a contemporary plant, the mountain avens, *Dryas octopetala*, which occupies the same limestone pavement and rarely flowers in cultivation as it does in nature. This is often due to the wide sheets of vegetative growth feeding on the highly nutritious soil at the expense of flower bud production. A lean soil should therefore be given to each of these subjects, and position plenty of large, flat stones under their expanding growth.

The dryas produces attractive oak-shaped leaves and large white flowers. Both the silene and dryas are typical representatives of this limestone habitat and can easily be propagated from cuttings.

Anemone baldensis
Photo by Ian Pryde.

It is hard to miss the special glory of these limestone screes along with the delicious fragrance of plants such as *Thlaspi rotundifolium*, which sends down deep into the shingles a well-anchored taproot, above which are tufted rosettes of dark green, oval leaves. The flowers consist of flattened heads of showy, rosy lavender flowers on short 2 cm stems. I have never succeeded with this lovely species in my garden and doubt that I can begin to reenact this deep scree environment. If seed is made available, have a go. In this instance, I can only create a picture of how it grows in its native habitat and wish the reader luck.

Easier of cultivation, but never likely to reach the heights of perfection in cultivation, is the outstandingly fragrant *Valeriana supina*. It would be possible to pass this plant by if it were not for its fragrance, as the completely prostrate mats cover areas in excess of a dinner plate with its dense clusters of pale pink flowers. It demands a spartan diet in full sun, but its strongest demand is the acute drainage it so craves in the wild. The rooted pieces can be detached to replenish stocks.

A plant that is characteristic of the high dolomite limestone screes is *Anemone baldensis*. For the reader who is familiar with the Himalayan *A. rupicola* or the North American *A. drummondii*, here is the European equivalent. It is immediately recognised in nature as it runs around in the limestone rubble with its underground stolons, sending up here and there tufts of fine, dark, three-lobed leaves. Graceful stems 7 to 12 cm in length each carry a solitary white, often blue-backed flower with yellow anthers. The flowers are followed by a woolly head of achenes that can be saved to increase stocks.

This is a species I am surprised not to have seen more often in cultivation, which asks only for an acutely drained, calcareous mixture with added pieces of limestone. It should be given an open, sunny aspect in an alpine bed, where it will certainly reward the grower when associated with subjects such as daphnes, *Primula auricula*, and campanulas.

When climbing or traversing up the typical limestone screes and boulders, such as the extensive moraines located under the impressive Langkofel Mountain (3181 m), there is another specialised habitat much favoured by alpine plants. A casual glance across the white rock terrain seems to reveal only the fleeting movement of snow buntings. But dotted about are large boulders the size of a garage with humus-filled ledges and crevices, each supporting a specialised flora. Two alpine willows are very often seen sprawling down from a humus-filled pocket created from a mixture of eroded silt and rotting vegetation. These deciduous shrubs create their own leaf mould that further enhances these growing conditions and allows other species to associate with them.

Salix reticulata

Salix reticulata, the netted willow, is one of the most desirable species for the garden, forming prostrate woody stems in dense mats. The rounded, net-veined leaves are a wonderful sight when they have newly emerged. The flowers on willows are upright catkins with the male and female flowers produced on separate plants. In the case of this species, the male catkins are a most attractive reddish colour and flower in the spring. *Salix reticulata* should be given room to spread to at least about 50 CM in diameter and loves to sprawl over rocks or down the side of a wall. It requires full sun but is not fussy about soil pH in the garden. Cuttings struck late on in the season will readily root during the winter period.

A more diminutive species but no less attractive is *Salix retusa* and its truly alpine cousin, *S. serpyllifolia*. This latter species forms tightly adpressed mats, appearing to be a compact from of *S. retusa*. It forms tiny, oblong, slightly notched leaves and pretty yellow catkins. An additional attribute of these alpine willows is their autumn colour, created as the leaves often pass to a golden yellow colour.

A closer inspection of these boulders reveals a number of treasures that really provide the gilt on the gingerbread. *Androsace hausmannii* is a member of the Aretian section endemic to the Dolomites. It is not going to excite the avid collector of androsaces, but it is a most welcome species when planted directly into a boulder of tufa rock. In its best forms, this short-lived species is most attractive forming a loose cushion of up to six rosettes. These rosettes appear almost hoarfrosted with their glaucous glands but are at their best when studded with deep pink buds. It is at this stage that I like to photograph them. Once open, the white flowers have a yellow eye, and if flushed pink they are most desirable. To propagate this spring-flowering species, seed should be saved and sown freshly.

Often growing beside the androsace are minute, congested rosettes of pointed, glaucous leaves belonging to *Gentiana terglouensis*. It is immediately recognised by its foliage and its consistent demand of growing on a limestone base. Rarely do these congested plantlets exceed 2 to 3 CM across, but when the flowers appear they demand a lengthy inspection. So often, because they climb to high altitudes between 1900 and 2700 M, the screes are enshrouded in a cloud mass and the flowers fail to open. But when they do, they are almost stemless, with 5 to 7 MM stalks, each topped with a deep blue flower often without a white eye. The gentian can either be planted in tufa or positioned between pieces of limestone on a trough. Plants should not be allowed to dry out during the growing season, and the plentiful seed set even from four to five flowers must be sown at once. It is a real treasure.

Throughout the Dolomites this habitat of stable scree with humus-filled outcrops is home to one of the most favoured alpine plants, *Rhodothamnus chamaecistus*. It is a surprising calcicole member of the heather family, Ericaceae. Although most members of this family are acid-loving plants, this is not to be seen as an outrageous exception, because, in common with other species such as *Erica carnea*, it is shallow rooting and generally forms a mat of roots that fan out within the shallow layer of accumulated neutral to acid humus. It is a native of the Eastern Alps but is most often seen in the Dolomites at altitudes ranging from 1300 to 2400 m. The best forms are encountered in open positions, but it is adaptable and can also be found within the subalpine zone in shaded positions amongst clearings of *Pinus mugo*. It scrambles over limestone boulders in the form of a low shrublet clothed with small, narrow, dark green leaves.

Rhodothamnus chamaecistus

When a well-flowered shrub is located at its pristine best, it wins all the plaudits possible from eager onlookers with its terminal clusters of saucer-shaped, rich pink flowers. It is quite simply stunning.

Over the years, I have met up with gardeners who exercise little in the way of patience. This can relate not only to the time a plant takes to flower, but also the duration taken to obtain a plant in the first place. If you fall into this category, then the lovely rhodothamnus is not for you. The best plants I have grown were raised from seed. This is in itself an art and requires skill, owing to the typically dustlike nature of the seed. Mike and Polly Stone of Askival, Fort Augustus, Scotland, are not only famous for their garden and range of plants grown, but Polly is known for her great ability to raise rare plants from seed. They have mastered the art of raising most notably ericaceous plants from seed sown onto desiccated sphagnum moss. The whole process of raising saleable plants can take many years (five or six) without the intervention of excessive fertiliser applications. So, quite naturally, the resulting plant will be expensive. Having spent our money, it loves to be planted on a trough. I would position it in partial shade in all but the coolest of gardens. It resents any form of drying out and will quickly succumb if exposed to summer scorch. Plants should establish well in a well-drained soil rich in peaty humus and wedged between pieces of magnesium limestone or dolomite. They flower in late spring.

In order to perpetuate stock, I hardly dare mention the word *seed* and a further wait of five or six years. Funny how many rock gardeners mention their yearning for an extra life!

Growing in the same location and habitat is the alpine bearberry, *Arctostaphylos alpinus* (synonym *Arctous alpinus*). This is a most lovely prostrate deciduous shrub deserving of a place on any raised bed or trough for its showy autumn colour. There is no finer sight in nature than a rock smothered with the bright red to orange hues created by this species in September and October. I have never seen a more spectacular plant (for its autumnal display) than the plants found on a different continent—in Hokkaido, Japan. It seems to benefit from magnesium-rich soils, and maybe it is this property common to dolomite rock that creates such a fine leaf colour prior to its fall.

Plants are slow to establish in the garden but are worth every effort we can afford it. Mature plants produce black berries, following the white flowers, from which the seeds can be extracted for subsequent sowing.

Returning to the spring again, I want to highlight a few classic Dolomitic species, which include those for which most alpine growers would wish to find a home.

One of the choicest, earliest to flower, and largest flowering of all the alpine species of saxifrage is *Saxifraga burseriana*. A member of the *Porphyrion* section and the subsection *Kabschia*, this saxifrage commemorates the early botanist Joachim Burser (1583–1639). This species is endemic to the Eastern Alps, where it is confined to limestone and dolomite formations. It is sometimes seen in rock crevices but more often on gravelly debris, or in humus-filled crevices on large boulders. Its altitudinal range is from 1500 to 2200 M.

Arctostaphylos alpinus

Surely this is the loveliest of all Kabschia saxifrages, represented in gardens in many geographic forms and variations along with still more lovely hybrids claiming it as one of the parents. The true species forms large cushions in nature with sharply pointed, glaucous leaves and solitary white flowers on reddish 2.5 to 5.0 CM stems. The flowers vary greatly in shape and size, and I will list a few of my favourite forms which have been introduced over a long period of decades, commencing with plants discovered by both Farrer and F. Sündermann. They are *Saxifraga burseriana* 'Clarissa', selected by Lincoln Foster in 1970; *S. burseriana* 'Crenata', with sculptured petals; *S. burseriana* 'Gloria'; and *S. burseriana* 'Mangart'. All have attractive white flowers produced in abundance.

Saxifraga burseriana

Some of the finest hybrids raised with *Saxifraga burseriana* as one of the parents include *S.* ×*boydii* (*S. aretioides* × *S. burseriana*), with 'Aretiastrum', 'Faldonside', and 'Sulphurea'; *S.* ×*elisabethae* (*S. burseriana* × *S. sancta*), with 'Boston Spa' and 'Millstream Cream'; and *S.* ×*irvingii* (*S. burseriana* × *S. lilacina*), with 'Jenkinsiae' and 'Lusanna'.

The true species, forms, and hybrids can happily be grown in a trough amongst pieces of tufa or planted directly into a boulder of tufa rock. Care should be taken to protect plants from the full glare of summer sunlight. The cushions should be carefully tended to remove moss, liverwort, and seedling weeds. There can be no doubt that each one of these recommendations will give untold pleasure to the grower. They can easily be propagated by cuttings taken during the dormant season and dibbled into pure sand with glass protection and a little bottom heat. The type species can be raised from seed with considerable variation in habit and flower to be expected.

Growing on limestone cliffs and in fissures formed in huge stabilised boulders is a real treasure, *Primula tyrolensis*, that prefers cooler positions away from the full glare of the sun.

I have only once been fortunate to time my visit to the Pala group of the Dolomites in early to mid-June. Having traversed a snowfield to reach the chosen habitat, I found the ledges and fissures lined with loose, sticky rosettes of

Primula tyrolensis
Photo by Jim Jermyn.

Primula tyrolensis

foliage. These rosettes were tucked in firmly to these fissures, often running horizontally and supporting a one- to two-flowered umbel on a 1 to 2 CM peduncle (stem). The flowers are highly variable, the best usually just out of reach of the camera! They are predominantly a lovely shade of rose-pink to lilac-pink, often with a white eye.

Primula tyrolensis is one of the more challenging primulas to flower. I have a plant growing rather well on a trough among *Campanula raineri* along with some saxifrages. Each of them flowers profusely but my primula, rarely and then sparingly. I have never been a great feeder of plants in the garden. I'm not quite sure why, since I manage obediently to tend to the needs of the indoor plants and hanging baskets around the house. Perhaps this shy-flowering species needs a gentle reminder to perform and would benefit from a weak liquid feed of tomato (or high potash) fertiliser. I know Harry Jans grows and flowers these Dolomitic rarities very successfully on his tufa pillars. Here is another alternative way of growing the primula rather than in a trough. If one can coax it into producing more than a few flowers, no doubt seed will be produced for further propagation.

A rare natural hybrid between *Primula tyrolensis* and *P. minima* is to be found in just one location in the southern Dolomites in an area where *P. minima* finds a suitable turf beneath limestone outcrops containing the *P. tyrolensis*. The hybrid, *P. ×juribella*, is a most desirable plant worth seeking out, showing all the attrib-

Leontopodium alpinum

Leontopodium alpinum
Photo by Jim Jermyn.

utes of both parents but happy to reward its grower with flowers in this instance.

Growing on boulders nearby *Primula tyrolensis* is a diminutive but most attractive form of *P. auricula*. It is *P. auricula* subsp. *balbisii*, and once again it is early-flowering. A visit to these parts in late June and early July will likely be too late to enjoy the tight effarinose rosettes of foliage, with many hairs on the margins and miniature 2 to 4 cm stems with an umbel of deep yellow flowers that

Daphne striata

bear no scent. It is a superb plant for a trough or boulder of tufa and flowers reliably early in the spring, producing plenty of seed.

A little later in the short growing season afforded to the species in this harsh environment are plants of *Ranunculus seguieri* and dwarf forms of the lovely edelweiss, *Leontopodium alpinum*. Often growing amongst these treasures in pockets of turfy terrain are low, fragrant bushes of *Daphne striata* that frequently prove disappointing in terms of flower quality, by comparison to the much more floriferous and easily grown *D. cneorum*.

The greatest surprise for me, though, when botanising around the famous Rolle Pass in the southern Dolomites was to find neat cushions of *Eritrichium nanum* growing in the characteristic dolomite limestone. Some readers may exclaim, "but so what?" Well, I had been brought up on the literary works of Farrer and often return to his vivid descriptions and motivating prose. In his exhaustive work *The English Rock Garden*, first published in 1919, he wrote of the eritrichium: "In the well-trodden ranges it may be taken as absolutely calcifuge", accepting that it may be obliged to put up with limestone in certain parts of the Eastern Alps. Not so! It thrives in the Rolle Pass on limestone and

Eritrichium nanum subsp. *jankae*
Photo by Jim Jermyn.

takes on a slightly different appearance, with slightly paler blue flowers than its calcifuge variant. This eastern variant of limestone formations should be called *E. nanum* subsp. *jankae*, and it reappears in the Carpathian mountains. It is worth mentioning that this subspecies is the one to try in the garden. If seed becomes available from a known origin, it can be sown *in situ* in a purpose-made hole in a boulder of tufa rock. Care should be taken to nurture the developing seedling that might, just might, turn into a neat little cushion with its truly unsurpassable blue flowers!

One of the Dolomites' most famous and most illustrious of inhabitants is *Potentilla nitida*. Although abundant on limestone boulders, pavements, and stabilised scree conditions in these parts, it is also found farther west in the calcareous mountains near Lake Como and much farther eastward into the

Potentilla nitida

Karawanken. It is undoubtedly the glory of its race, and once seen in its wide mats and silvery carpets of trefoiled foliage it is never forgotten. One cannot help but pat these solid cushions with their downy surface. It is in this state that many visitors have come to recognise this beautiful plant, including myself, for it often begins to flower well into July and August in nature.

For those who have witnessed a well-flowered carpet of the rose-pink flowers showering down over a boulder of limestone, it is quite breathtaking. I recall taking a lift up from San Martino di Castrozza to the mighty limestone towers of the Rosetta (2743 м). As the cabin lift rose (rather swiftly, for my needs) up the mountain, I kept my eyes glued to the passing cliff faces and boulders. In fact, this form of lift can create rather an alarming experience, for just as you forget that you are in a lift and become totally immersed in the passing flora, the whole contraption reaches a supporting pylon, at which point there is a sudden jerk as the cabin swings for a moment and you are left regaining your composure and wishing you hadn't enjoyed that extra Pilsener or piece of plum tart. It is all part of the fun in these parts, but on this particular occasion I remember suddenly spotting a vast mat of *Potentilla nitida* suspended over a great buttress of rock completely covered with deep reddish pink flowers. I knew I could not get any-where near to the plant again, and to this day I have never witnessed such a form. What a view, and what a selection of unique plants the chamois goats must experience!

Campanula cochlearifolia   *Campanula cochlearifolia*

The potentilla is easily grown in the garden and should be treated in the same manner as *Dryas octopetala* and planted at the edge of a large piece of limestone, over which the flat carpets of foliage can spread. A free-flowering plant, blooming in mid and late summer in cultivation, is a just reward for the grower and a fitting reminder for anyone who has visited the Dolomites late in the growing season. It is easily propagated by stem cuttings removed after flowering.

The potentilla is variable in flower colour, and although a soft pink is the normal shade, it can be obtained as *Potentilla nitida* var. *rubra*, with deep reddish pink flowers, or *P. nitida* var. *alba*, with pure white flowers.

During late July and August, the true alpine campanulas are to be seen flowering at their best. When driving up over the high passes, the roadsides' protective walls are often home to fine stands of the showy and ubiquitous *Campanula cochlearifolia* either in its customary pale blue form or a pure white one. When transported to our gardens, it should be imprisoned between rock boulders, for it spreads gallantly. It is such a lovely plant, though, for its late colour and masses of thimblelike flowers. It is also represented in cultivation with a pale slate-blue–flowered form, *C. cochlearifolia* 'Miranda'.

Often found in cooler situations growing in rock fissures is the closely related *Campanula scheuchzeri*, with its deeper blue bells. Once again, this is easily grown in the garden and is of good constitution. Both campanulas are easily

lifted and divided after flowering if such a require-
ment is deemed necessary.

The real pride and joy of the Dolomites, though,
involves another campanula, this time a true
endemic and saxatile member of this illustrious
race. It is *Campanula morettiana*. I found my first
plants when visiting the very same spot where I had
found the *Primula tyrolensis*, growing on huge boulders strewn in an open valley. Here I was, two full
months later in the season with a good friend of
mine, showing him some of the wonderful scenery
in the Dolomites. Whilst working on the side of
Lake Garda, a number of friends who visited me
sought the glamour that went with the lakeside
social life. I, though, felt they ought to enjoy the real
Dolomitic landscape!

Growing in little chinks and minuscule hollows in
the ice and water-riven rock face were neat tuffets
of hairy, heart-shaped foliage with a little posy of

Campanula morettiana
Photo by Jim Jermyn.

perfectly created violet-blue bells, hanging on short 2 to 4 CM stems. I called my
friend and after some inevitable protestation managed to get him to support my
weight as I carefully reached up and photographed the campanula.

It is a rare plant confined to limestone cliffs and boulders at altitudes up to
2300 M, and it flowers there during late July through August. Its name commemorates the Italian botanist, G. Moretti (1782–1853) of Pavia. I can recommend this specialised plant to be grown in a boulder of tufa rock in a cooler
position. Here it should be safely out of the watchful reach of the native slug
population that will make a quick meal of its hairy tufts. Seed is the only sensible means of propagating this choice species, but if the reader feels inspired to
try it in the garden, why not roll the boat out and seek to purchase the pure white
form as well, *Campanula morettiana* var. *alba*?

From time to time in the history of modern alpine gardening, an artificial
hybrid of outstanding beauty is created either by chance or by careful hand-pol-
lination. Many of the finest plants raised are created by chance, and it was by this
method that one of the finest of all hybrid campanulas was raised. It occurred in
the 1970s at the famous Broadwell Nursery in the Cotswolds, England. The
hybrid arose when a passing bee transferred a dollop of pollen from *Campanula
raineri* and deposited it on the ripe stigma of *C. morettiana*. Once the seedlings
flowered from within the pan of *C. morettiana*, a distinct seedling was spotted,

with its shallower flowers and typical *C. raineri* leaves. Once isolated, it grew vigorously and in its second year flowered continuously from June until September. What a discovery! The colour of the bells was a lavender-blue, and here was the birth of a fine hybrid named *C.* 'Joe Elliott' to commemorate its raiser, and what a fitting plant by which to remember him. It has the same running habit as *C. raineri* and can therefore be propagated by both division and from cuttings. Plants can be grown in a trough or raised bed and are best protected from winter wet with a cloche cover. This outstanding hybrid received an AM in 1978 followed by an FCC in 1981—quite an accolade.

This one, along with the true species, is the ultimate of treasures emanating from this, the richest of all regions in the Alps. The Dolomites are totally accessible, easy of terrain, and as Farrer so aptly stated, "Of one thing I am sure, if words of mine help to allure you to the Dolomites you will return again and again" (1913). I can assure readers he is right again. Once you have a taste for these rich and diverse habitats from woodland to meadows, to marshes and up into the alpine screes and turfs, you will wish to return.

I hope the reader will feel confident to grow some of its exciting endemics. Most are easy of cultivation and a few are close to impossible. That is why both gardening and a trip to the Alps go hand in hand.

The Julian Alps

These mountains form the most easterly part of the Eastern Alps before entering the Balkans. They lie within the ever-developing, friendly Republic of Slovenia, formerly part of Yugoslavia and earlier part of the Austro-Hungarian Empire, whose capital is Ljubljana.

The flora is not dissimilar to that of the Dolomites and is made up largely of calcicole plants. The mountains are centred on the highest mountain of this state, Mount Triglav, 2863 M. The Kranjska Gora povides an ideal centre for the walker and the plant hunter, and a visit to these parts in May and June should reward the visitor with fine stands of the local lily, *Lilium carniolicum*. It is often found growing on limestone outcrops and in alpine meadows. It extends southward into Greece and the Balkans and is there represented by the form *L. carniolicum* subsp. *jankae*. The type species produces reddish orange flowers with orange anthers. The southern variant has yellow flowers and orange anthers.

I have already lamented the confusion that surrounds the naming of alpine linums. I will here stick with the familiar name for a lovely subspecies frequently found in grassy meadows in the Julian Alps. It is *Linum alpinum* subsp. *julicum* that I am particularly partial to—indeed, any of the numerous subalpine forms of this pale blue–flowering flax. From deciduous perennial clumps arise a mass of 30 to 45 CM stems, clothed with linear leaves and branched clusters of pale to sky-blue flowers over a long period from late spring through the summer. It can be propagated from cuttings or from seed and is best given space in the rock garden or alpine bed in full sun.

One of the most delightful and easily grown of the alpine pinks is *Dianthus monspessulanus* subsp. *sternbergii*. Long before one finds this species, while scrambling across the limestone shingles beneath the mighty Triglav, its sweet fragrance will send a greeting. Its underground stolons race around beneath and between the stones, forming grasslike clumps of growth with a fine show of 9 to 15 CM stems with pretty, fringed flowers from pale to deep pink. It is a superb plant for the scree garden or when positioned between limestone rocks in full sun. I find that seed-raised plants are preferable, and the best colour forms can be selected.

A plant rarely seen in gardens but deserving to be better known is *Primula carniolica*. It is restricted to a small area in the southern Julian Alps, growing at a low altitude of around 900 to 1000 M. It can be found in light woodland or stony pastures in pockets of soil between boulders of limestone, preferring shady aspects. It belongs to the subsection *Brevibracteata* and is an attractive plant, forming a congested rosette of shiny green leaves. The purplish pink flowers are held in an umbel of around five flowers on a 6 to 10 CM stem. The only farina on the plant forms a ring around the throat, giving the impression of a white eye. I have not found this species easy in cultivation and recommend growing it in a humus-rich soil in a little shade.

In sharp contrast to the foregoing is another primula species, this time one which is easily grown and more widely available in the trade, either as plants or from seed. It is *Primula wulfeniana* from the subsection *Arthritica*, occurring between 1800 and 2100 M exclusively in limestone areas. This species prefers to grow in humus-rich meadow slopes and can form large, dense mats with sheets of colour. The rosettes are tight and upright with leathery leaves so typical of this subsection. The upper surface is dark green and shiny, while the undersides are pale green. The umbel contains up to three flowers on 1 to 7 CM stems and can be a quite spectacular violet-pink to reddish violet with a white eye. It is an easy primula to please if one can provide the calcareous substrate it desires. Planted in full sun in a moisture-retentive mixture, it should perform well and can be replenished either from division or from seed.

In the western parts of the Karawanken mountains, *Primula wulfeniana* meets with *P. minima* to produce a very fine hybrid, *P. ×vochinensis*, intermediate between the two parents. It produces vivid flowers of a deep rose-pink over neat,

Primula wulfeniana
Photo by Gilbert Barrett.

toothed rosettes. In my experience, this is a sterile hybrid which must therefore be increased vegetatively.

A locally endemic species of alpine buttercup found in limestone scree well irrigated from the melting snow water is *Ranunculus traunfellneri*. In its best forms this is a fine plant closely akin to *R. alpestris*, with more acutely cut foliage. A large-flowered form would be well worth planting in a trough with other lime-loving species, where it will provide a fine show of white flowers in late spring. Freshly sown seed is the best way to propagate it.

I am always on the lookout for improved forms of any alpine alyssums, and in the Eastern Alps some good ones are to be found. One in particular is *Alyssum ovirense*, which grows in fine scree at altitudes of up to 2400 m, where it forms neat, little wiry shrublets with solid heads of golden-yellow flowers in the spring. It is a valuable plant for a trough or raised bed and should not be given too rich a mixture. The best forms should be selected from seed.

A rather special plant endemic to this part of the Eastern Alps is *Gentiana froelichii*. It is a rare species with a limited distribution from the Carnic and Julian Alps to the Karawanken. It grows at altitudes from 1800 to 2400 m in screes, stony turf, and humus overlying limestone. It sometimes associates with *Primula auricula*, *G. terglouensis*, *Silene acaulis*, and *Potentilla nitida*.

It is very distinct from other species of European gentian, with the exception perhaps of a diminutive form of *Gentiana clusii*. *Gentiana froelichii* forms a tufted rosette of upright, narrow, lanceolate leaves, a paler green than *G. clusii*. The flower stalk is about 2 cm long and bears a large, solitary blue flower. A

Gentiana froelichii in cultivation
Photo by Klaus Patzner.

well-flowered clump of this species is a wonderful sight and takes considerable skill to cultivate. It is quite happy in the open garden in a cool position planted between pieces of limestone. I would certainly recommend covering the plants with a cloche during the winter months. Flowering as late as midsummer, it is useful for its summer colour, and care should be taken to watch the ripening seed capsules which rapidly shed their seeds when ripe. This is the only means of propagation, and the neat rosettes of foliage should not be disturbed. To alleviate risk of a fungal attack through the decaying foliage, I would remove it carefully and top dress the plant with added grit. This is a very exciting species from a celebrated genus.

A personal favourite of mine from these mountains is the geographic variant of *Viola calcarata* from the Eastern Alps, *V. calcarata* subsp. *zoysii*. It is a fine plant for a trough and produces glossy, orbicular leaves and short, single-flowered stems with large yellow flowers. I find that, in common with other species, it is a hungry feeder and quickly exhausts itself in this position. This is yet another

Viola calcarata subsp. *zoysii*

Campanula zoysii

reminder for me to be a little more generous with my Haws watering can and the liquid feed. A careful watch after flowering for ripening seed capsules will ensure a few are collected before their sudden dispersal.

The most famous plant from this part of the Eastern Alps is surely the curious and most beloved campanula of all, *Campanula zoysii*. I have yet to witness this alpine gem in nature but can well imagine the scene as it fills vertical limestone crevices, spilling out with trailing stems and a myriad of bottle-shaped flowers a delicate shade of blue.

Campanula zoysii is found fairly widespread in the Karawanken and Julian Alps between 1800 and 2300 M. It is easily raised from seed and, if the seedlings can be kept away from the attention of slugs, will quickly mature into fine plants for a trough or boulder of tufa rock. The actual germination of the seed may take place the second spring after sowing, so the seed pots should not be discarded in frustration. I have found that, like *Viola calcarata*, it can quickly become exhausted after a major burst of flowering. It should therefore be rejuvenated with a top dressing of gritty compost and regular liquid feeding. It flowers during the summer months, and great care must be taken to protect plants from slugs that cherish this valuable plant. Many growers recommend a generous 5 to 7 CM layer of top-dressing material to deter slugs and encourage free drainage around the neck of the plant. This is an excellent tip and as well provides winter protection against excessive wet.

A number of good colour variants will arise from seed, and one that deserves special mention is *Campanula zoysii* 'Lismore Ice', raised by the very fine grower and propagator of alpine plants, Brian Burrow, who spotted this seedling in the mid-1980s. His eagle eyes have identified a number of excellent plants, both in the wild and from self-made hybridisation, and his work has been a great influence in the horticultural trade in recent years.

This is a very fitting plant to conclude this major chapter on the Eastern Alps. The range of plants from this area alone would suffice for most keen alpine gardeners, but it serves well to lead us into the penultimate region known simply as the Balkans.

7: The Balkans

I t is my intention to be highly selective in my choice of plants from this vast area that straddles Europe and Asia Minor. The main remit of this book is to describe a selection of European mountain plants that are accessible to the alpine gardener and, where possible, available from specialist nurseries and seed catalogues. I will therefore restrict my recommendations to those plants that have been well-documented and are known to most keen alpine gardeners. For the reader who feels disappointed at my oversight regarding a few favourite species, I hope that my bibliography will point to some further reading and make amends for any compelling omissions.

This range will be broken down into smaller components comprising the Central Balkans, including the former Yugoslavian independent states, Greece, and Bulgaria.

The Central Balkans, Including the Former Yugoslavian States

Gardening can often provide a few fruitful surprises; one that I experienced involved a well-filled trough of *Gentiana verna*. When casually passing by the trough in February or March, I noted a little rosette battling away for space between the gentians, amongst which were a few very pretty pink flowers. What could it be, and how did it get there?

It was in fact a seedling of *Androsace hedraeantha*, apparently dispersed by a bird or perhaps simply carried over in some retained compost. This is a popular and uncomplicated species belonging to the section *Aretia*, subsection *Dicranothrix*. It occurs only in the central Balkans from the Albanian mountains eastward into the Rila mountains of Bulgaria.

The folly of war and its aftermath has been brought home recently with the images beamed across the world by satellite—of atrocities and pillaging carried

Primula kitaibeliana

out in the Balkan states. The result is that many of its beautiful mountainous areas, those that are both politically sensitive and provide strategic vantage points, are heavily mined. This has left the local inhabitants with a seemingly lasting legacy of extreme danger and a great loss in terms of potential revenue from tourism.

One of the botanically richest mountains is Mount Korab (2764 M) on the Albanian frontier. Some of the highlights of the upper alpine meadows here include *Wulfenia baldaccii*, *Edraianthus graminifolius* subsp. *niveus*, *Geranium subcaulescens*, and great quantities of *Androsace hedraeantha*. What a thrilling collection of plants! The androsace prefers schistose or volcanic rocks of an acidic formation and forms a neat dome of closely packed rosettes with bright green leaves. The apple blossom–pink flowers are held in an umbel on short 10 to 20 MM stems. Having found a self-sown seedling (by whatever means of dispersal) in my trough of gentians, I saved the seed and raised a stock of young plants that would supply stocks for many years to come.

The mountains in this area are home to many more exciting plants, including some from Albania, Macedonia, and neighbouring Bosnia-Herzegovina. These include *Convolvulus boissieri* subsp. *compactus*, *Ranunculus crenatus*, the Balkan form of *Gentiana verna* subsp. *tergestina*, and *Primula kitaibeliana*.

Primula kitaibeliana is a beautiful species all too rarely seen in cultivation. I remember fine stands of it in the Schachen Alpine Garden and also recall meeting one of my Dutch customers (whilst running Edrom Nurseries) enthusing about it, too. It is a rare species belonging to the subsection *Rhopsidium* of the section *Auricula* and is restricted to the southern Velebit mountains of Croatia and Mount Prenj in Bosnia-Herzegovina. It is not a species of high altitudes and rarely exceeds 2000 M, choosing to inhabit moist, grassy limestone rock faces. The flattish rosettes are made up of pale green leaves strongly aromatic from the sticky glandular hairs. An umbel of one to five flowers is held on a 2 to 5 CM stem, and at their best can be a bright magenta-rose. My recollection is of paler pink variations, but their being of a large proportion relative to the subsection to which they belonged.

Every effort should be made to reintroduce this attractive species and to popularise it further, for there is no reason to assume that its rarity brings with it any difficulty of cultivation. A well-organised seed-collecting trip is required to reintroduce to gardens some of eastern Europe's most desirable alpine plants. In the case of this primula, it is a calcicole species which will grow perfectly well in a trough or raised bed.

Macedonia is an ancient kingdom rich in its flora and home to two notable plants of great value to alpine gardeners. I spent some time writing about the growing requirements for the Pyrenean endemic, *Ramonda myconi*. In doing so, I alluded to the fact that, despite its undoubted beauty and value to gardeners, its Balkan cousins were more desirable for their floral excellence.

Due west of the Macedonian capital, Skopje, there rises a rich mountain range called the Sar Planina. Close by is the Vardar river, which runs through some impressive gorges. It is within this locality that *Ramonda nathaliae* is to be seen at its best. It inhabits

Ramonda nathaliae
Photo by Jim Jermyn.

damp, partially shaded or (more rarely) sunnier limestone slopes and embankments. It may be seen at its best during May, when in some spots the congested leathery rosettes grow so thickly as to stain the gorge-side with their lavender flowers. Having grown and admired this species for many years in my own garden, I can only imagine the awesome beauty this natural picture creates for those fortunate enough to have experienced it. It can be grown either on the flat in a cool, moist, humus-rich bed or, perhaps to show off further its unique beauty, in a vertical wall or block of tufa rock. It flowers in mid to late spring in cultivation and sets plenty of seed, which should be treated in the same way as for *R. myconi*.

Ramonda serbica is another very special and more locally distributed species found in this part of the Balkans, closely related to *R. nathaliae*. The two can be distinguished by the following characteristics: *R. nathaliae* has broadly ovate leaves with regular teeth along the margin. The flowers are more flat with yellow anthers. *Ramonda serbica* has spathulate, deeply toothed leaves whose margins are upturned. The flowers are more cup-shaped with blue anthers.

Ramonda serbica can be given the same treatment in the garden as the preceding species, but the true plant will need to be more diligently sourced. It inhabits shady, mossy crevices on limestone cliffs in a locality due west of Skopje.

Close by, growing in slightly more open, sunnier aspects, is perhaps the

Saxifraga federici-augusti subsp. *grisebachii*

showiest of Europe's Engleria saxifrages, *Saxifraga federici-augusti* subsp. *grise-bachii*. If only there were a simpler way of naming such a distinct and impressive plant!

It grows mainly between 500 and 1700 M on limestone rock and is a Balkan endemic, flowering in nature from May to July, depending on altitude. This outstanding species produces a flat, glaucous rosette, sometimes singly or more normally three to six together, forming a tight clump. The flowering stems can extend from 7 to 20 CM and are densely covered with glandular hairs as well as attractive cauline leaves varying in colour from bright cherry-red to purplish crimson. The inflorescence is made up of about 20 flowers of a striking crimson-red.

This is an alpine plant we gardeners simply cannot afford to have missing from a trough or boulder of tufa rock. I tend to choose a cooler position affording plenty of light but away from the intense summer heat that tends to cause severe scorch. Young seedlings are best planted direct into the tufa or wedged

Edraianthus graminifolius
Photo by David Millward.

between pieces of limestone. Although I am sure I will have offered to my former customers on many occasions single-rosetted plants with a flower stem, I would prefer to choose a multirosetted specimen. Although the plant is not monocarpic, the flowering rosette will expire after flowering, having set copious amounts of seed.

Perhaps the best-known cultivar of *Saxifraga federici-augusti* subsp. *grisebachii* is *S.* 'Wisley', which has a particularly brightly coloured inflorescence. Since most of the stock offered in the trade is seed-raised, it can only be called Wisley Group. The best forms could be raised vegetatively and given a clonal name. Whichever form is chosen, most are very beautiful and flower as early as midspring.

A genus deserving all the plaudits that are given to it is *Edraianthus*, a distinctive member of the campanula family. All of its members are native to the Balkans, with a concentration of species from Croatia, including the Velebit mountains and the Planina Biokovo.

The taxonomy of the genus is fairly complex, but most readers will not require a detailed description of the species. Alpine gardeners have been greatly indebted to the endeavours of Vojtěch Holubec and his recent seed collections from this part of the Balkan region, including a number of edraianthus species.

I will now describe a few of my particular favourites amongst this calcicole group of bellflowers. *Flora Europaea* (Tutin 1964) has played safe and brought together a number of closely related species into the *Edraianthus graminifolius* group. It includes three bellflowers I would recommend the reader look out for: *E. graminifolius* subsp. *croaticus* as well as the stunning white-flowered *E. graminifolius* subsp. *niveus* and *E. tenuifolius*. Each of these species and their subspecies grow in limestone crevices and form compact cushions with flowers held in terminal clusters in the form of large, sessile, upright, violet-blue bells, while the subspecies *niveus* has pure white flowers. The stems may vary in length and in the case of *E. tenuifolius* are an attractive reddish colour.

They can all be positioned in a trough between pieces of tufa rock in full sun. Each one of these species flowers during the late spring and early summer and produces plentiful seed.

The next group is of equal horticultural merit, the *Edraianthus pumilio* group, which encompasses the species *E. pumilio*, *E. dinaricus*, and *E. wettsteinii*. The first of the three can easily be obtained in commerce and is found growing in limestone crevices in the locality of Biokovo, Croatia, at 1700 M. It forms compact, silvery cushions up to 12 CM in diameter in nature, consisting of short, greyish, needlelike leaves with involute margins. The sessile flowers are produced singly in a tight posy and are a wonderful shade of blue.

Edraianthus pumilio
Photo by Jim Jermyn.

Edraianthus pumilio is a perfect trough plant but can easily be grown in any well-drained position in full sun. The delving taproot greatly benefits from a cool root run and is best wedged between pieces of tufa or limestone. The other two are equally desirable and should be looked out for in specialist seed lists.

My final choice is the striking *Edraianthus serpyllifolius*, again growing in limestone crevices from the Biokovo at 1750 M. It forms very compact cushions, 2 to 8 CM across, with short, glabrous, reddish stems radiating out from the cushion. The flowers appear in the early summer months and are the deepest purple-blue bells. It associates well with *Dianthus haematocalyx*.

The long-established cultivar *Edraianthus serpyllifolius* 'Major' is a vigorous, free-flowering form often offered in the trade which can be propagated sparingly by cuttings taken from around the central rosette in mid to late summer. The best results can be achieved when nursing a mother plant by pinching out the flowering buds and strengthening the vegetative

Edraianthus serpyllifolius 'Major'
Photo by Klaus Patzner.

growth. The 10 MM cuttings should be cut away with sharply pointed scissors and inserted into a container of moist rooting medium consisting of equal parts washed sand and perlite. The pot or tray should then be kept in a polythene tent to encourage rooting. At any stage during the propagation, a careful watch must be kept out for slugs, as the cuttings are particularly prone to attack. Once rooted, they can be hardened off and potted up ready for their eventual planting out in a trough or alpine bed.

Degenia velebitica is a plant that I first came to understand relative to both its native habitat and its cultivation requirements as a result of my trips to the Czech Republic. It is a rare member of the crucifer family native to the Velebit mountains, where it grows in limestone scree. Its name commemorates the Hungarian botanist Arpad Degen (1866–1934), who first made an in-depth study of the Velebit flora. It makes a compact tuft of silvery rosettes of linear foliage. The flowers are bright citron-yellow and held in clusters on short stems of 4 CM in length. It grows well when directly planted into tufa or planted vertically in crevices between pieces of limestone. It likes a sunny position but resents winter wet, and I would recommend protection from the elements during the winter months. After flowering, care should be taken to collect any viable seed in order to replenish stocks.

Campanulas feature strongly in the Balkans and a careful choice should be made to locate the most rewarding and attractive from a diverse race. A reliable one that is found in the Velebit mountains, this time at around 1600 M, in fissures

Degenia velebitica

of vertical limestone, is *Campanula waldsteiniana*. It forms a tight, overwintering cushion that produces a number of erect, wiry stems some 4 CM high, clothed with spathulate leaves and wide open purple-blue bells. It is a valuable late-flowering specimen for a trough or raised bed, blooming in late summer and early autumn. It can be increased either from seed or cuttings taken from newly emerged shoots before they have initiated flower buds. Once they have rooted, the growing points must be nipped out to prevent flowering.

The closely related *Campanula tommasiniana* (also from limestone fissures in the Croatian mountains) can be differentiated with its more tubular flowers. Both are worthy of a place in the alpine garden.

A plant for which I have great respect is *Euphorbia myrsinites*. It is a vigorous, fleshy perennial forming trailing woody stems that radiate from a central crown, dressed with narrow, fleshy, glaucous leaves. The inflorescence consists of showy heads of yellow bracts and flowers in the early summer. It is best planted in a sunny wall to allow room for the trailing stems.

Great care should be taken when propagating this plant from cuttings (from nonflowering shoots) taken in mid to late summer to avoid getting any of the milky sap on any part of the skin. I once failed to take the necessary precautions and suffered from some unusual symptoms, hence the respect!

An outstanding dianthus species found in the Sar Planina in Kosovo is

Dianthus scardicus
Photo by Margaret and Henry Taylor.

Dianthus scardicus. For some time, the Taylors have been growing this dwarf plant and disseminating seed. It has bright pink flowers on 3 to 5 CM stems and is ideal for a trough, and it does not seem fussy about soil pH.

Summer-flowering alpine species are of particular value, as previously noted, because of the inevitable glut of spring-flowering subjects already adorning our gardens. *Geranium subcaulescens*, sometimes lumped into *G. cinereum* subsp. *subcaulescens*, is one of the most rewarding of late-flowering alpine species. It is widely distributed in the Balkan region, occurring in Macedonia, Albania, and Greece. It extends still farther and seems indifferent to either limestone or serpentinite substrates. It certainly is not at all fussy when we come to choosing a site in the garden. All it requires is a well-drained, spacious site in full sun. In nature it is variable in habit with some miniaturised forms growing on ridge tops, where the flowers are almost sessile. I would like to trial seed-raised plants from such a locality to see if they would retain such a habit in lowland conditions.

Geranium subcaulescens surely represents one of the showiest of all alpine plants. The deeply cut, greyish green leaves and their radiating stems are clothed with huge upturned flowers, a wicked vibrant reddish crimson with a distinct black eye. The recent Alpine Garden Society seed-collecting expedition to northern Greece in 1999 introduced some fine forms, including pink-flowering forms, each with the acronym MESE (Macedonia and Epiros Seed Expedi-

Geranium subcaulescens and *G.* 'Ballerina'

tion). I would alert readers to look out for these introductions.

There can be no finer sight than a generous planting of mixed geraniums, including *Geranium cinereum* and the hybrid *G.* 'Ballerina', in an open, expansive alpine bed or rock garden. The colours will compete with any of the North American alpine phlox and outlast any other species for its period of flowering. The best forms can be propagated from cuttings taken during the dormant season and inserted in a mix of 75 percent sand and 25 percent perlite. On the other hand, if a mixed bag is acceptable, seed is a fun way of increasing stock.

To conclude this richly diverse part of the Balkan region, I want to extol the virtues of one final cyclamen species. It was never my intention to expend much ink on bulbous species or orchids, which have been so well documented both from a taxonomic and horticultural dimension through specialist monographs. Yet I cannot bypass the best known and most widely planted of all autumn-flowering bulbs, *Cyclamen hederifolium*. It occurs here in the former Yugoslavian republics and much more widely throughout the Balkans as well as the Mediterranean region.

It has been in cultivation at least since the 16th century and became a naturalised species in Britain, too. It is a woodland plant as well as growing in open scrub and on rocky slopes up to an altitude of 1300 M. Many gardeners will be familiar with its large, globose tubers extending up to a diameter of 15 CM. These become corky and fissured with age and often become exposed when established in the garden.

In recent years, here in the U.K., we have been treated to regular displays from Ashwood Nurseries at the Royal Horticultural Society's Flower Shows held in Westminster, London. Their details will feature in my list of recommended nurseries, for they offer a wide range of superbly grown plants. They are well known for both their spring and autumn displays of cyclamen. I have always loved *Cyclamen hederifolium* as an autumn-flowering tuberous plant, but more recently I have been captivated by the extreme variation exhibited within the shape and colour of its foliage. The leaf lamina varies from broadly heart-shaped with a lobed margin to oval or elliptic. Some of these extremes are astounding, but it is the variation in leaf pattern that is most striking—from plain to slight marbling, to creams and silver colouring.

The flowers often appear in late summer and continue on throughout the autumn, and it is not exceptional for a mature tuber to exhibit up to 50 flowers at the same time. Most forms in cultivation show little in the way of fragrance, but in the wild scented forms are not uncommon. Once again, modern selection of seed strains has produced some wonderful colour breaks, from deepest pink through to purest white.

In the garden, I prefer to plant this species around the base of deciduous or coniferous trees, but there is no reason, other than choice, to do so. It is equally at home in the open or in dappled shade. It seems indifferent to soil pH. The tubers prefer a well-drained, medium loam with added leaf mould, and a regular top dressing of leaf mould is strongly recommended during the summer months before flowering.

Raising cyclamen from seed can soon mushroom from a balanced hobby to an obsession—beware! Freshly sown seed gives little short of 100 percent germination in around eight weeks, whilst older seed will take up to six months to germinate.

This is a truly widespread species in nature and deserves all its accolades in the garden. It is the easiest and certainly the finest cyclamen for the open garden.

Greece

My discussion of Greece will feature alpines growing on Mount Smolikas, Mount Kajmakcalan, and Mount Olympus.

Mount Smolikas

Mount Smolikas (2637 M) is the second highest mountain in Greece and features as a prominent peak in the northern Pindus Mountains. Perhaps owing to the underlying rock component of serpentinite, this mountain supports a very rich alpine flora.

Above 1700 M, *Pinus heldreichii* (once known as *P. leucodermis*), the Panzer pine or Bosnian pine, is predominant within the wooded zone and then peters out above 1900 M as the alpine zone emerges. The serpentinite ridge is home to some plants of great horticultural significance. Let me describe a few of those that I have grown successfully.

Although some very fine forms of the previously described *Geranium subcaulescens* predominate, there are fine stands of perhaps the most attractive of the truly alpine dianthus species, *Dianthus haematocalyx* subsp. *pindicola*. I have

Dianthus haematocalyx subsp. *pindicola*
Photo by David Millward.

grown this plant for many years in an open, sunny, gritty alpine bed and it is uncomplicated and free-flowering. It received an AM as early as 1947, soon after its general introduction to gardens. It is a distinct form of the species owing mainly to its compact nature, with short, silvery grey leaves which are gathered into compressed tuffets. The flowers are almost stemless and are a rich rose-pink with a buff reverse, being the more striking because of the purple-brown calyces.

It is easily grown in any well-drained position in full sun and prefers a lime-free soil. This subspecies breeds true from seed, and since cuttings also root easily there is no difficulty with its propagation.

During my early days in the alpine plant trade I became aware that to the uninitiated public, a rock garden plant began with the letter *a*, such as alyssum, arabis, or aubrieta. As a result, I rather tended to keep clear of them, at a cost to my appreciation of their finer attributes. One of them is an endemic to this mountain range, *Aubrieta glabrescens*, and what a valuable garden plant it is. A truly chasmophytic (a crevice dweller) species, it forms a tight clump up to 15 CM across in partly shaded rock faces with lilac-purple flowers. A superior form of any species within this popular genus, which commemorates French botanical artist Claude Aubriet (1668–1743), should be propagated from cuttings taken after flowering. This particular species is well worth seeking out for a sunny wall as an alternative to the more widely offered *A. deltoidea* which is widespread in southern Europe.

Aubrieta deltoidea

I have described a number of fine viola species suitable for the alpine garden in my travels from west to east, and my final choice is the Balkan native *Viola albanica*, first described from this mountain. It is locally abundant here and very much approaches the beauty and habit of its French cousin, *V. cenisia*. It has a pink flower with a yellow eye and clearly enjoys the serpentinite gravels as it nestles between stones, sending out a mass of suckers. The orbicular, grey-green leaves add to the beauty of this alpine viola wholly suitable for a trough or raised bed. A careful watch for ripening seed will provide the simplest means of increase.

Perhaps the best known endemic to these parts is *Campanula hawkinsiana*. It is a species happily growing in shaly banks in subalpine woodland clearings as well as within the alpine zone on the serpentinite screes. It is in fact a serpentinite endemic and represents a challenge to the open gardener. Not being prepared to submit to alpine house culture, I would plant this treasure in a trough, wedged in between pieces of an acidic rock. It requires an acutely drained substrate and winter protection to give the rather susceptible central rootstock a chance of establishment. A successful grower will be able to admire its compact mounds of ascendant growth, topped with wide-open bells of violet-blue with a white eye. A well-flowered plant should set seed and therefore provide an insurance policy.

A little more on this unique serpentinite rock may be helpful. I encountered this rock from time to time in Japan and it always supported a rich flora. This material is often known as soapstone, is typically dark green to black in colour, and is made up of serpentine minerals. When dampened, the rock surface is somewhat soapy to touch. What is significant about it from the gardener's point of view is that it contains a significant amount of magnesium, iron, and certain trace elements. Having analysed the pH of such a soil in the Smolikas, the results will indicate a high alkalinity. This should not, though, be confused with a high level of calcium. This little bit of geological detail may help the gardener who wishes to seek the very best conditions for these challenging species.

Mount Kajmaktcalan

Mount Kajmaktcalan (2524 M) consists mainly of metamorphic schistose rocks along with gneiss and areas of peaty soil. It is in these peaty flushes that the eastern European native member of Ericaceae, *Bruckenthalia spiculifolia*, is found. It forms low bushes 10 to 15 CM tall, with terminal leads of small, open pink bells. It is a stoloniferous plant which will grow well in a damp, acidic, boggy condition in the garden, accompanying such plants as *Parnassia palustris* and *Primula farinosa*.

A very attractive member of the legume family, *Genista depressa*, is found near the summit and represents a most attractive alpine member of this extensive genus. It forms a prostrate shrub, sending out underground runners just below the soil level. The flowers are a stunning golden yellow reminiscent of our own gorse or whin, with its erect pea flowers, only this time in miniature. This is an easy species to please in a sun-baked position between rocks. The seed capsules need to be watched carefully to catch them before popping.

A rather challenging species is also found on this mountain growing in peaty soil with running water at its feet. *Ranunculus cacuminis* grows here at an altitude of 1900 M and up to the summit, thriving in a similar fashion to the Spanish endemic *R. acetosellifolius*. No surprises—it is equally difficult to please in the garden. If fresh seed can be obtained, or a young plant, then every effort should be made to please it well, perhaps according it a deep trough containing a well-drained, humus-rich material. It should be kept covered during the dormant season and both fed and watered during the growing season. The reward? An exciting white buttercup with large open flowers nestling amongst deeply dissected foliage—in fact, a rather special one. Having produced a few flowers, there will possibly be a seed set, which should be immediately collected and sown.

A plant that I have often attempted to grow and clearly not yet mastered is *Dianthus myrtinervius* subsp. *caespitosus*. I suspect I have been growing the type species but have never flowered it well enough to be sure of its true identity.

Dianthus myrtinervius subsp. *caespitosus*
Photo by David Millward.

Recent collections from this area (most notably the 1999 Alpine Garden Society MESE one) have finally introduced this outstanding subspecies. In nature, it all but resembles an Aretian androsace or the closely related *Dianthus microlepis* from Bulgaria. It forms tight cushions producing masses of nearly sessile deep pink flowers over a mat of densely overlapping leaves. It is certainly a plant for an alpine bed made up of gravel and sand to encourage it to maintain its true character. Plants may be increased by seed or from cuttings, and it flowers from early summer onwards.

The turf-covered ridges of this mountain come alive with the local speciality, *Gentiana verna* subsp. *balcanica*—another exciting variation to look out for and deserving of a special position in a trough. A wonderful association with the gentian would be one of the dwarfer yellow linums such as *Linum* 'Gemmell's Hybrid', a cross between *L. elegans* and *L. campanulatum*. The former is widely distributed in the Balkans and represents one of the finest yellow-flowering dwarf species.

Mount Olympus

Mount Olympus is the highest mountain in Greece, at 2911 M, and lies just inland from the Aegean Sea along the east coast, where Thessaly borders Macedonia. Seven major peaks are higher than 2500 M on Olympus, and they are barren looking and made up of a pale limestone.

There can be no doubting that the most charming and famous of the Olympus endemics is *Jankaea heldreichii*. This is a highly specialised member of the family Gesneriaceae and closely related to the ramondas. It is a rare plant growing within the national park status, so collecting is strictly forbidden. Despite its rarity and the myths surrounding its difficulty of culture, it is now available from a number of commercial sources, and I hope the following tips will encourage the reader to have a try!

Jankaea heldreichii

The monotypic genus is named in honour of Victor de Janka (1837–1890), a Hungarian authority on the flora of eastern Europe. It is almost exclusively found in crevices in vertical cracks of the endemic limestone. It will also grow on flat mats of humus resting on rock ledges, often protected by an overhang. I hope that this picture of its native habitat gives the reader a clue as to how to grow it in the garden. If in nature it is not growing entirely in the shade, then it receives direct sunlight for perhaps only an hour in the first part of the day and another hour at the conclusion of the day.

I have from time to time visited friends who garden amidst an old, disused quarry or who have natural outcrops of rock. What a treat, affording an opportunity for growing many plants in either natural or manmade crevices. For most of us, though, we will have to import boulders of our own endemic rock or transport a costly load of tufa rock to create the specialised habitats such plants as the jankaea desire. A pillar of tufa is just the right material for this species. Young plants, when they become available, are best planted as small propagules of no more than 2 to 3 CM in diameter directly into a boulder of tufa.

I have never travelled to Mount Olympus, but I wish to draw attention particularly to those who have, most notably the valuable observations of Marjorie Brough (who wrote in the AGS bulletin in 1953). Clearly, the plants grow in shade; how, though, do they receive their necessary water? The long roots at the base of the woody trunk act primarily as a means of anchorage and not as water collectors. The plants gain most of their moisture from the rosettes themselves and the adventitious roots growing in the rosettes. It now becomes clear how important it is to preserve the old and decaying leaves around the rosettes. In nature, the young offsets feed on these old, dead leaves—they provide the very humus they require for their survival. Indeed, when vegetative propagation is the desired method, the little offsets can be carefully detached and sufficient roots will come away with them.

When it comes to the planting, I would do so in early spring. The hole created for the propagule should be as tight as possible. The best material to accompany the roots in its hole is an equal mixture of well-rotted leaf mould and tufa dust. The piece of tufa in which the jankaea is planted should be resting in a shallow basin of water that should be kept replenished year-round or alternatively be partly buried in the soil. The ambient atmosphere within which the boulder is situated should be cool and humid. It may be positioned behind a shady wall or in the shade beside a pond, for example.

It seems that much time has been spent on this one species, *Jankaea heldreichii*, but I hope that the effort afforded to it is deemed well worthwhile. The flat rosettes of rounded leaves are shining, with a lovely silvery felt of white down, followed by the crystalline, lavender-blue bell-shaped flowers. This is the reward for such attention to detail.

A number of plants are found within close proximity to the jankaeas, including *Campanula oreadum*, *Viola delphinantha*, and a most attractive columbine, *Aquilegia ottonis* subsp. *amaliae*. The columbine can be found within both the

Jankaea heldreichii

Viola delphinantha

subalpine and alpine zones from 400 to 2300 M. It is also distributed across other mountains within the Balkan range.

I have raised this species on a number of occasions and find it a valuable addition to an alpine bed. Flowering stems may reach 20 to 30 CM, and during late spring and early summer the bicoloured flowers of purplish blue and white are most attractive. It is best situated in a cool, partly shaded spot, and I would allow it to self-sow and then control it accordingly.

A crevice dweller of great beauty is *Campanula oreadum*, which flowers on Olympus from late June onwards. It has distinct shiny leaves with long, tubular bellflowers of a deep purple-blue. This is another subject for a tufa garden or any sunny spot, where it can be planted between pieces of limestone in a freely drained mixture. It can be increased from seed. It associates with further kindred species, including *Saxifraga marginata* var. *rocheliana*, with its short panicle of up to eight white flowers, and *Edraianthus graminifolius*.

One of the ultimate treasures of the Olympus range is *Viola delphinantha*, which Wilhelm Schacht once described as "the finest alpine I have ever seen". It is a rare, shrubby viola somewhat akin to its Spanish counterpart *V. cazorlensis*. It is found in nature wedged into sunny limestone crevices, forming a gnarled, woody rootstock and wiry stems clothed with thin leaves. At the time of blooming, the most wonderful twin-spurred flowers of a rose-pink are produced.

There can be no doubt that this is a plant for direct planting into tufa, and it requires complete protection from the elements from the autumn through until spring. If one is successful with flowering this challenging species, the plant should be watched very carefully for the fattening seed capsules.

This viola, along with its compatriot jankaea, from lower, shadier elevations, is prominent amongst an exciting flora from Greece. I will now describe a few desirable species to treasure in the garden from the Bulgarian mountains.

Bulgaria

The Bulgarian mountains considered here are the Rhodopes, Pirins, and Rilas.

Rhodope Mountains

The Rhodopes form the second largest mountain range in Bulgaria. They consist of a beautiful labyrinth of numerous peaks, ridges, and deep forested valleys within which are cliffs and rocky walls. Featuring mainly of gneiss and granite, in many places great intrusions of limestone occur. The highest mountain is Goljam Perelik (2191 m).

The highlight from this range of mountains is the subalpine gesneriad, *Haberlea rhodopensis*. At elevations from 200 to 900 m, this species inhabits the northern and eastern cliffs and rock walls, forming hanging masses of strap-shaped foliage and myriads of blue-violet flowers.

So here is a plant which in the garden requires a cool, shaded wall where the large clumps of congested rosettes, the size of a dinner plate, have room to expand and display their glorious flowers in late spring. The rosettes are made up of wide, hairy leaves and drooping umbels of flowers on 8 to 15 cm stems. To increase this species, it is an easy matter to dislodge a few side rosettes, which will have fine root hairs at their base. These should be potted up into a loose humus mixture and kept in a cool, shaded position until well-rooted.

Plants are best positioned in a dry stone wall, where a good 15 cm of soil can be backfilled in which to position young plants vertically. They very

Haberlea rhodopensis
Photo by Jim Jermyn.

often shrivel up during a hot, dry summer and can quickly be revived with a good watering late at night.

Some botanists recognise the variety *Haberlea rhodopensis* var. *ferdinandi-coburgii* from the Lovech area in central Bulgaria. It is differentiated by having large flowers with a wider mouth. I am currently growing a distinct clone related to this variety named 'Connie Davidson', which received an FCC in May 2003. It commemorates the late Connie Davidson of Edinburgh, who collected this plant with her husband, Dr. James Davidson, in this part of Bulgaria. It is

Haberlea rhodopensis 'Virginalis'
Photo by Jim Jermyn.

an extremely vigorous clone with wide, bright green foliage and masses of heavy trusses of deep lilac flowers with even deeper purple markings within.

I am also very partial to the less-vigorous clone displaying white flowers, *Haberlea rhodopensis* 'Virginalis'. Each of these clones, along with their parents, represents one of the great classics of all subalpine plant species, and what a bonus to be able to find such a lovely plant to associate with miniature ferns on a shaded wall.

Other choice species from this area include the rather curious *Saxifraga stribrnyi*, *Iris reichenbachii*, and the golden yellow–flowered *Linum rhodopeum*, which *Flora Europaea* (Tutin 1964) wisely accords as a variety of *L. flavum*.

Pirin Mountains

This mountain range is situated in the southwest corner of Bulgaria and contains 60 peaks in excess of 2900 M. The highest peak is Mount Vichren (2915 M). Geologically, the range consists mainly of crystalline slate and granite, but the northern parts are made up of marble. The abundance of high mountain lakes in this range, along with its botanical treasures, make it a most attractive area to visit. I will describe a few of the choicer species that will settle down well in the lowland garden.

The Munich Botanic Garden has fine stands of the showy Kabschia saxifrage, *Saxifraga ferdinandi-coburgii*, which in nature forms large, solid cushions with masses of bright yellow flowers at the end of June to the beginning of July. It grows in light calcareous soil on stony outcrops, forming mats up to 1 M across

Saxifraga ferdinandi-coburgii

at altitudes up to 2900 M. Thousands of cushions are in full flower as soon as the snows recede. What a thrill to experience this sight.

These cushions are made up of crowded rosettes with greyish needlelike leaves, and the flowering stems are reddish, from 3 to 12 CM, and topped with a cyme of 3 to 15 bright yellow flowers. This species is easy to please on a trough or raised bed and is best given space to spread out over and amongst pieces of tufa in a moisture-retentive calcareous soil in an open position. It flowers in late spring in lowland gardens.

Saxifraga ferdinandi-coburgii is parent to a favourite hybrid saxifrage in the section *Porophyllum*. It is *S.* 'Zlatá Praha' ('Golden Prague'), whose other parents are *S. marginata* and *S. stribrnyi*. This cultivar flowers over a long period from mid to late spring, forming a tight cushion, with 4 to 6 CM stems and a racemose cyme of 9 to 20 yellow to orangey salmon-coloured flowers. Both the recommended species and the hybrid can be increased from cuttings taken during the dormant season and inserted into a mix of sharp sand with a little added perlite.

Another saxifrage found in the limestone crevices on Mount Vichren is *Saxifraga spruneri*. It, too, belongs to the section *Porphyrion*, subsection *Kabschia*, and was discovered by Spruner in 1842 and sent to the Boissier Herbarium in Geneva, Switzerland. It is a species easily distinguished within its subsection by the glandular hairy surfaces on its leaves. It has a superficial resemblance to species of the Mossy group. From the firm, green cushions, the 3 to 8 cm flowering stems arise with a terminal cyme of 4 to 15 pure white flowers in early summer. It is easily accommodated in a cool, partly shaded trough, and the cushions like to be positioned between pieces of limestone or tufa. It is best increased from seed.

To add to the flavour of this calcicole flora, the summit limestone supports still more exciting species, including the already described *Gentiana orbicularis* and *Leontopodium alpinum* subsp. *nivale*, along with sheets of *Dryas octopetala* and wide mats of *Saxifraga oppositifolia* with golden yellow *Alyssum cuneifolium* var. *pirinicum*. One final subject that I wish to describe is the precious little alpine cornflower, *Centaurea achtarovii*.

Even without flowers, *Centaurea achtarovii* makes a most attractive foliage plant, with its densely white, tomentose leaves formed into a symmetrical rosette. When I first set eyes on these felty rosettes, I could see "death by winter wet" written all over them. But with care, it can be grown in a deep trough with winter cover. Here, the plant will produce a deep taproot that must delve down between stones and a gritty mixture preferably containing limestone. The flowers are borne singly on a 4 to 5 cm stem and consist of a large violet-blue cornflower made up of many ray florets in the early summer. In nature, it associates with *Daphne kosaninii* and *Saxifraga ferdinandi-coburgii* at elevations of about 2200 m. With great care, a few seeds may be saved, and to my knowledge this is the only way to propagate this lovely plant. A bit of a challenge, but the next area to be covered introduces some age-old favourites.

Rila Mountains

These spectacular mountains are situated some 55 km to the south of the Bulgarian capital, Sofia. With more than 100 peaks taller than 2000 m, the highest is Mount Moussalla (2925 m), which is also the highest mountain in Bulgaria.

There must still be great potential from this vast mountain range, as its flora seldom features in botanical works. It is my view that a number of its endemics will rank amongst the most distinguished of all alpine plants. A number of individuals have written about their botanical trips to the Rila mountains, and both the late Gilbert Barrett and the Czech plantsman Josef Halda have given us a greater insight into its intimate flora. A fine time to botanise in these mountains is the beginning of July, where it will be observed that the underlying rock is predominantly acidic.

Having broken free from the subalpine zone, one ascends to meet low bushes of *Pinus mugo* underplanted with *Bruckenthalia spiculifolia*. The meadows begin to display an exciting flora above 2000 м, with *Campanula alpina* showing off its deep blue bells. The highlight here, though, are the myriads of little dense, compact tufts belonging to *Dianthus microlepis*. This is one of my firm favourites within this celebrated race of plants. It is so variable in flower colour that it is hard to find two identical plants. For those of us who have not visited the Moussalla, imagine the picture. The little plants dotted in the turf are amassed with pink flowers in every shade, to carmine, rose-violet, and pure whites. The white ones usually have a darker centre. The petals are also variable in shape; some are rounded, entire, while others are dentate. The foliage varies, too, from pale green to dark green and even silvery leaves. The first impression is of flowering cushions akin to *Silene acaulis*.

At long last, this superb plant is gaining the recognition it justifiably deserves. It is easily grown in any sunny alpine bed, trough, or raised bed, where it will flower in the late spring. I would choose a lime-free, gritty mixture and plant a

Dianthus microlepis

Dianthus microlepis
Photo by Ronald Bezzant.

Aquilegia aurea

number of seed-raised plants together with *Gentiana brachyphylla* amongst small pieces of stone. The trough would benefit from winter protection. I have noticed that some of the variants, either named or haphazardly raised from seed, featuring glaucous leaves, tend to prove more robust and long-lived.

The most widely grown cultivar is *Dianthus microlepis* 'Rivendell', a seedling raised by Brian Burrow from an original collection made by Dieter Zschummel. It displays large deep-pink flowers over a long period. Dr. Keith Lever has also raised some fine forms at his Aberconwy Nursery in North Wales, including *D.* 'Conwy Silver' and 'Conwy Star', both of which feature silvery leaves and deep pink flowers.

The species can easily be raised from seed, while the named cultivars should be propagated from cuttings taken after flowering from healthy new growth. The little cuttings are best inserted into a mix made up of equal parts sand and perlite. Great care should be taken to protect plants from an attack of aphis.

Two plants that deserve to be grown more widely in gardens are both endemic to these Bulgarian mountains. They are *Aquilegia aurea* and *Geum coccineum*. The first time I saw the latter, it was growing in the Munich Botanic Garden by a narrow stream which was racing down underneath a tufa cliff covered with large pads of haberlea and ramondas. The shrill, reddish orange flowers were quite outstanding on tallish stems so typical of the more robust, herbaceous species of geum. It prefers a damp position in the garden.

Aquilegia aurea is one of the rarest amongst its European counterparts and the only yellow-flowering columbine native to Europe. It is a beautiful plant that is best supported amongst dwarfer subshrubs such as the sprawling salix species. The stems rise to about 30 to 38 CM with large creamy yellow flowers in late spring. I have found it to be a little short-lived and in the future will try to offer it a more freely drained soil. Once established, it sets a modest amount of seed that should either be allowed to self-sow or be saved as a means of increase.

In the vicinity of the Moussalla hut at 2389 M, some other special plants are to be found. They include *Ranunculus crenatus* with its huge white cups amongst

Soldanella pusilla and *Primula minima*. But the real treasure found at about 2400 м and higher is *Gentiana pyrenaica*. How strange it is to find it more than 1600 км away from its well-known location in the eastern Pyrénées. The turf in which it is growing here is not always as damp as in the Pyrénées, although it is again found above 2500 м in wetter places alongside brooks amongst sphagnum moss. The gentian forms neat clumps here with its deep purplish blue, upright flowers.

At this elevation of 2500 м and above is another special endemic and a firm favourite of mine, *Primula deorum*. It was first described at the end of the 19th century by Czech botanist Velenovsky, who died in 1949. He named it after his god, Allah, whose name the mountain Moussalla also commemorates. This spectacular primula is found only in wet places, where it thrives amongst cotton grass (*Eriophorum vaginatum*), *Pinguicula leptoceras*, and *Gentiana pyrenaica*. It is locally abundant here, growing in hollows of dark, humus-rich soil. The solid clumps are made up of sheaflike rosettes of erect foliage with a glabrous upper surface. The flowers are held typically on 8 to 12 см stems in a one-sided umbel. They are a rich, reddish violet-purple in colour and are easily differentiated from *Primula glutinosa*, with which it shares the subsection *Cyanopsis*.

Primula deorum

Pinguicula leptoceras

Cultivating this species presents no difficulty in any lime-free, humus-rich soil, given the extra provision of moisture; it is the flowering of it that proves more challenging. I have found that it both grows and flowers consistently when planted in a cool spot with live sphagnum moss incorporated both around its roots and the neck of the plant. I would recommend raising fresh stock from seed and leaving the plants undisturbed. It is one of the real treasures of the Rila mountains and shows just how diverse and specialised the European alpine flora is.

A fitting conclusion to this rich mountain range is provided by a most unusual species of gentian that is all too rarely seen in gardens but should be given every chance to succeed. At an elevation of around 2300 M on Moussalla, *Gentiana frigida* is growing in open, rocky terrain and flowering too late in the year for the early season walkers. It is seen flowering at its best from July through to early September. I have seen only forms with lemon-yellow flowers, but they vary (much in the same way as the circumpolar *G. algida*) from pure white through yellow shades to pale blue and violet.

Gentiana frigida is regarded by some botanists as a geographical race of *G. algida*, but it is sufficiently distinct to merit sound specific status. It occurs in the Styrian Alps, the Carpathians, and the Tatra mountains, always choosing a lime-free soil. The older clumps may reach up to 10 CM across with up to 20

Gentiana frigida

flowers that are held in an erect, terminal cluster of one to three in number. The basal foliage is narrow, but the short 5 to 7 CM stems carry stem leaves that are thick in texture.

It is a very choice plant for an acid trough or raised bed, where the roots should be kept cool by being wedged between stones and planted in an open gritty mixture. The only means of increase is by seed, which ripens late on in the season.

While writing this penultimate chapter, it has rekindled memories of plants I have grown over the years and then subsequently lost, very often owing to a lack of attention to detail. This further reminds me how valuable the specialist seed collectors are, both in the furtherance of conservation and replenishing the needs of horticulture. Many of these collectors have an intimate knowledge of the terrain covered in this chapter and yet, owing to the political upheaval in these parts, they may take considerable risks when collecting in the field.

Many of these mountains I have highlighted belong to unspoilt regions of great beauty and attract little in the way of major tourism. They will undoubtedly be home to further discoveries, but for now we gardeners have a surfeit of varied plants from which to choose.

Pulsatilla halleri subsp. *slavica*

8: The Carpathians, Including the High Tatra Mountains

This remote mountain range extends from the northern Czech Republic to central Romania, with the highest peak, Gerlach, reaching 2655 M in the High Tatra Mountains. I will commence my description of plants from this region with one of the most popular and easily grown of all daphnes. It is *Daphne arbuscula*, which is an endemic of the karst mountain range, made up of dolomite limestone and known locally as the Muran mountains. Here are steep cliffs, often in excess of 1400 M high, with steep valleys between. It is on ledges and crevices in this dolomite and conglomerate rocks from 700 to 1300 M where the daphne grows, sometimes along with *Primula auricula*, *Pulsatilla halleri* subsp. *slavica*, and *Clematis alpina*.

Daphne arbuscula forms somewhat trailing, multibranched, dwarf evergreen shrublets of 10 to 30 CM in height. In nature, it flowers during May and June. The young branches have a reddish tinge and the foliage is generally a dark shining green, almost glabrous. Some forms, most notably the white-flowering form, have finely pubescent foliage and are more difficult to root from cuttings. The flowers are sweetly fragrant and produced in dense terminal clusters of 5 to 30 in number.

This is a most rewarding alpine daphne and perhaps the easiest of the dwarf species to establish in any sunny, well-drained bed, and also the most obliging to root from cuttings. Care should be taken in the hottest of climates to adapt accordingly and provide a cooler spot. I have learned to my cost never to allow the branching stems to be touched by neighbouring plants. During any damp spell, when the foliage of, for example, a geranium is touching the daphne, there appears to be an inducement of a fungal attack. This quickly spreads and the whole plant can collapse within weeks. So this daphne, including other dwarf species, should be given plenty of air. Position a few pieces of limestone underneath the stems and top dress annually with a coarse chipping or gravel. This top dressing will form a good medium into which the spreading stems can send down roots, and I often find that in July and August it is possible to remove rooted branches for propagation or relocation.

Plants flower during the late spring to early summer and are easily propagated from semiripe cuttings inserted into a mix of equal parts sharp sand, fine Cambark (or another finely graded, pine-based medium), and perlite. The lower leaves of the cuttings should not touch the base of the compost, as this may also induce a fungal rot.

A visit to the Blackthorn Nursery in Hampshire or to Arrowhead Alpines nursery in Fowlerville, Michigan, will send any genuine plantsperson into a frenzy, such is the range of daphnes on offer. Two cultivars I would strongly recommend from this species are *Daphne arbuscula* forma *alba* and *D. arbuscula* 'Muran Pride', with exceptionally large flowers.

Over the years, much confusion has arisen and many articles have been written about the legendary *Pulsatilla* 'Budapest'. The plant under this name received an FCC in 1963 when exhibited by Valerie Finnis. She had originally been given the plant by Wilhelm Schacht. Shortly before his death, I was sitting with him in his home in southern Germany, reminiscing about some long lost plants. One that featured in our conversation was this pulsatilla. He recalled getting to know a man from Budapest who enjoyed raising and hybridising pulsatillas. Wilhelm obtained this plant from the man and passed it around; the rest is history, as the awarded plant immediately died before being increased. Apparently, fairly close to the Hungarian capital of Budapest are hills that support some very fine pulsatillas with flowers varying from pale mauve to blue.

I think it will be abundantly clear to the reader by now that I am not a scientist but am very much a down-to-earth gardener. However, we all clamour for new plants, and there needs to be a degree of order with regards to their taxonomy. There is no doubt that the original name *Pulsatilla* 'Budapest' is now invalid. Whatever the real origin of these plants, they are highly variable from seed and often exhibit lovely, shaggy flowers in shades of lilac to pale blue. They are quite special and currently should be named *P.* 'Budapest Blue'.

In the Carpathian range a form of *Pulsatilla halleri* subsp. *slavica* can be found in the spring, and it, too, deserves a special place in our gardens, where it will adorn itself with immense flowers of violet-purple in the early spring.

Whilst working in the Schachen Garden, I was greatly aided by the geographical layout of the garden. One of the systematic rock gardens that featured the Carpathian flora surrounded an old arolla pine, *Pinus cembra*. At the time of my studies on the Schachen, it also included a fine little gnarled shrublet of *Rhododendron myrtifolium*, now correctly named *R. kotschyi*. It is native to the Bucegi Mountains of Romania, which are composed of limestone and conglomerates.

Rhododendron kotschyi
Photo by Gilbert Barrett.

So, here again, as with *Rhodothamnus chamaecistus*, is a calcicole member of Eri-caceae. This one is easily the most beautiful of the European species and forms low-spreading bushes growing up to 20 CM in height. At about 2000 M, it is found growing abundantly in humus-rich turf along with *Vaccinium uliginosum*

Scorzonera rosea

and *Loiseleuria procumbens*. It produces fine trusses of flowers varying from deep pink to bright carmine-rose and a few whites.

Seed is occasionally offered of this rarely seen dwarf rhododendron, and I have flowered seedlings after five to six years. It is not fussy in the garden but is happy in an alpine bed, perhaps wedged between pieces of dolomite rock and gnarled logs.

At one time, rock gardens across Europe were adorned with generous plantings of the most prolific of campanulas, *Campanula carpatica*. It seems to have dropped in popularity for some reason, but it still proves to be such a rewarding plant for its late-summer colour. Both the type form and *C. carpatica* var. *turbinata* are well known in gardens, the latter distinguished by its flatter flower cups. A number of popular cultivars also exhibit their huge flowers, from shades of darkest blue to ice blue and albinos. For a plant that is so adaptable in gardens, it is intriguing to note that in nature it inhabits partly shaded limestone rocks. It is very much a crevice plant, and the beauty of its immense cup-shaped flowers is further enhanced by the grey background of limestone. It is not a high alpine plant of the *C. morettiana* or *C. zoysii* type, but how satisfying to enjoy growing an uncomplicated plant from an austere habitat.

The best forms of this campanula can be divided and replanted as the new growth appears in midspring; seed-raised plants may vary from the original parent but will provide fine, strong plants.

A very pleasing member of the family Compositae is *Scorzonera rosea* that I also met up with the first time on the Schachen. It is a plant of the subalpine meadows, where it resembles a dwarf gerbera with rose-pink flowers. It has narrow, lance-shaped leaves and a tuberous root system. It flowers in the summer and is best planted in association with taller subjects and allowed to seed around.

Another two taller growing species which I am always keen to locate are deserving of the reader's awareness, both with showy blue flowers. They are members of the buttercup family: *Aquilegia transsilvanica* with its deep blue columbine flowers and the strong and dwarf-growing *Delphinium oxysepalum*. I have grown the delphinium from stock I purchased from Josef Holzbecher in

Brno, Czech Republic. It forms a robust herbaceous clump in an open, sunny, well-drained soil and in early summer produces a fine show of dark blue flowers with a black eye. Both of these endemic species can be increased from freshly sown seed.

At higher altitudes in the Bucegi mountains some of the true alpine species associate together to form a spectacular sight, flowering predominantly in late June and July. Eritrichium is found in its calcicole form, *Eritrichium nanum* subsp. *jankae*, growing with the diminutive and attractive *Androsace villosa* var. *arachnoidea* with its woolly rosettes.

The most distinct plant endemic to this mountain range is the calcicole relative of *Dianthus glacialis*; I will refer to it as *D. gelidus*, but it has also been described as *D. glacialis* subsp. *gelidus*. It grows in crevices, forming neat little cushions made up of dense tufts of dark green leaves over a deep taproot. The near stemless flowers are far superior to its calcifuge cousin, being somewhat larger and more variable in colour, from rose-pink to salmon-pink. I have found it to be a more permanent plant that grows well positioned in a trough amongst pieces of limestone in a well-drained mixture. A careful watch should be made for seed in order to bulk up stocks. It is a most valuable garden plant, endemic to the Carpathians.

If one is a collector of a particular genus of alpine plants (I guess that most of us usually succumb to this practice), then why not build up an aggregate of soldanellas? Although some of them may prove challenging to flower, success guarantees the most satisfying and compelling rewards.

The last one I will describe is native to the Polish Tatra mountains. *Soldanella carpatica* resembles *S. alpina* in appearance, although the former generally carries more flowers to a stem. The foliage is typically rounded with a reddish underside, and the flowers are more of a purplish blue than those of *S. alpina*. It is easily grown in a dedicated trough and should be given a humus-rich soil with added pieces of limestone—with a warning to keep the slug population at bay.

Of the various species of dianthus found in the Carpathians, the most beautiful is *Dianthus callizonus*. From the first time I saw this species flowering in the Schachen Garden, I was smitten by its extravagantly marked flowers. In its native Transylvania, it is known as the Königstein pink, since it occurs on the mountains of the same name, Königstein, or in Romanian, Piatra Craiului (2239 m). This mountain consists of a long white ridge of limestone between the Bucegi and Fagaras mountains. The outstanding treasure of this mountain is *D. callizonus*. It forms loose, sprawling clumps with narrow, grey-green leafy shoots. During June and July, these bear large rose-pink flowers with a central zone of intricate markings and spots.

Dianthus gelidus
Photo by Jim Jermyn.

Dianthus callizonus

Having obtained the true species from a reputable source, the plant should be given space in a calcareous soil with added pieces of limestone, around which the dianthus will send its underground roots to find a cool haven of protection. Aerial shoots will pop up in various places when it is happy, but at no time should the soil be allowed to become waterlogged. I am currently growing it in a trough, as I wish to enjoy the flowers near to the house, but with this position there is the added risk of drying out and becoming exhausted.

It will not tolerate a sun-baked position and prefers a cooler spot, but not too shaded. I am rarely without seed, which germinates readily. A number of growers enjoy hybridising members of this genus, and when *Dianthus callizonus*, *D. alpinus*, and *D. gelidus* are planted in close proximity, some of the resulting seedlings are well worth saving.

I have often grown the hybrid *Dianthus ×boydii*, commemorating the late William Brack Boyd of Melrose, Scotland, who raised it. This hybrid is likely to be the progeny of *D. callizonus* and *D. alpinus* and has lovely, deep pink, fringed flowers over lime-green foliage.

Another hybrid, this time of recent origin, showing great promise is named *Dianthus* 'Pudsey Prize'. It was first spotted by the keen plantsman Alan Spenceley of North Yorkshire, England, when visiting the former Lismore Nurseries. It is a seedling of *D. glacialis* that had been growing in close proximity to *D. alpinus* and *D. callizonus*. The showy flowers have toothed petals of a bright carmine-pink colour. One to look out for that received an RHS Preliminary Commendation in June 2000.

My final choice from the Carpathians, and indeed the last plant to be described in this book, is in fact rather appropriately the last species to flower in my garden before the winter season. It is *Crocus banaticus* that, in nature, generally commences its flowering well into October. The flowers are large and consist of delicate, long-tubed, bluish purple petals. The three inner segments of the flower are conspicuously shorter than the three outer ones, which sets it apart from other species. It also has a distinct lilac-coloured, finely divided stigma. In nature, the plants grow in both meadows and woodlands at around 500 м. In the garden it is easily pleased. I have corms planted in an open, gritty bed as well as in a woodland bed, and both sites suit it well. As with many plants I have described, it produces a very fine albino form, the best of which currently is *C. banaticus* 'Snowdrift', with immense white flowers and distinct yellow anthers with white feathery appendages.

It is fun to allow congested clumps of corms to seed around, and this they will do if one is not too zealous a weeder. The fruits mature and ripen in the spring and should be given a light top dressing to encourage their multiplication.

Crocus banaticus

It is fitting to conclude the chapter with this rarely described region in Europe and highlight some of its plants. Indeed, it has been a great pleasure and privilege to travel across this continent from west to east and draw the reader's attention to many of my favourite alpine plants.

During this lengthy excursion, I have inevitably been reminded of many plants which I no longer grow, ones which I will eagerly seek to relocate and plant in a more favourable position than the last time I tried. The real fun of growing both subalpine and truly alpine species in the open garden is the knowledge that some of them will prove too challenging, but in the process of failing there is always potential for learning. The next time we may just succeed. Another observation I have noted from this hobby is that there is also a great deal of camaraderie within the alpine gardening world.

I have been privileged to travel throughout Europe meeting fellow gardeners and plantsfolk; the same has been true when travelling in the United States, Canada, and Japan. There are few barriers between gardeners, and I have learned a great deal on my travels, as various friends and new acquaintances pass on their experiences and tribulations.

Some people find plantsfolk a trifle unorthodox! I was reminded of this recently whilst botanising in Austria with Dieter Schacht and Klaus Patzner. I found a bluff of silicaceous rock covered with perfect specimens of *Primula glutinosa* interspersed with *P. minima*. I was naturally overjoyed, as the scene was simply spectacular, each clump surpassing the next. I wriggled uneasily and impatiently on my front trying to gain the perfect vantage point for a picture with full depth of field and the blue sky behind. Unbeknown to me, a passing group of Italians had stopped, perhaps to see if I needed help! I temporarily forgot myself and began to wax lyrical in German about these plants. They smiled politely, nodded, and on they went, presumably to enjoy the wonderful air, the panoramic views, and the exercise. We plantsfolk enjoy all these things, too; we have, though, grasped something that few others even think about. Is it not true that we are greatly privileged not only to appreciate the alpine flora but also to have the opportunity to grow these plants in our lowland gardens? I hope we will never, never take this enormous privilege for granted. It's no wonder that people may look at us and wonder if all is well, but it is they who are missing the very essence of what stimulates us. For those readers who are not able to visit the mountains of Europe, I hope I have painted a modest picture of their allure and evoked a desire to keep persevering with their endemic plants or perhaps to try them out for the first time.

Well-constructed rock garden at Munich Botanic Garden

9: A Practical Guide to Alpine Gardening

In this busy world in which we live, few of us have the time to dedicate to growing alpine plants to the degree that we would perhaps like. Those who are retired or who do have the time will no doubt grow many of their choicest and more demanding plants in pots. The shelter that can be given to a frame full of pot-grown plants and the amount on control the grower can give these plants is much greater than is possible in the garden setting.

Troughs fall somewhere between the pot and the open garden, and their capacity is small enough to permit full attention to detail. I have therefore given numerous recommendations to this form of alpine gardening because I see it as a compromise, and I am also aware that troughs have become more freely available in recent years and at more affordable prices. Lack of moisture is easily rectified with a watering can, and autumn and winter excesses can be avoided with cloche covers. Liquid feeding may prove highly beneficial.

Once we move out into the open garden, all sorts of opportunities open up, and these are dependent on space and the amount of time and cost one is prepared to commit to each project.

Many articles have been written in great detail outlining specialised aspects of, for example, tufa cliffs and crevice gardening. There will no doubt be further highly innovative ideas being brought into the open in the coming years, thus raising the level of expertise in this form of gardening.

My advice is always to speak to experienced gardeners and see, in practice, how they achieve their success. It is also highly enlightening to study and enjoy these plants in the wild and learn from nature's perfect means of survival.

Throughout this chapter I include some of Duncan Lowe's outstanding line drawings to give a visual guide to some practical ways of growing alpine plants. He was the master of the raised bed and its construction and grew a wide range of plants on them, including some tricky ones. He has influenced both me and many other alpine gardeners in the way we approach the art of cultivation. I am

indebted to David Mowle of Lancaster, England, for making these line drawings available.

I will now outline a few suggestions that have worked for me and from which
many friends have also derived great success and enjoyment.

The Raised Bed

A raised bed is, in essence, a wall enclosure holding an appropriate soil mixture
for growing plants. Its obvious advantages are that it provides an immediate
improvement in the drainage due to its elevation and depth, and it provides ease
of maintenance and viewing.

Providing walls for planting vertically offers contrasting positions of full sun
or shade. Here are a few tips regarding its construction and subsequent planting.

Although my first crack at gardening was in the home of my parents in Hertfordshire, England, I first studied and practised the growing of alpine plants at
Ingwersen's wonderful nursery in that beloved of English counties, Sussex.
Although at that time, in the early 1970s, my first love was the game of cricket,
growing alpine plants was a very close second. My digs were located in a pretty
little village called West Hoathly, within cycling distance of the nursery and
neighbouring Gravetye Manor (the home of that great doyen of gardening,
William Robinson). It was also within a few miles of Wakehurst Place, Sheffield
Park Gardens, and many more superb gardens. Perhaps more importantly, it
was home to my village cricket club. Little known to those readers unfamiliar
with these parts is the fact that the underlying rock in this area is the famous
Sussex sandstone. This is the very material, quarried close by, which was especially sought for the RHS Wisley's rock garden. I purchased a lorry-load of this
rock, and along with a stone mason with whom I shared a beer or two in the
local Cat Inn, transported both to my home in Hertfordshire.

We created a raised bed, some 6 M by 1 M, and 60 CM in height. The finished
article was modelled on the construction shown in figure 2.

This type of sandstone is particularly easy to cut with a club hammer and cold
chisel due to the strata of the rock. The walls were built and regularly backfilled as we progressed. I have since learned a great deal in my later discussions
with Duncan Lowe regarding the ideal formula for growing a wide range of
choice alpine plants. Needless to say, my first efforts needed some refinement.

With subsequent experience, I can therefore recommend the following soil
mixture: Make up equal quantities (by volume) of sterilised loam, peat (or sterilised leaf mould), coarse grit, and chippings. I prefer utilising good loam, as it
acts as a buffer (stabilising the pH of the mix and providing a measure of safety

Figure 2. A typical raised bed

from certain nutrients) and in my experience creates a longer life for the bed. Prior to filling up the raised bed, it is important to point out that unless the drainage of the underlying soil is adequate, some graded rubble should be placed at the base of the bed. As the mixture is shovelled between the walls, it should be carefully firmed in to avoid creating pockets of air behind the rock walls. What is the preferred height of such a raised bed? In my view, a height of about 40 to 50 CM would be ideal for the raised area, allowing sufficient drop for trailing plants.

Here is an important tip which I have learned from Duncan Lowe, particularly so for the cultivation of cushion-forming androsaces: The surface of the bed should be topped with a layer of very coarse, washed grit, chippings, or shale to a depth of at least 25 MM and preferably 50 MM. This may seem excessive, but I can assure readers that it is this part of the equation that is most important. The type of topping may vary according to the type of plant chosen and whether it prefers an alkaline or acidic substrate, also allowing it to blend in with the chosen rocks.

It may be that with the climate change experienced by many gardeners across the globe, there is a case for incorporating leaky pipe or an alternative type of irrigation system at the time of construction. If, due to the width of the bed, it is not going to be possible to reach the centre with ease, both for planting and subsequent maintenance, a few decent-sized slabs should be carefully placed as stepping stones to facilitate these tasks. I would also strongly recommend that the choice of soil mixture be adapted according to the reader's own climate—for example, a more moisture-retentive mixture in a drier climate and by contrast a more freely drained mixture for a damper climate.

As far as the walls are concerned, rock looks just the part, but it is not quintessential. I have worked with railway sleepers, logs, and other biodegradable materials, each one with its own merits and serving the purpose of creating height for a well-drained bed that is easy of access for the regular attention such choice plants demand.

In his book on androsaces (Smith and Lowe 1977), Duncan Lowe states that most species can be satisfactorily grown in the open garden. He also adds that "some overhead winter protection is given to the more difficult species". I would go a step further and say that all the cushion-forming species need to be protected from a Scottish winter! How useful it would be to experience a regular winter cover of snow. This is now a rare occurrence, and weeks of stop-start rain, frost, rain, frost is the bane of an alpine plant's overwintering period of dormancy. I therefore strongly recommend the provision of a stabilised glass cover (or a substrate plastic material), allowing free movement of air around plants (see figure 3).

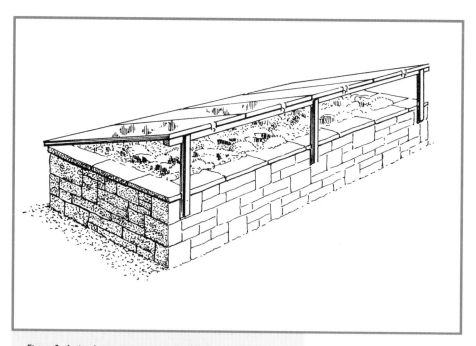

Figure 3. A simple way to cover a raised bed

Tufa in the Garden

It is hard to put a value on tufa as a material utilised by the alpine gardener. To suggest, as we often do, that it is akin to gold dust may sound a bit dramatic. But it is that useful. In fact, a number of plants simply will not perform naturally or as satisfactorily on any other material—to name a few, *Primula allionii*, *Jankaea heldreichii*, *Daphne petraea*, *Campanula morettiana*, *Campanula zoysii*, and a number of *Saxifraga* species.

Tufa is relatively lightweight, extremely porous in nature, and holes can be bored into its surface with relative ease. It is a calcareous rock that has been created over centuries. The name *tufa* comes from the Latin *tofus*, meaning a soft stone. The excellent drainage afforded by this material allows many of the plants I have described to be planted directly into the rock without protection.

Like many students who were privileged to train at Ingwersen's Nursery in Sussex, I was able to experience growing alpine plants in the great boulders of tufa sitting in the upper tier of the nursery below the car park. Large pieces of exposed tufa can be susceptible to drying out, owing to its porous nature. For this reason it is best to bury at least one-quarter of the rock in the soil; this allows capillary action to aid the moisture levels. Some growers will feel that this is an awful waste of rock and planting space. If this is the case, small pieces of tufa can be positioned (having cut the base to fit) in a saucer 35 cm diameter by 5 cm deep. The saucer should have at least five holes of 12 mm in diameter drilled in the part of its base that will not be obscured by the base of tufa rock. Having prepared a roughened surface in the central base of the saucer, a fairly stiff mix of cement—three parts sand to one part cement—should be prepared as a base for the tufa. In further preparation, the saucer and the tufa should be wetted prior to the cement being spread over the base of the saucer to a depth of 6 mm. Place the tufa on the cement and firm gently. Allow this to dry slowly before handling. Whether we are aging a trough or a piece of tufa, a variety of materials can be mixed together to speed up the process—diluted cow manure, yoghurt, and soot can be used.

Planting tufa

Planting a piece of tufa is a time of heightened excitement. I would carry out the planting in early spring to allow a full season for root establishment. Late autumn planting does not allow time for the plants to settle satisfactorily. First of all, drill the holes at 45 degrees (figure 4) to the vertical in order to retain the plant and compost. Then, having created holes about 25 mm in diameter to a depth of 7 to 9 cm, the fun commences. Have a tray close by to retain all the tufa dust and particles.

Figure 4. A tufa boulder set in a trough;
inset shows the manner of planting

Before planting, the tufa should be thoroughly soaked. I would prepare a lean compost made up of equal parts John Innes compost No. 2 and gritty sand (of which the latter is made up of 50 percent graded tufa debris and sand). The small plants should have been well watered prior to planting and allowed to settle, and then they can be carefully knocked out of their pots. Shake them gently, and carefully place the roots in the hole without forcing. It may be helpful to lay the roots on the back of a pointed, concave tool to ease the roots into the hole. Before back-filling with the compost, make sure the neck of the plant is in the correct position. Carefully add the compost, a teaspoon at a time, and firm gently with an appropriate stick. This part of the operation must be carried out gradually and efficiently to ensure there are no pockets of air or damage to the roots.

Having planted the boulder, water carefully but well; thereafter, the watering process is the key to success of the planting. During the growing season, the tufa may need to be watered once every five days and every month during the dormant season. This, of course, is only a guideline and depends on the natural rainfall if the boulders are left open to the elements.

Why go to all this effort, then? This is not just art form in the garden, but a practical and pleasing way of growing a number of tricky species very successfully, including *Primula allionii*. Choose a piece of tufa roughly 30 to 35 CM in diameter and up to 60 CM long. On such a piece we can accommodate up to 30 plants—a mini-garden all on its own, full of treasures.

A number of readers may have visited the tufa mountains created by two highly innovative gardeners, Tim Roberts of Lancashire, England, and Harry Jans, who gardens in The Netherlands. Their work has taken the whole process to another dimension. Tim's tufa mountain rises to 2 M in height and is three-sided, creating all sorts of possibilities for a variety of plants. The same is true of Harry's tufa pillars, which abound with exciting plants thriving in an outdoor environment that cannot be achieved with a conventional rock garden, raised bed, or trough. Having three sides to these tufa mountains or pillars provides different aspects or exposures, so valuable for particular species. For example, one can experiment with sunnier positions for saxifrages, campanulas, and primulas, while jankaea, ramondas, and ferns can favour the shadier aspects.

Perhaps this type of garden is the future towards which we will all be moving, along with the current craze for crevice gardening. I have attended many Alpine Garden Society and Scottish Rock Garden Club shows over the years and admired the wonderful pan-grown specimens, but to witness a perfect specimen in nature presents a new challenge to the grower. What connection was there between a perfectly flowered clone of *Primula allionii* exhibited in a large pan to the neat posy hanging on a cliff in its native haunts? For me, very little. My goal is therefore to attempt to grow these treasures according to their true character in the garden. I am certainly not alone; hence, the challenge to create an ideal microenvironment in the garden that is also pleasing to the eye.

I have just given a brief foretaste to the whole subject of gardening with tufa. The specialist journals of the Alpine Garden Society, Scottish Rock Garden Club, and the North American Rock Garden Society are just a few which will add flesh to the bones to which I have introduced the reader.

A Trough Garden

When I took over Edrom Nurseries, in Berwickshire, Scotland, in 1978, a collection of well over 50 troughs, several measuring in excess of 2 M by 1 M by 60 CM, came with the business. I was naturally thrilled, not only with the individual troughs, with many of them being naturally hand-hewn out of stone, but also with the contents. I was able to dedicate certain troughs to an individual species of plant or even a group of plants each requiring identical soil requirements.

What, then, are the advantages of alpines in a trough? The potential for creating a perfectly drained soil and incorporating a particular type of soil to meet the individual demands of a plant species or group of plants is one benefit. Troughs also offer ease of maintenance, including winter protection. (See figure 5 for Perspex covers as piloted by Ian and Maggie Young of Aberdeen, Scotland.

Figure 5. Individual Perspex plant covers (submitted by Ian Young)

Perspex is the brand name for a lightweight, tough, acrylic sheet of plastic.) Troughs also offer the pleasure of viewing, and in some cases, they are easy to transport. It is significant that a small trough, perhaps typically, 75 CM by 35 CM by 25 CM, can be the focus of our attention. This allows us to pay more attention to detail than we may perhaps afford to a larger rock garden, scree, or raised bed. The result is that the plants benefit from our closer observation; we will tend to watch more closely for the plants' needs with regards to watering, feeding, and weeding.

The most frequent cause of failure with alpine plants in a trough is a lack of depth, causing plants to become quickly exhausted and rapidly dry out. For this reason, I would recommend that a choice of trough should allow for a minimum depth of compost of 20 CM—preferably a little more.

A trough dedicated to a particular species or group of plants might include, for example, *Campanula alpestris*, *Gentiana verna* (or one of its cousins), and *Ranunculus parnassifolius* 'Nuria', along with other calcifuge species.

Let me now outline the planting of just such a trough for a special planting of *Campanula alpestris*.

I would choose a trough at least 35 CM in depth, with the general dimensions 50 CM by 35 CM. Above the drainage holes, I would recommend the following mixture: A selection of broken pieces of clay pots, slate, or flat stones placed above and around the drainage holes. A square of perforated zinc cut to cover the hole will also work admirably. A 5 to 10 CM layer of loose humus, including some very well rotted manure and leaf mould, will provide a cool substrate into which the roots will search. This layer also serves as a buffer, preventing the finer soils from working into the drainage holes and causing a blockage. The soil mixture that makes up the bulk of the trough's contents should consist of a humus-rich, well-drained mixture reflecting the need of the particular type of species to be planted. I will assume (for the purpose of this description) that I have obtained plants of the calcareous form of *Campanula alpestris*, so my soil mixture will consist of equal parts (by volume) of a John Innes type potting compost (No. 2 in the U.K.); sterilised leaf mould or sphagnum peat; and a coarse, gritty sand. When filling the trough with this compost, it is important to compact the contents as each 8 to 10 CM or so of material is added. This can be achieved by gently firming with the hand into the corners of the trough to ensure there will be no pockets of air. At no time should the compost be so severely compacted that the subsequent drainage is impaired, however. The trough should be filled a little above the rim to allow for sinkage.

At the time of planting, I would have a collection of some 6 to 12 stones of various sizes, according to the dimensions of the trough. These should be placed tastefully and in such a way that a good proportion of the stone remains below the surface of the soil, allowing an additional cool root run for the plants as well as the interior walls of the trough.

In a trough with the dimensions of 50 CM by 35 CM by 35 CM to be dedicated to some superlative form of *Campanula alpestris*, I would select six to eight plants and position them around the trough and between the rocks. A layer of up to 5 CM of coarse, washed limestone chipping (the colour and type of which will be chosen so as not to clash with the rocks) should be placed around the plants. Finally, the plants should be thoroughly watered.

Such a dedicated trough could be chosen for any number of our favourite plants, whether they be gentians, saxifrages, or other genera.

A Crevice Garden

Many articles have been written specifically about the construction and success of crevice gardening (see my Bibliography), so I will not write at length about it. I have, though, often referred to positioning, or wedging, plants between stones in a horizontal or vertical crevice. This is perhaps one of the most exacting

Figure 6. Creating a crevice between rocks

requirements for an alpine plant and assumes that the root run beneath the crevice is made up of a perfectly drained compost. Diagrams at figures 6 and 7 demonstrate the way to create such a crevice and its subsequent planting.

Outstanding example of a modern crevice garden by Ota Vlasak, Czech Republic
Photo by Jim Jermyn.

Figure 7. Planting a crevice

A Scree Garden

I make few references to a scree or moraine garden and include this type of innovative garden in my alpine bed. It is very often created on a naturally sloping part of the garden, often a cooler spot in my garden. I see no reason to pay too much attention to the position but simply state that most alpine plants do require good, uniform light.

The mixture incorporated into a scree is basically the same as that chosen for a raised bed, and the approach to surfacing is identical. My predecessor at Edrom

Figure 8. The simple scree bed

Nurseries, Alex Duguid, had a strong belief that the scree should be made up of richer mixture. As a result of this view, he dug out the soil to a depth of 45 to 60 cm and incorporated a layer of well-rotted manure in the base, prior to adding the well-drained soil mixture as prescribed for the raised bed.

There are clearly advantages with the ground level scree or alpine bed, in that taller plants can be incorporated in the landscape to good effect. It is also possible to make good use of a gently sloping aspect in the garden and incorporate a few large boulders to create the affect of a rock outcrop (see figure 8).

It now remains for me to wish the reader every success in the quest to grow a wide range of European alpine plants.

Sources of Choice European Alpine Plants and Seed

Societies and Seed Exchanges

The Alpine Garden Society
AGS Centre
Avon Bank
Pershore
Worcestershire WR10 3JP
England

The Scottish Rock Garden Club
P.O. Box 14063
Edinburgh EH10 4YE
Scotland

The Saxifrage Society (England)
membership@saxifraga.org

The North American Rock Garden Society
PO Box 67
Millwood, New York 10546
U.S.A.

European Nurseries

Aberconwy Nursery
Graig
Glan Conwy
Colwyn Bay LL28 5TL
Wales

Ardfearn Nursery
Bunchrew
Inverness-shire IV3 6RH
Scotland

Ashwood Nurseries Ltd.
Ashwood Lower Lane
Kingswinford
West Midlands DY6 0AE
England

Blackthorn Nursery
Kilmeston
Arlesford
Hampshire SO24 0NL
England

Christies Nursery
Downfield
Main Road
Westmuir
Kirriemuir
Angus DD8 5LP
Scotland

Edrom Nursery
Coldingham
Eyemouth
Berwickshire TD14 5LD
Scotland

Hythe Alpines
Methwold Hythe
Thetford
Norfolk IP26 4QH
England

Mendle Nursery
Holme
Scunthorpe
North Lincolnshire DN16 3RF
England

Pottertons Nursery
Moortown Road
Nettleton
Caistor
Lincoln LN7 6HX
England

Tough Alpine Nursery
Westhaybogs
Tough
Alford
Aberdeenshire AB33 8DU
Scotland

Ger. Van den Beuken
Zegersstraat 7
5961 XR Horst (L)
Netherlands

North American Nurseries

Arrowhead Alpines
P.O. Box 857
Fowlerville, Michigan 48836
U.S.A.

Beaver Creek Greenhouses
Box 129
Fruitvale, British Columbia VOG ILO
Canada

Mount Tahoma Nursery
28111 112th Avenue
East Graham, Washington 98338
U.S.A.

Siskiyou Rare Plant Nursery
2825 Cummings Road
Medford, Oregon 97501
U.S.A.

Wrightman Alpines Nursery
RR #3
Kerwood, Ontario NOM 2BO
Canada

Sources for Newly Introduced Seed of European Alpine Plants

Jim & Jenny Archibald
Bryn Collen
Ffostrasol
Llandysul
Dyfed SA44 5SB
Wales

Euroseeds
Mojmir Pavelka
P.O. Box 95
741 01 Novi Jicin
Czech Republic

Vojtěch Holubec
Sidlistni 210
CZ—165 00
Praha 6
Czech Republic

Glossary

achene: a one-seeded fruit, usually one of many in a fruiting head

adventitious: of a structure, such as a root, which develops at an unusual position

AGM: Award of Garden Merit, the Royal Horticultural Society's symbol of excellence given to plants of outstanding garden value

AM: Award of Merit, the second highest award granted by the Royal Horticultural Society

anther: the part of the stamen containing the pollen grains

axil, axillary: the point of connection between the leaf and stem, hence axillary flower or bud

basal: leaves which arise from the base of the stem

biennial: a plant requiring two years from seedling to flowering, after which it dies

blade: the expanded, flattened part of a leaf

bract: a modified leaf below a flower

bulbil: a small bulb which can be detached from the larger bulb on which it grows and forms an independent plant

calcareous: of rocks made up mainly (as in limestone) or partly of calcium carbonate

calyx: the sepals collectively

crenate: with rounded teeth, as distinct from dentate, which is with angular teeth

cyme: an inflorescence formed of axillary branches terminating in a flower, the central flowers maturing first

dentate: with angular teeth, as distinct from crenate, which is with rounded teeth

entire: without lobes

epiphytic: growing on other plants but not parasitic on them

farina (farinose): a mealy or powdery covering to an organ (for example, a primula)

FCC: First Class Certificate, the highest award granted by the Royal Horticultural Society

filament: the slender stalk of the stamen which bears the anthers

follicle: a dry, podlike fruit splitting down one side only

genus: a group of closely related species

glabrous: not hairy

glaucous: grey or blue colour

granite: a hard, igneous rock showing no trace of layering

herbaceous: plants without woody stems, dying down each year or season

heterostylous: with thrumb- and pin-eyed flowers (for example, *Douglasia vitaliana*)

hirsute: hairy

hybrid: result of cross-breeding between two different species of plants, the offspring possessing some of the characters of each parent

hybrid swarm: groups of plants of varying shapes and colour derived from a number of different species

igneous: of rocks that have been subjected to melting and recrystallisation

inflorescence: the part of the plant on which the flowers are borne

lanceolate: shaped like a lance, with the broadest part nearest the base

leaf axil: the point at which the leaf stalk joins the stem

lobed: rounded divisions at the edge of a leaf but not completely dividing it

marble: a hard, crystalline metamorphic rock resulting from the recrystallisation of limestone

monocarpic: plants which take a number of years to reach flowering, but die afterwards (for example, *Campanula thyrsoides*)

mycorrhiza(l): an association of a fungus and a higher plant in which the fungus lives within or on the outside of the roots, forming a symbiotic or parasitic relationship (for example, with *Cypripedium*, *Pryolaceae*)

node: a point on the stem from which one or more leaves and or buds arise

ovary: the part of the flower containing the ovules and later the seeds

panicle: a branched flowering stem

parasitic: living and feeding on another organism

pedicel: the stalk of a single flower

peduncle: the section of flower stalk below the umbel

perennial: living for more than two years or theoretically living indefinitely

perianth: the outer ring of petals

petiole: leaf stalk

pin-eyed: primula flower in which the style is long, so that the stigma appears at the mouth of the corolla and the anthers are inserted in the corolla tube

pinnate: the regular arrangement of leaflets in two rows either side of the leaf stalk

polycarpic: living for many seasons or not dying after flowering

polymorphic: the occurrence of more than one form of individual in a single species within an interbreeding population

pubescent: hairy or downy, usually with small, fine hairs

raceme: a simple inflorescence in which the flowers appear on short, nearly equal stalks

rhizome: an underground modified stem, often swollen and fleshy

rootstock: the topmost part of the root system from where it begins to branch to where it becomes the stem

rosette: an arrangement of leaves radiating from a crown or centre, often spreading over the ground

saxatile: specially adapted to growing in rock fissures

scape: flowering stem without leaves

schistose, schistlike: schist is a crystalline (igneous) rock whose components' minerals are oriented in a continuous succession of thin parallel planes—in sharp contrast with granite

sepal: one of the outer set of perianth segments

sessile: stalkless

silicaceous: of rocks which contain no calcium carbonate (limestone) and thus give rise to acid soils

species: the basic unit of classification; plants having similar characteristics and in which the individuals breed freely with each other

spike: a slender, elongated cluster of numerous flowers

stamen: one of the male reproductive organs of the flower which bears the pollen

stigma: the part of the female organ which receives the pollen

stolon (stoloniferous): a runner—that is, a branch which grows close to the ground and develops adventitious roots (for example, *Geum reptans*)

style: the more or less elongated part of the female organ which bears the stigma

subspecies (subsp.): group within a species showing certain minor differences

symbiotic: an association of two dissimilar organisms, usually to their mutual advantage

taproot: the main descending root

terminal: at the apex—that is, at the end of a stem or branch

thrumb-eyed: primula flower in which the style is short, so that the stigma is included in the corolla tube and the anthers are positioned at the mouth of the flower

tomentose: a feltlike covering of downy hairs on leaves or other plant parts

tuber: a swollen portion of a stem or root, usually below ground

umbel: flat-topped inflorescence in which all the flower stalks arise from a single point

variety: a subordinate rank to species and subspecies

whorl: more than two organs of the same kind arising from the same level around the stem

Bibliography

Almond, L., and M. Almond. 1989. Plant Portraits. *Journal of the Scottish Rock Garden Club* 84: 286.

Bacon, L. 1979. *Mountain Flower Holidays in Europe*. Woking, Surrey: The Alpine Garden Society.

Barrett, G. E. 1970. The Carpathian Mountains. *Bulletin of the Alpine Garden Society* 161: 253–261.

———. 1972. Moussalla. *Bulletin of the Alpine Garden Society* 169: 231–240.

Bevington, H. 1993. Alpine Walks. *Bulletin of the Alpine Garden Society* 254: 391–397.

Blanchard, B. 1990. *Narcissus*. Woking, Surrey: The Alpine Garden Society.

Bland, B. 2001. A New Dimension (Saxifrages). *Bulletin of the Alpine Garden Society* 284: 187–196.

Brinkley, S. 1997. Clusius, Renaissance Man. *Journal of the Scottish Rock Garden Club* 100: 237–249.

Brough, M. A. 1953. *Jankaea heldreichii* in cultivation. *Bulletin of the Alpine Garden Society* 92: 102–111.

Erskine, P. 1989. *Viola cazorlensis* in the garden. *Bulletin of the Alpine Garden Society* 236: 133–134.

Farrer, R. 1911. *Among the Hills*. London: Waterstone.

———. 1913. *The Dolomites*. London: Cardigan Books Ltd.

———. 1919. *The English Rock Garden*, vol. 1 and 2. London: Jack.

Ferns, F. 2001. Aspects of the Picos de Europa. *Journal of the Scottish Rock Garden Club* 106: 51–59.

Fouarge, J. G. 1996. *Primula allionii* in the wild. *Bulletin of the Alpine Garden Society* 265: 313–321.

Grey-Wilson, C. 1988. *The Genus Cyclamen: Kew Magazine Monograph*. Portland, Oregon: Timber Press.

Grey-Wilson, C., et al. 2001. Special European Issue. *Bulletin of the Alpine Garden Society* 285.

Halda, J. 1973. Plant Hunting in the Bulgarian Mountains. *Bulletin of the North American Rock Garden Society*, 31: 152–158.

Hills, L. D. 1950. *The Propagation of Alpines*. London: Faber and Faber.

Horny, R., K. M. Webr, and J. Byam-Grounds. 1986. *Porophyllum Saxifrages*. Stamford: Byam-Grounds Publications.

Howes, J. 2003. Saxifrages of the Maritime Alps. *Journal of the Scottish Rock Garden Club* 110: 22–43.

Ingwersen, W. 1949. *The Dianthus*. London: Collins.

———. 1978. *Manual of Alpine Plants*. Eastbourne: Will Ingwersen and Dunnsprint.

Jans, H. 1999. Growing Jankaea successfully. *Bulletin of the Alpine Garden Society* 275: 200–204.

Lowe, D. 1995. *Cushion Plants for the Rock Garden*. Portland, Oregon: Timber Press.

Mathew, B. 1989. *Hellebores*. Woking, Surrey: The Alpine Garden Society.

Mathew, B., and C. Grey-Wilson. 1971. Some Flowers of Yugoslavia. *Bulletin of the Alpine Garden Society* 164: 107–120.

Murfitt, R. 2004. Tim Roberts and his Tufa Mountain. *Bulletin of the North American Rock Garden Society*, vol. 62, no. 2: 112–131.

Page, J. 2003. Crevice Gardening. *Bulletin of the Alpine Garden Society* 293: 257–278.

Philbey, D. 2001. Miniature Tufa Gardens. *Bulletin of the Alpine Garden Society* 286: 443–453.

Rasetti, F. 1980. *I Fiori della Alpi*. Rome: Accademia Nazionale dei Lincei.

Richards, A. J. 1996. A summer visit to the Sierra Nevada, Spain. *Bulletin of the Alpine Garden Society* 266: 468–472.

Richards, A. J., et al. 2000. Northern Greece. *Bulletin of the Alpine Garden Society* 281.

Rolfe, R. 1998. A summit circuit. *Bulletin of the Alpine Garden Society* 272: 195–206.

———. 2004. *Viola* Section *Melanium*: A scattershot survey. *Journal of the Plantsman* 3: 154–161.

Schacht, W. 1936. The Rock Gardens of Vrana, *Bulletin of the Alpine Garden Society* 23: 14–23.

Smith, G. F., and D. B. Lowe. 1977. *Androsaces*. Woking, Surrey: The Alpine Garden Society.

Smith, G. F., B. Burrow, and D. B. Lowe. *Primulas of Europe and America*. Woking, Surrey: The Alpine Garden Society.

Stone, M. A. 1995. A quest for *Pulsatilla* 'Budapest Blue'. *Journal of the Scottish Rock Garden Club* 95: 155–158.

Taylor, H. 1977. A tour through the Maritme Alps. *Journal of the Scottish Rock Garden Club* 60: 217–220.

Taylor M., and H. Taylor. 1982. Europe's Choice Alpines. *Journal of the Scottish Rock Garden Club* 69: 303–311.

———. 1988. Plant Portraits. *Journal of the Scottish Rock Garden Club* 82: 84.

———. 1990. Plant Portraits. *Journal of the Scottish Rock Garden Club* 86: 53.

———. 2002. Three New Primulas in Northern Italy. *Journal of the Scottish Rock Garden Club* 109: 306–317.

Tutin, T. G., et al. 1964. *Flora Europaea*, vol. 1–5. London: Cambridge University Press.

van Zwienen, K. 1998. Alpine Plants of the Cantabrian Mountains. *Journal of the Scottish Rock Garden Club* 101: 363–368.

———. 2003. *Saxifraga oppositifolia* and its cousins. *Journal of the Scottish Rock Garden Club* 111: 31–43.

Webb, D. A., and R. J.Gornall. 1989. *Saxifrages of Europe*. Bromley, Kent: Christopher Helm Ltd.

White, R. 2002. *Daphne ×hendersonii*, a high ranking hybrid. *Bulletin of the Alpine Garden Society* 290: 492–498.

Wilford, R. 2000. Some Perennial Adonis. *Bulletin of the Alpine Garden Society* 282: 429–434.

Zvolanek, Z. 2003. Crevice Gardens. *Journal of the Scottish Rock Garden Club* 110: 71–84.

Conversion Tables

inches	cm		feet	m		miles	km
1/10	0.3		1	0.3		1/4	0.4
1/6	0.4		2	0.6		1/2	0.8
1/4	0.6		3	0.9		1	1.6
1/3	0.8		4	1.2		2	3.2
1/2	1.3		5	1.5		3	4.8
3/4	1.9		6	1.8		4	6.4
1	2.5		7	2.1		5	8.0
2	5.1		8	2.4		6	9.7
3	7.6		9	2.7		7	11
4	10		10	3		8	13
5	13		20	6		9	14
6	15		30	9		10	16
7	18		40	12		20	32
8	20		50	15		30	48
9	23		60	18		40	64
10	25		70	21		50	80
20	51		80	24		60	97
30	76		90	27		70	110
40	100		100	30		80	130
50	130		200	60		90	140
60	150		300	90		100	160
70	180		400	120		200	320
80	200		500	150		300	480
90	230		600	180		400	640
100	250		700	210		500	800
			800	240		600	960
			900	270		700	1,100
			1,000	300		800	1,300
			2,000	610		900	1,400
			3,000	910		1,000	1,600
			4,000	1,200		1,500	2,400
			5,000	1,500		2,000	3,200
			6,000	1,800		2,500	4,000
			7,000	2,100			
			8,000	2,400			
			9,000	2,700			
			10,000	3,000			
			15,000	4,600			

Index of Plant Names

Photographs are indicated by **boldfaced** page numbers.

A

Achillea clavennae 236
Achillea oxyloba 236
Adonis cyllenea 49
Adonis distorta 187
Adonis pyrenaica 61, 89, 91–93, **92**, 187
Adonis vernalis 50, **50**
Allium insubricum 121, 122, 160, **161**
Allium narcissiflorum 121–122, **121**, 160
Alyssum alpestre 127
Alyssum cuneifolium 93, 184
Alyssum cuneifolium var. *pirinicum* 276
Alyssum ovirense 252
Alyssum serpyllifolium 127
Amelanchier ovalis 172
Androsace alpina 11, 70, 139, 141, 150–152, **151**, 153, 195
Androsace ×*aretioides* 152
Androsace brevis 70, 159, 162
Androsace carnea 70, 73, 84
Androsace carnea ×*pyrenaica* 72, 73
Androsace chamaejasme 70, 225
Androsace ciliata 61, 68, **69**, 70
Androsace cylindrica 61, 70, 72, 73
Androsace cylindrica ×*hirtella* 71, 72, 74
Androsace hausmannii 70, 239
Androsace hedraeantha 70, 152, 255, 256
Androsace ×*heeri* 152
Androsace helvetica 22, 70, 139, 152, 200–202, **201**
Androsace hirtella 70, 72, 73
Androsace laggeri 70, 73, 84
Androsace laggeri 'Andorra' 84, **84**
Androsace obtusifolia 70, 152, 225
Androsace pubescens 70, **127**, 128
Androsace pyrenaica 70, 72, 73
Androsace vandellii = *Androsace argentea* 70, 120, 152–154, **153**
Androsace villosa **54**, 56, 70, 93, 186, 210
Androsace villosa var. *arachnoidea* 287

Androsace wulfeniana 70, 71, 159, 202, **202**
Anemone baldensis 130, 140, 237, **237**
Anemone drummondii 237
Anemone ×*lipsiensis* 40
Anemone ×*lipsiensis* 'Seemannii' 40
Anemone narcissiflora 80, 96, 167, **168**, 224, **225**
Anemone nemorosa 39
Anemone nemorosa 'Allenii' 40
Anemone nemorosa 'Lady Doneraile' 40
Anemone nemorosa 'Vestal' 40
Anemone ranunculoides 39
Anemone rupicola 237
Anthyllis vulneraria 219
Antirrhinum sempervirens 80
Aquilegia alpina 15, 132, **133**, 225
Aquilegia aurea 278, **278**
Aquilegia jonesii 132
Aquilegia ottonis subsp. *amaliae* 271
Aquilegia pyrenaica 61, 77, **78**, 225
Aquilegia transsilvanica 286
Arctostaphylos alpinus = *Arctous alpinus* 241, **241**
Arenaria purpurascens 79
Arnica montana 219
Asperula hirta 63
Asphodelus albus 80
Aster alpinus 91, 219
Astragalus alpinus 219
Aubrieta deltoidea 266, **267**
Aubrieta glabrescens 266

B

Bruckenthalia spiculifolia 268, 277
Buglossoides gastonii = *Lithospermum gastonii* 77

C

Callianthemum anemonoides 181, 196–198, **198**, 208
Callianthemum coriandrifolium 206, **207**
Callianthemum kernerianum 180, 181–183, **182**, 187, 196, 198, 208
Campanula alpestris = *Campanula allionii* 121, 122–124, **122**, **123**, 125, 138, 156, 300, 301

Delphinium oxysepalum 286

Dianthus alpinus 14, 125, 126, 210–212, **211**, 289

Dianthus alpinus 'Adonis' 212

Dianthus alpinus 'Joan's Blood' 212

Dianthus alpinus 'Millstream Salmon' 212

Dianthus ×*boydii* 289

Dianthus callizonus 18, 19, 211, 287–289, **288**

Dianthus 'Conwy Silver' 278

Dianthus 'Conwy Star' 278

Dianthus gelidus = *Dianthus glacialis* subsp. *gelidus* 287, **288**, 289

Dianthus glacialis 125, 193, **194**, 287, 289

Dianthus haematocalyx 260

Dianthus haematocalyx subsp. *pindicola* 265, **266**

Dianthus 'Inshriach Dazzler' 108

Dianthus microlepis 269, 277, **277**

Dianthus microlepis 'Rivendell' 278

Dianthus monspessulanus subsp. *sternbergii* 251

Dianthus myrtinervius subsp. *caespitosus* 268, **269**

Dianthus pavonius = *Dianthus neglectus* 8, 106–108, 106, 125, 138, 211

Dianthus 'Pudsey Prize' 289

Dianthus scardicus 263, **263**

Dianthus simulans 18

Dianthus sylvestris **207**, 208

Diapensia lapponica 22, 102

Doronicum grandiflorum 144

Douglasia vitaliana = *Vitaliana primuliflora* 93, 105, 125, 128, **129**, 186, 307

Douglasia vitaliana var. *chionotricha*. See *Vitaliana primuliflora* var. *chionotricha*

Douglasia vitaliana subsp. *praetutiana*. See *Vitaliana primuliflora* subsp. *praetutiana*

Draba dedeana 56, **57**

Dryas octopetala 27, **27**, 76, 140, 210, 236, 248, 276

E

Edraianthus dinaricus 260

Edraianthus graminifolius 256, 259, **259**, 272

Edraianthus graminifolius group 260

Edraianthus graminifolius subsp. *croaticus* 260

Edraianthus graminifolius subsp. *niveus* 260

Edraianthus pumilio 260, **260**

Edraianthus pumilio group 260

Edraianthus serpyllifolius 260

Edraianthus serpyllifolius 'Major' 260, **261**

Edraianthus tenuifolius 260

Edraianthus wettsteinii 260

Eranthis cilicica 32

Eranthis hyemalis 29, 32, **33**, 34

Eranthis hyemalis (Tubergenii Group) 'Guinea Gold' 32, 33

Erica arborea 59

Erica australis 59

Erica carnea 44, 216, 240

Erica carnea 'Myretoun Ruby' 44

Erigeron frigidus 120

Erinacea anthyllis 118

Eriophorum vaginatum 279

Eritrichium nanum 7, 22, 25, 68, 78, 135, 139, 202, 231, **232**, 246

Eritrichium nanum subsp. *jankae* 246, **246**, 287

Eryngium bourgatii 81

Erysimum helveticum 137, 138, **139**

Erysimum pumilum 138

Erythronium dens-canis 35–36, **36**

Erythronium dens-canis 'Frans Hals' 36

Erythronium dens-canis 'Pink Perfection' 36

Erythronium dens-canis 'Snowflake' 36

Euphorbia myrsinites 262

F

Fritillaria camschatcensis 80

Fritillaria lusitanica 119

Fritillaria pyrenaica 59, 61

Fritillaria tubiformis = *Fritillaria delphinensis* 96, 167, **168**

Fritillaria tubiformis subsp. *moggridgei* 96

G

Galanthus 'Bertram Anderson' 34

Galanthus elwesii 32, 33

Galanthus 'Mighty Atom' 34

Galanthus nivalis 32, 33, **33**, 38

Galanthus plicatus 33, 34

Galanthus 'Spindlestone Surprise' 34

Galanthus 'S. Arnott' 34

Genista depressa 268

Gentiana acaulis 8, 80, 88, 136, 145

Gentiana algida 280

Gentiana alpina 86, **87**, 88, 120

Gentiana angustifolia 16, 57, 115, 125–126, **125**

R

Ramonda myconi 61, 66–68, **66**, 257

Ramonda nathaliae 66, 257, **257**

Ramonda serbica 257

Ranunculus abnormis 116

Ranunculus acetosellifolius 120, 268

Ranunculus alpestris 171, **171**, 252

Ranunculus amplexicaulis 60, 88, 118

Ranunculus ×arendsii 118

Ranunculus ×arendsii 'Moonlight' 118

Ranunculus bilobus 167, 169, 171, 181, 210

Ranunculus cacuminis 268

Ranunculus crenatus 171, 210, 256, 278

Ranunculus ×flahaultii 89, 91

Ranunculus ×flahaultii 'Noufonts' 91

Ranunculus glacialis 15, 24, 120, 135, 141–143,
    143, **144**, 151, 195, 231

Ranunculus glacialis forma *rosea* **143**

Ranunculus gramineus 117, 118

Ranunculus gramineus 'Pardal' 118

Ranunculus parnassifolius 24, 88, 141, 166, **167**,
    186

Ranunculus parnassifolius 'Nuria' 8, 88–90, **89**,
    166, 300

Ranunculus parnassifolius 'Pena Prieta' 59, **60**

Ranunculus pyrenaeus 89, 90, **90**

Ranunculus seguieri 24, 121, 122, 140, 141, 143,
    144, 245

Ranunculus seguieri subsp. *montenegrinus* 143

Ranunculus traunfellneri 171, 252

Rhododendron ferrugineum 22, 91, 225, **226**

Rhododendron hirsutum 22, **22**, 225

Rhododendron kotschyi = *Rhododendron myrti-
    folium* 284, **285**

Rhodothamnus chamaecistus 14, 27, 166, 239,
    240, 285

S

Salix reticulata **238**, 239

Salix retusa 239

Salix serpyllifolia 239

Saponaria 'Bressingham Hybrid' 194

Saponaria caespitosa 194

Saponaria ×olivana 194, **195**

Saponaria oxymoides 194

Saponaria pumilio 193

Saxifraga ×anglica 'Myra Cambria' 75

Saxifraga aretioides 75

Saxifraga biflora 154

Saxifraga ×boydii 242

Saxifraga ×boydii 'Aretiastrum' 242

Saxifraga ×boydii 'Faldonside' 75, 242

Saxifraga ×boydii 'Sulphurea' 242

Saxifraga burseriana 162, 241, 242, **242**

Saxifraga burseriana 'Clarissa' 241

Saxifraga burseriana 'Crenata' 241

Saxifraga burseriana 'Gloria' 241

Saxifraga burseriana 'Mangart' 241

Saxifraga callosa 100, 133

Saxifraga callosa subsp. *callosa* var. *australis* =
    Saxifraga callosa var. *lantoscana* 66, 100, 101,
    102

Saxifraga callosa subsp. *callosa* var. *callosa* =
    Saxifraga callosa var. *bellardii* 100, 101, **101**,
    102

Saxifraga callosa 'Limelight' 101

Saxifraga 'Cloth of Gold' 103

Saxifraga cochlearis 102

Saxifraga cochlearis 'Minor' 102

Saxifraga cotyledon 160, 162

Saxifraga diapensioides 102, 103, 176

Saxifraga ×elisabethae 242

Saxifraga ×elisabethae 'Boston Spa' 242

Saxifraga ×elisabethae 'Millstream Cream' 242

Saxifraga federici-augusti subsp. *grisebachii* =
    Saxifraga grisebachii 258, **258**

Saxifraga federici-augusti subsp. *grisebachii*
    'Wisley' 259

Saxifraga ferdinandi-coburgii 274, 275, **275**, 276

Saxifraga florulenta 100, 104, 105

Saxifraga granulata 11

Saxifraga hostii 162

Saxifraga ×irvingii 242

Saxifraga ×irvingii 'Jenkinsiae' 242

Saxifraga ×irvingii 'Lusanna' 242

Saxifraga ×kochii 154

Saxifraga ×kochii 'Firebrand' 154

Saxifraga longifolia 61, **61**, 63–65, **65**, 66, 95,
    102, 133

Saxifraga marginata 275

Saxifraga marginata var. *rocheliana* 272

Saxifraga ×megaseaeflora 'Karel Capek' 75

Saxifraga oppositifolia 132, 154, 191, **191**, 276,
    311

Saxifraga oppositifolia subsp. *blepharophylla*
    191, 192